Tokyo-Brussels Partnership

Security, Development and Knowledge-based Society

P.I.E. Peter Lang

Bruxelles · Bern · Berlin · Frankfurt am Main · New York · Oxford · Wien

Takako UETA & Éric REMACLE (eds.)

Tokyo-Brussels Partnership

Security, Development and Knowledge-based Society

« International Insights »
No.7

This volume is the result of a joint research project between the International Christian University (the 21st Century Center of Excellence Program – CoE), the TEPSA (Trans European Policy Study Association) and the Université libre de Bruxelles (ULB) (Institut d'études européennes – IEE).

1 avenue Maurice, 1050 Brussels, Belgium
info@peterlang.com; www.peterlang.com

ISSN 1780-5414
ISBN 978-90-5201-043-4
D/2008/5678/61

Bibliographic information published by "Die Deutsche Bibliothek"

"Die Deutsche Bibliothek" lists this publication in the "Deutsche Nationalbibliografie"; detailed bibliographic data is available in the Internet at <http://dnb.ddb.de>.

CIP available from the British Library, GB and the Library of Congress, USA.

Contents

PART 2. UNIVERSAL AND REGIONAL SECURITY AND DEVELOPMENT CHALLENGES

Foreword

Christian FRANCK

Secretary-General TEPSA,
Professor Université catholique de Louvain

In the foreword he dedicated to the special issue of Studia Diplomatica on *Japan-EU cooperation: Ten Years after The Hague Declaration*, Ambassador Kimura wrote:

> Since 1991, we have witnessed considerable deepening and widening of our relationship... However, if we consider the economic weight of the EU and Japan in the world, and their corresponding political responsibility on the global stage, it is clear that our mutual relations have much room for further advancement.[1]

Precisely, the 2001 Action Plan for a Decade of Japan-EU cooperation has paved the way to closer links between EU and Japan.

In short, it is necessary to recall to what extent the EU-Japan relationship has got narrower and wider since 1991. Since the mid-1970s to the late 1980s, this relation was mainly based on trade. EU suffered a unequal trade: The EU-Japan relationship was mainly characterised by trade disputes on issues such as cars, steel, video recorders, a forced dumping, and non-tariff barriers. As Christophe Piening pointed out in his *Global Europe: the European Union in World Affairs*, "the trade imbalance has tended to dominate the EU's ties with Japan, simply because there has not been other dimension on which to build"[2]. A parallelism can be drawn between the concerns deriving from Japan's exports inspired in those times with the reaction to the current Chinese exports' pressure.

The turning point in the EU-Japan relationship has coincided with the end of the Cold War. The Hague Declaration was made less than

---

1 Takako Ueta and Éric Remacle (eds.), *Japan-EU cooperation: Ten Years after the Hague Declaration*, edited by *Studia Diplomatica*, Vol.LIV, 2001, No.1-2, Preface.

2 Christophe Piening, *Global Europe: the European Union in World Affairs*, Boulder, Lynne Rienner, 1997, Chapter 7, *the EU and Asia*, p. 150.

two years of the fall of the Berlin Wall. Not only trade, investments, but also monetary, scientific and technologic cooperation, cultural and political dialogue on worldwide political issues became part of the EU-Japan partnership.

The focus of this partnership made a shift from concerns about trade issues to cooperation in order to face common global challenges. Regarding political and security issues, Professor Takako Ueta wrote that: "since the fall of the Berlin Wall, no diplomatic relations of Japan have undergone such dramatic development as Japan-Europe political relations"[3]. First, the ties between Europe and Japan have strengthened while covering a larger amount of activities. Those ties also got wider due to the cooperation of Japan with the European Union in the promotion of a regional stability in Asia as well as in Eastern Europe; this has also something to do with common efforts in promoting multilateralism within the WTO and the UN.

According to Robert Cooper, the Council's External Relations Director General, who has recently published a very stimulating book entitled *The Breaking of Nations, Order and Chaos in the Twenty-First Century*[4], the European Union and Japan belong to the "postmodern world." It is opposed to the pre-modern world where the states failed in reaching their goals, and to the modern world, in which prevails the Westphalian paradigm of balance between power, State's sovereignty, separation of domestic and foreign affairs; the post modern world does not primarily rely on balance of power but rather on cooperation and multilateralism. It does not emphasise mainly on sovereignty or on fight against external meddling with internal affairs but on the management of interdependence and mutual interference which stems from connections between civil societies.

In Asia, Japan is the only State which belongs to this post modern world, as much as the European countries. This common pattern is a solid starting point for an improvement in the EU-Japan relationship at global scale.

Since 1998, on the initiative of the International Christian University of Tokyo and of the Université libre de Bruxelles (ULB), in partnership with Trans European Policy Studies Association (TEPSA) or with the Groupe d'études politiques européennes / Studiegroep voor Europese Politiek (GEPE-SEP), with the regular and decisive support of the Japan

---

3 Takato Ueta, "Japan and the european security institutions", in *Japan-EU cooperation: ten years after the Hague Declaration*, *op.cit.*, (see footnote 1), p. 131.

4 Robert Cooper, *The Breaking of Nations, Order and Chaos in the Twenty-First Century*, London, Atlantic Books, 2004.

Foundation along with the active participation of the Japanese mission in the EU, a yearly seminar has been held in Brussels on the EU-Japan relationship. The frequency of the conferences has enabled Japanese, European Scholars, diplomats, politicians, experts, students and TEPSA Friends people attending these activities, to get to know better each other. TEPSA, as a network of research institutes working on European policies, has been especially interested in managing this project which involves the relationship between the EU and Japan, in the broader context of *regional security, development and knowledge-based society*[5]. This serie of yearly conferences is all the more relevant for TEPSA as it contributes to the establishment of a permanent community of scholars dealing with all the dimensions of the EU-Japan relationships. As TEPSA Secretary General, I am especially delighted to introduce this book.

The publication of our yearly meetings will invite any reader to review the EU-Japan relationship in the context of the global economy in fields such as foreign policy, security, and cooperation for world stability. It will also emphasise how much the EU and Japan are promoting a competitive, dynamic and knowledge-based economy. On that respect, it is known that the European Union is lagging behind and that the Lisbon strategy, which aims at reducing the gap with Japan and the USA, is only providing questionable results.

5 All programmes of previous conferences are annexed.

Preface

Éric REMACLE & Takako UETA

Professors respectively at Université libre de Bruxelles (ULB) and International Christian University (ICU), Tokyo

It is our great pleasure to publish this third book, which is a collection of papers from the annual Japan-EU Cooperation Conference in Brussels. This volume mainly includes papers from the 8th conference in 2005 as well as a few papers from the 9th conference in 2006.

The first book, *Japan-EU Cooperation: Ten Years after the Hague Declaration*, was published under the direction of Takako Ueta and Éric Remacle. The Royal Institute of International Affairs (IRRI-KIIB) in Brussels kindly included it in the *Studia Diplomatica* series in Vol.LIV (2001, No.1-2). The second book, which is titled *Japan and Enlarged Europe. Partners in Global Governance*, came out in 2005 and was co-edited by us and published by P.I.E. Peter Lang. These books reflect the development of Japan-EU cooperation in various fields.

The Japan-EU Cooperation Conference has been mainly co-organised by: the Trans European Policy Studies Association and its Belgium branch, the Study Group on European Policies (SEP-GEPE); the Université libre de Bruxelles (ULB) (its Institute for European Studies, Solvay Business School and the Réseau d'études en politique internationale, or REPI); the Garnet-Globalisation and Regionalism Network (Network of Excellence, EU Commission 6th Framework Programme on R&D); and the International Christian University (its Japan's Social Science Research Institute and the Centre of Excellence Programme). The last eight conferences and the 2006 conference were significantly supported by the Japan Foundation and the Japanese Mission to the European Union. We thank them for their continuous contributions to this project.

In this volume's annex, we have included the programs of the last eight conferences, which serve to show how many common interests Japan and the EU have. Through these conference activities, exchanges of views on Japan-EU relations among scholars, diplomats, practitioners, students and citizens have been multiplied.

For many years, the external policy of Japan has become more and more value-driven, which means that Japan has attached increasing importance to democratic values, market economy, and human security. The EU has defined Japan as a "strategic partner." In the meantime, the EU has developed its "actorness" in the field of its external relations.

When adopting the European Security Strategy in December 2003, the European Council has pleaded for a multidimensional holistic approach to security, involving fight against poverty, support to regional integration, addressing global challenges and fighting against transnational threats.

In his policy speech at the Centre for Strategic and International Studies in Washington, D.C. on May 3rd in 2006, "Working Together for a Stable and Prosperous East Asia – Lessons of the Past, a Vision for the Freedom to Dream," Foreign Minister of Japan Mr Taro Aso pointed out three priority objectives in the region in order to establish a multilateral regional framework:

1. Promote freedom, democracy, market economy, the rule of law, and respect for human dignity;
2. Fight against narrow-minded nationalism;
3. Increase transparency and trust, and thus predictability in the fields of economic, political and military affairs in Asia.

Living in a less secure world, Japan-Europe intellectual dialogue and research is useful not only in the field of hard and soft security but also in social, economic, and trade dimensions, since both are facing the same problems as having the same political and economic systems.

This volume covers the EU "Lisbon Agenda," which is relevant to Japan. We have a very clear overview of Japan in view of the Lisbon Agenda. We thank Ambassador Takekazu Kawamura for contributing his insight on this issue as well as the "EU and Japan as Strategic Partners" which was his speech on the occasion of the ninth Japan-EU Cooperation Conference in November 2006. Besides the Lisbon Agenda, this book includes chapters on societal, economic, trade, currency, and security dimensions. We hope that this book will be useful for faculty, students and practitioners to better understand Japan-EU relations and their future.

PART 1

GLOBAL ECONOMIC TRANSFORMATIONS AND THE IMPACT OF KNOWLEDGE-BASED SOCIETY

Opening Address on the "Lisbon Agenda and Japan" at the Trans European Policy Studies Association (TEPSA) International Conference[1]

His Excellency Takekazu KAWAMURA

Ambassador of Japan to the European Union

1. Introduction

It is a great honour and pleasure for me to address such a distinguished group of academics and experts and attend this TEPSA international conference only one month after I came to Brussels as the Ambassador of Japan to the EU. May I first express my sincere appreciation to Professor Remacle (ULB), Professor Ueta (ICU) and Professor Franck (UCL) for their joint efforts in making this event happen.

Common Challenges

For introductory remarks of the first session, I was given the theme of the "Lisbon Agenda and Japan." I would like to take this opportunity to touch upon challenges that prompted the Lisbon Agenda in Europe and reforms in Japan.

Two such challenges, that are often discussed, are: global competition; and ageing populations with declining fertility.

With regard to global competition, China and India enjoyed annual growth rates of 9.5% and 6.7% in 2004 respectively[2]. Japan and the EU, on the other hand, saw their rates stagnating at 2.7% and at 2.4%[3]. In 2004, Japan's birthrate fell to 1.29, while the EU Member States experi-

---

1 On 28 November 2005

2 European Commission, *Economic Forecasts Spring 2005 Statistical Annex Table 55*, 4 April 2005.

3 *Ibid.*

enced similar scales of decrease in general (the average in the EU: 1.48, Italy: 1.29, Germany: 1.34 in 2003)[4]. In respect to ageing populations, it is expected that, in Japan, the population ratio of those over 65 years old will increase from 19.5% in 2004 to 28.7% in 2025. In the EU, the ratio is projected to reach 22.6% in 2025 from 16.4% in 2004[5].

The Similar Goals

Against such a background, the Lisbon Agenda in Europe aims to create "the most dynamic and competitive knowledge-based economy in the world" by 2010. Japan too, is struggling to achieve similar goals to the EU.

2. Japan's Reforms

Since the bursting of bubble at the beginning of the 1990s, Japan had been suffering from continuous deflation and negative growth due to a considerable extent of non-performing loans. Upon his appointment in 2001, Prime Minister Koizumi has been engaged in dynamic structural reforms with his principles of "No Gain without Reforms," "Shift from Public to Private Sectors" and "Shift from Central to Local Government." As a result, the ratio of non-performing loans decreased down to 2.9% in 2005 from 8.4% in 2002[6]. At the same time, the unemployment rate fell from its peak of 5.5% in the beginning of 2003 to 4.2% in September 2005[7]. Looking at these figures, one could say that the Japanese economy has gathered its momentum of recovery. And the Government has begun to shift its policy from "defensive reform" to "offensive reform" for even greater growth.

Japan's efforts on reforms, which somewhat resemble efforts on the Lisbon Agenda, have been taking place in five areas among others. These are: 1) Stimulating R&D; 2) Promoting Intellectual Property; 3) Advancing IT technologies; 4) Making the Government smaller; and

---

4 Ministry of Health, Labour and Welfare, Government of Japan, *Vital Statistics 2004*, Tokyo, 1 June 2005. Eurostat, *Population in Europe 2004*, Luxembourg, 22 September 2005. National Institute of Population and Social Security Research, *Population Statistics of Japan 2005*, Tokyo, 15 April 2005.

5 National Institute of Population and Social Security Research, *Population Projection for Japan (estimated January 2002)*, Tokyo, January 2002; Eurostat, *Population Projections 2004-2050*, Luxembourg, 8 April 2005.

6 Financial Services Agency, Government of Japan, *Statement by the Minister for Financial Services: Normalization of the NPLs Problems of Major Banks*, Tokyo, 25 May 2005, http://www.fsa.go.jp/en/announce/state/20050525-1e.html.

7 Ministry of Internal Affairs and Communications, Government of Japan, *Labour Force Survey*, Tokyo, 2005.

5) Streamlining Employment, Pension and Medical Care. I would like to take a concise, but closer look at each of them.

Stimulating R&D

Universities Closer to the Market

In Japan, the necessity of strengthening linkages between universities and business had long been recognised. The Government promoted, for example, the establishment of "Technology Licensing Organisations." Through these organisations, it aims to make universities able to obtain and utilise intellectual property rights more easily. Nowadays, universities are closer to the market: The total number of University Based Venture Enterprises increased from 98 in 1995 to more than 1,000 in 2004. The number of patent applications increased, and the royalty revenue of universities boosted 150 times as big as 5 years ago; that is from 140,000 Euro (20 Million Yen) in 1999 to 20 Million Euro (2.9 Billion Yen) in 2004[8].

University Reform

Furthermore, the Government implemented university reform in 2004. All of the 99 state-run universities became independent from the Government. The aims of the reform are; 1) to enable universities to carry out activities of their choice; 2) to enhance their attractiveness through competition among universities; 3) to help the universities conduct their R&D and other academic activities, to respond to the needs of society and economy in a more flexible manner.

Tax Incentives for R&D

In addition to the university reform, the Government introduced the R&D tax credit system in 2003, which benefits enterprises by around 10% of their total research expenses. As a result, enterprises are encouraged to undertake more R&D and so their R&D expenses increased by 6.2% in 2004 from the previous year[9].

Government Expenditure on R&D

At the same time, the Government itself has expanded the R&D investment for further development of Japan's science and technology

---

8 Ministry of Economy, Trade and Industry, Government of Japan, *Survey on Technology Licensing Organisations*, Tokyo, 2005.

9 Ministry of Internal Affairs and Communications, Government of Japan, *Report on the Survey of R&D in Japan*, Tokyo, 2004.

capabilities. The Government aims to increase its 5-year R&D expenditure to 170 Billion Euro (24 Trillion Yen) by the end of 2005[10].

Promoting Intellectual Property

In today's world, value-added creativity and originality are increasingly important in economic activities. The competition each enterprise faces is not only about the price, but more importantly about innovative and dynamic technologies.

With the purpose of enhancing Japan's international competitiveness, the Government started focusing on 3 elements of Intellectual Property Rights, namely creation, protection, and its effective exploitation[11]. It was decided to set up the "Intellectual Property Strategy Headquarters" in 2003 with the Prime Minister as its Head. Initiatives taken by the headquarters include: the establishment of the Intellectual Property High Court; the improvement of court procedures; more speedy patent examination; and strengthened measures against counterfeit goods.

As a result, public awareness on the importance of intellectual property is growing in Japan, and the enterprises are strengthening their intellectual property strategies. The royalty balance of patents turned into surplus in 2003[12], and is expanding, while the number of confiscation of counterfeit import products in 2004 tripled in 3 years[13].

Advancing IT

Internet

To "make Japan the most advanced IT nation in the world," the Government adopted the "e-Japan Strategy"[14] in 2001. Following this Strategy, the Government adopted laws and regulations in order to encourage competition through new entries. Following this, within just four years, the price of high-speed and ultra high-speed internet fell by one-third, and Japan successfully achieved the "highest" speed broad-

---

10 The Science and Technology Basic Plan (2001-2005): decided by the Government of Japan on 30 March 2001.

11 *Basic Law on Intellectual Property, Article 1.*

12 Bank of Japan, *Balance of Payments.*

13 The Customs and Tariff Bureau, Government of Japan, *Situation of Import Prohibition of Products Infringing Intellectual Property Rights in 2004*, Tokyo.

14 IT Strategy Headquarters. Government of Japan: http://www.kantei.go.jp/foreign/it/network/0122full_e.html.

band environment with the "lowest" price in the world[15]. The number of subscribers to such broadband internet services quadrupled and reached 20 Million in June 2005[16]. That means 40% of the total households in Japan have the most advanced internet access, and some of households are enjoying 100 MB per second with FTTH. In Belgium for example, the most common internet is ADSL, with only 4 MB per second.

Mobile Phones

I should also mention that the evolution in the area of mobile phone usage is remarkable in Japan. In March 2005, the users of mobile phones increased to 91 Million, of which over 70% have camera installed and over 80% have connection to the internet[17]. Moreover, due to the development of mobile terminals, a Japanese mobile phone enables, not only access to the internet, but also TV broadcast, electronic payment and e-ticket.

Making Government Smaller

In the face of the ageing population, the top priority of Japan's economic and fiscal policy is to reduce the government spending and make the government small and effective.

Japan, in fact, has been continuously reforming its government structure for quite some time if you think about the privatisation of both Telephone and Telegram field and national railway network in 1980s. The benefit the de-regulations since 1990 brought to the Japanese people is estimated to be 100 Billion Euro (14 Trillion Yen) per year, or 800 Euro (110,000 Yen) per person[18].

Nevertheless, Japan's fiscal position is still problematic: at the time of June 2005, Japan's general government budget deficit for the year 2004 accounts for around 6%[19] of the GDP, and the gross debt of the central government is expected to reach 160%[20] of the GDP. Japan thus cannot meet the criteria to introduce the euro. With the aim of achieving

---

15 ITU, *The Portable Internet*, September 2004, Ministry of Internal Affairs and Communications, *Price Comparison Report as of February 2004*, 31 August 2004.

16 Ministry of Internal Affairs and Communications, Government of Japan, *Statistics of Broadband Service Subscription*, Tokyo, September 2005.

17 Ministry of Internal Affairs and Communications, Government of Japan, Statistics of Mobile *Service Subscription*, Tokyo, September 2005.

18 Cabinet Office, Government of Japan, *Economic Benefit of Deregulations since 1990*, Tokyo, 2003.

19 Organisation for Economic Co-operation and Development, *OECD Economic Outlook* 77 (2005), 24 May 2005.

20 *Ibid.*

sustainable finance, in other words, to avoid leaving burdens to the next generation, the Government aims to achieve a surplus in the primary balance early in the 2010s[21].

After the outstanding victory of the LDP in the general election held this September, the Postal Privatisation Law was passed. The number of affected postal service officers, who have actually a status of government employee, is estimated to be 270,000. For further downsizing of government, it was also determined that more than 5% of a total of 690,000 government officials, excluding those postal service people, is to be cut within 5 years[22].

I should note that the recent economic recovery we are witnessing in Japan has different characteristics from the past. It was mainly achieved through private sectors' dynamism, rather than with the help of government spending. In order to facilitate this dynamism even more, re-thinking about roles of the public sector may become an increasingly important agenda for Japan.

Employment, Pension and Medical Care

Due to the rapidly declining and ageing population, social security expenditure in Japan reached 17.5% in relation to the GDP in 2001. In order to reduce the financial burden, the Government started implementing reforms in 2002 in the Medical Insurance System in that the youngest age eligible for medical care for the elderly people would be raised from 70 to 75 years old. The Government also started reforming the Pension System, such as by restraining the future premium level.

Moreover, in response to the declining population, the Government is striving to achieve a society where women and the elderly can work comfortably. For example, the Government is promoting parental leave and aims to increase such leave from its current 64% to 80% for all working women, and from 0.3% to 10% for men. It is also facilitating to raise the retirement age up to 65 from 60 years old[23].

Here in Europe, the Lisbon Agenda is also setting the same goal of increasing the female employment rate. I personally and strongly believe that without the active involvement of women in workforce, "the

21 Cabinet Office (Council on Economic and Fiscal Policy), Government of Japan, *Reform and Perspectives – FY2002 Revision (Cabinet Decision)*, Tokyo, 24 January 2003.

22 Basic Direction on Personnel Cost Reform: decided by Council on Economic and Fiscal Policy, Government of Japan on 14 Nov. 2005.

23 Ministry of Health, Labour and Welfare, Government of Japan, *Annual Report on Health, Labour and Welfare 2003-2004*, Tokyo, 21 June 2004.

most dynamic and competitive knowledge-based economy" would be very difficult to achieve. The Japanese Government's efforts have shown certain effects since the number of female members in the Government Councils doubled within ten years, and new female employees working in the Government on a managerial course increased to over 20% of total new employees for the first time[24]. In addition, the female employment rate reached 57.4% in 2004, which is higher than 55.7%, the average rate in the EU[25].

3. Conclusion: Japan-EU Cooperation

Japan and the EU have a lot in common. We share the basic values of society as well as many similar challenges. For further and sound development of the world economy, both Japan and the EU can contribute more, and the two sides should solidify our partnership even more. In that respect, the continuation of implementing existing frameworks such as the Regulatory Reform Dialogue, the EU-Japan Business Dialogue Round Table, the Intellectual Property Rights Dialogue is essential. Moreover, cultural and academic exchanges such as the series of the "EU-Japan Year of People to People Exchanges," including this conference, should continuously take place.

It is also from this same perspective that I applaud the efforts of the organisers of this conference, namely, the Trans European Policy Studies Association, the International Christian University, the Université libre de Bruxelles (ULB), the Garnet-Globalisation and Regionalism Network, and its sponsor, the Japan Foundation.

I extend my best wishes for the success of this session and the conference as a whole.

Thank you very much.

---

24 Cabinet Office, Government of Japan, *Annual Report on Gender Equality 2005.*

25 Organisation for Economic Co-operation and Development, *Employment Outlook 2005.*

The Knowledge-based Society, the New World Economy

Implications for Japan and Europe

Kálmán DEZSÉRI

Senior research fellow, Institute for World Economics
Hungarian Academy of Sciences, Budapest
Assistant professor Central European University, Budapest

It is commonly thought all over the world that knowledge is and will certainly become, in the future, the most important driving force to achieve prosperity as well as long-term and sustainable development. Moreover, knowledge became the main factor, which determines the international competitiveness of economies and countries. The qualitative and quantitative differences in the way of accessing and using the knowledge are the contentious point between societies and countries in the world. Therefore, one of the most important development challenges for institutions in charge of national and global governance is the acceleration of accessibility and the improvement in the affordability of knowledge; consequently, the divisions about the global knowledge can be reduced. Unless these efforts succeed, the gap between the forerunner countries and those lagging behind in terms of economic development will increase further. This fact deeply influences the way the new world economy is shaped. Europe and Japan have to tackle a complex package of issues in order to create a thorough and balanced knowledge-based society. The global competition compels countries to take the necessary steps with far-reaching impacts.

1. Knowledge-based Economy and Society

The knowledge-based economy and society are a very complex and broad phenomenon. Its analysis needs for multidisciplinary methods. They imply various dimensions and aspects.

a) The knowledge-based economy has a very powerful driving force – in terms of technology – that means a rapid growth of information and telecommunication technologies (ICT). Due to this technological revolution in the information and telecommunication technology, information has become easy to access, to transfer, to replicate. However, information and knowledge are not placed on an equal footing: knowledge has remained a long and costly process to create and to get access to.

b) Under these new conditions, telecommunication and networking have got into all the spheres of human life and activities. The new technology forced the human beings to work in a radically different way and created new spheres of activities, which were unimaginable up to now. The information society has become true.

c) The speed of the technical development is justified by the fact that every 3 to 5 years a new generation of ICT appears on the market and within the laboratories. It has microeconomic implications. The ICT companies are among the largest corporations and the ICT sector has grown at the highest rate in the economies.

d) Knowledge, based on information and supported by cultural and spiritual values, has become an independent force and the most decisive factor of social, economic, technological and cultural transformation. The most important specific features of the knowledge-based society, that societies, institutions and economic players must adjust to, are the following:

- the dramatic decrease in time and space;
- the dramatic acceleration of technological development;
- the increase in R&D costs and the reduction of commercial life-cycles of newly developed products;
- the increasing importance of networks;
- the need for well-managed alliances between the providers of knowledge, the players that exploit knowledge and the skilful people that participate in both processes.

e) The emerging knowledge-based economy has been influencing other spheres and areas of societal activities everywhere in the world. These spheres and areas include institutional and innovation systems, human resource development, and so on. The knowledge-based economy provides the possibility to speed up the economic development and social progress in countries of the world. If a country is developed, it is endowed with a developed knowledge-based economy; however, if a country is lagging behind, a knowledge-based economy only constitutes a small fraction of its economy. Under such conditions, one of the most important challenges and opportunities for emerging countries put forward by the changing business environment is the classical division of labour between more and less developed countries. Knowledge and knowledge-based economy provide an opportunity to depart from the path to development suggested by models of traditional dependency.

f) The accumulation of knowledge as a factor of production and competitiveness, which is different from any other accumulation processes the economic history has ever witnessed. Knowledge as an infinitely renewable resource, is subject to rapid changes the education system is expected to foresee when developing the curricula.

g) The role of the nation states has to be re-assessed, re-considered in knowledge-based economies. Their role in managing a public education system, and in determining the adequate mixture between social cohesion and competition needs to be thoroughly analyzed; moreover, when it is necessary, their competence should shift to upper levels (e.g. international or integration, like EU) and to intermediate (regional) levels.

h) When decision-makers in the field of economic policy point out that – within the human capital of a knowledge-based economy – skilled people are the most important factors of competitiveness, they have to restructure and not only invest in the education system; but they must also reform the regulations thereof and make additional and long-term investments in the health care institutions.

Knowledge in a knowledge-based economy and society cannot substitute the two other factors of production, namely labour, capital and the economic and entrepreneurial infrastructure. However, knowledge has become, a key factor for the increase in efficiency of the others; it has turned to be the major source of competitive advantages.

From the microeconomic perspective, knowledge is only a necessary but insufficient condition for market success. Knowledge is valuable for firms when it is useful for achieving marketable technological innovation. Firms must be able to finance new technology ventures, to hire and train skilled scientists, engineers, managers and production workers, and then they can attempt successfully to be accepted by markets. Firms increasingly depend on specialised knowledge in a number of areas to provide endlessly a renewable source of competitive advantages. It is increasingly necessary for firms to be involved in a complex array of cooperative arrangements.

Under the new conditions, leading companies develop holistic models of corporate cultures built upon shifting duties, team structures, and high levels of expedient personnel turnovers. The traditional efforts to manage workers shift to the management of relationships with increasingly demanding customers. The unit of analysis for innovation is neither a product nor a technology, but a business concept[1]. Business concept innovation, and not only technology, enables to create new wealth.

We must bear in mind that new technological advances have diminished transportation, telecommunications and computational costs, while increasing the global flows of information. In the meantime, globalisation is expanding the movement of goods, services, capital investment (portfolio and direct), people, ideas and the spread of technology itself. In a globalised world, successful firms, notwithstanding their size, will be allowed to join the global network and meet global production standards. On this basis, the location would become irrelevant in a world of global input-factor arbitrage. Global networks enable industries to locate more efficiently labour, materials and supplies while reducing the cost. The knowledge-based society has been shaped in the context of globalisation, while always encountering stiff competition. However, global cooperation will bring efficiency and mutual benefits.

Innovation is supposed to follow a linear model. It implies that innovation sequentially proceeds from new scientific discoveries to new process, product and services. Innovation can take many forms, including incremental improvements to existing products or processes, applications of existing technologies to new markets and the use of new technologies to serve existing markets. Science and knowledge play key roles in innovations but are not necessarily the main drivers of new processes, products and services in all the areas. The new ideas grasped for innovations result from many sources. Nevertheless science and knowledge became necessary in the fields of innovation and product development process, and particularly in information technology and biotechnology.

The progress made in the implementation of knowledge-based economy and society is very unequal according to the countries of the world. The very high concentration of R&D, which characterised the 20th century, is still prevailing. The ongoing and overwhelming role of about twenty four countries in R&D activities still persists. The prevailing roles are played by the USA, EU (especially the UK, Germany, France), Japan and Russia. China and India are increasingly devoting resources to R&D activities in absolute and relative terms, as well. We also notice a handful of small, albeit technically advanced countries, which belong to the "group of 20" and which are quickly catching up with the most advanced countries. The competition between these countries has been

---

1 Hamel, 2000.

increasingly stiff and the countries are endlessly challenging the positions of each other.

2. Challenges and Implications for Japan and the European Union

In the 1990s, ICTs proved their capabilities to be a powerful motor of economic growth and competitiveness. Business and consumers in the USA have not wasted any time to benefit from the technological revolution. As a result, USA's business became more competitive and its economy reached high and unprecedented growth rate. Japan and the EU had to recognise that both economies must become much more digitalised and that the further economic development should be based on a much more efficient use of knowledge. The Japanese and the European economies have to face the demands of the time, the challenges of globalisation and the creation of a knowledge-based society. As far as the EU is concerned, there are some additional tasks. Some work still remain to be done for the member states to achieve the single market, to help countries which lag behind in order to catch up with the average EU level. These tasks cannot be fully separated from the general goal of creating a knowledge-based economy in Europe. It means that the European system of goals is much more complex than Japan's.

The expression 'information society' was first formulated and the phenomenon was first described in Japan. This expression is a translation of the Japanese *joko shakai*. It was introduced into the social science in the early 1970s by Yojeni Masuda who published a book entitled *The Information Society as Post-industrial Society* and based on the complexity of this issue in 1980. In this book, the information society is said to be the successor of the industrial society. He referred to information society as the highest stage of societal evolution, while drawing an analogy with the biological evolution. In the early 1990s, the Institute of Information Studies, made up of the Aspen Institute and other agencies in the USA, published an almanac for 1993-1994. It was entitled *The Knowledge-based Economy: The Nature of the Information Age in the 21st Century*. The United Nations immediately endorsed the term afterwards, and gave it a clearer definition in 1996. It defines a knowledge-based economy as an economy whose key elements are the possession, control, production and usefulness of knowledge and intellectual resources.

The expression 'knowledge-value society' was also introduced[2] in Japan. The term was defined as 'a society where the value of knowledge

2 By Taichi Sakaiya in his book written in 1985.

is the primary source of economic growth and corporate profits'. During the 1960s and 1970s, the Japanese society was making all possible efforts at shaping an industrialised society, based on the mass production of standardised goods. The education system was built up to foster highly patient and cooperative people while giving less importance originality and creativity so that those people perfectly fit to the work in standardised mass-production industries. Moreover, the media and other information sources were centralised in Tokyo; the products – which were manufactured according to the same standards – spread throughout the society under the dispatch of similar information.

If we look at the economic history of Japan, this conclusion should fit everybody: as a result of the process of fast industrialisation in the 1960s and 1970s, the revolution in the Japanese knowledge value was delayed. This is due to the careful development by the Japanese society of a government administrative organisation, an industrial structure, a financial system, employment practices, an education system, and an information environment that were appropriate for a standardised mass production society[3]. However, this pattern of development did not really meet the prerequisites of a knowledge-based society. In a knowledge-based society, creative labour is a major factor and the economy mainly includes intellectual enterprises, high-tech parks in which the entrepreneur is also the scientist. Such a society is characterised by a positive synergistic interaction of information, knowledge and effect. To achieve these new conditions, the Japanese society has also to implement several and sometimes deeply rooted changes or reforms through adequate policy steps.

As mentioned above, the task of Europe is more complex. In the EU, substantial changes are necessary such as a quick integration of the huge intellectual resources of the economies in transition into a European intellectual pool, stimulating the development of the participating countries, so that the goal of creating the knowledge-based integrated economy could be achieved. Every country can benefit from the development of a knowledge-based economy to become a participant on a more equal footing in the global development process. The success will influence and determine the quality of life and the working conditions of every citizen in the member states as well as the overall competitiveness of their industries and services. To do so, the European Council at the Lisbon meeting in March 2000 set a new and very ambitious goal for the EU member states: to achieve the most prosperous and competitive knowledge-based society and economy in the world by 2010.

---

3 Sakaiya, 2000.

Many experts and critics of the current situation argue that the requirements for creating a knowledge-based economy make the restructuration of the EU budget necessary. Currently, the EU budget is characterised by the protection of national interest: about half of the budget is aimed at financing the common agricultural policy and must be radically and urgently changed. Without cross-border centres of excellence, the EU will be nothing more than the addition of 25 countries. In this case, Lisbon targets will never be fully reached, and the USA and Japan will be far ahead within a decade.

The main goals of the European countries in the near future are:

1. The member states should boost investment in research on information and communication technologies (ICT) by 80%. Europe lags behind in ICT research, only investing EUR 80 per head as compared to EUR 350 in Japan and EUR 400 in the USA. The member states should put more money into ICT research and get more out of it, by doing more to encourage the commercial take-up of promising applications.

2. The member states should promote the development of an inclusive European information society. They should help to bridge the gap between the information society namely "haves and have-nots," and share the best practices in electronically-enabled public services. To do so, the European Commission takes flagship initiatives on technologies for an ageing society, clever vehicles and digital libraries.

3. The member states should create an open and competitive EU single market for information society and media services within the EU. This includes an efficient management of radio spectrum: the purpose of it is to free up common wave bands for obtaining promising new applications; to modernise the "TV without Frontiers" rules to meet the needs content consumption on-demand[4]; and update the EU telecom rules, by reducing the cost of using mobile abroad.

Moreover, it includes that the EU's main competitors devote over one third of their total public and private research spending on ICT, while Europe spends around 20%. Europe can become more globally competitive if the share of research spending on ICT R&D increases. It is of utmost importance that the role of private industries should increase. Investment in ICT can support the most effectively future growth and jobs. Now, the gap in ICT research investment makes up about half of the whole gap in research spending between the EU and the USA. The European Commission suggested to allocate EUR 1,822

---

4 Content consumption is distribution of digital content (e.g. music, photo, film, text, information, game, etc.) through information technology instruments (e.g. internet, mobile phone, etc.).

million annually to ICT research. This would represent an 80% increase in Community ICT research support.

The facts show that the European industry has a huge potential to innovate and deploy new ICTs, but the industry needs to invest in the incorporation of these technologies in its products, so as to sharpen their international competitive edge. For example, nearly half of the 100 biggest European companies do embed systems R&D and most of the top 25 European R&D spenders rely on them. These are not only ICT firms – they come from the automotive, aerospace, consumer electronics, medical systems, industrial automation and energy sectors too. Embedded electronics and software are expected to make up 33% of the value of medical equipment by 2009. Embedded systems research has a pervasive impact on industrial innovation generally. Industrial research investment in embedded systems in Europe is estimated at around EUR 15-20 billion per year, and firms that get involved in cooperative research are well-placed to benefit from its applications.

The use of ICT technology and the knowledge-based society must have and will have far reaching impacts on the European society. ICT technology should provide the opportunity to get a better health care and education, a better quality of life, some security and social inclusion. They should be made as widely available as possible in the EU. By 2010, European citizens and businesses should be able to use secure and convenient electronic identification to access public services in their country or in any other member state. Today's incompatibility of public sector electronic identification and authentication systems prevents from using public services across borders; it questions the access to a public service in another country such as electronic health prescriptions, or pan-European services such as jobs portals. Electronic government is moving beyond online information to fully transactional, citizen-centric and personalised services that deliver the high added value that citizens expect everywhere in Europe.

To do so, the research and innovation in egovernment are to be more systematically supported. It is commonly accepted in the member states that egovernment should be characterised by user-centred design, user satisfaction, and support for deploying large-scale pilot projects in electronic identification and electronic public procurement. The egovernment 2010 Action Plan which was recently presented looks at the further challenges: ensuring social inclusion, making efficiency and effectiveness true, strengthening participation in a democratic decision-making, delivering high impact applications, and putting key enablers in place.

ICT will and can play a crucial role in reaching the Lisbon goals. The common success will depend on how much the member states are committed to it through national plans and will contribute in delivering a sustained growth and skilled jobs. All the member states prepared national reform programmes (NRPs), which deal with the issue of ICT. In some of these NRPs, the ICT play a prominent role. The main areas listed for action are e-government, broadband and digital literacy. Many NRPs refer to the EU I2010 framework; they recognise therefore common objectives. The main tools proposed for achieving NRP goals are legislation and public funding. Other levers, such as the creation of new institutional frameworks, co-operation networks among ICT players or the promotion of standardisation efforts, are also considered. There are also other aims, which are to be achieved through upgrades of the existing infrastructure. Many NRPs propose e-literacy and e-skills programmes to improve human capital. Plans in this area have the purpose of introducing the ICT knowledge into school curricula, providing on-line libraries and addressing the digital divide, in particular between better and less educated and between urban and rural residents.

3. Comparison of the Current Situations in the EU and Japan

The EU member states and Japan have made so far lot of efforts to meet the challenge of creating their knowledge-based economy and society. They compete against each other and in the meantime, they compete with the USA, which has made more progress in this field. Their achievements should be measured and compared. A comparison should include a collection of some indicators, which can characterise a knowledge-based society[5]. Data of the EU member states and Japan need for additional data about the USA to provide an evaluation of the relative positions of these countries.

Generally speaking, the knowledge-based society has arrived in some parts of Europe and not everyone has benefited from it. In other EU member states, the movement has been slower which makes the EU very heterogonous in that respect too. The main division line has not always been between the old and the new member states. A north-south

---

5 It is partly based on available statistical information and on indicators of the SIBIS project (Statistical indicators benchmarking the information society, www.sibis-eu.org). This project carried out a large-scale representative survey of the population in all the 15 EU and 8 prospective member states and the US in 2002. This report gives a brief description of the current situation and past developments concerning major dimensions of the European knowledge society, such as economic, social and technological development, quality of work and life, etc.

distinction about a knowledge-based society can still be observed in Europe, with the Nordic countries and the Netherlands leading on nearly all of the knowledge-based society indicators. The gap is particularly strong on ICT aspects. The southern countries (Portugal, Greece, Spain and partly Italy and France) lag far behind the other countries. This digital division is in line with a strong economic north-south divide. In comparison with Japan and the USA, the EU member states and the EU average figures showed a very mixed picture. As the distinction between the best and the worst performing EU member states was often substantial, the EU average in comparison with the USA and Japanese figures not usually superior but just the opposite.

Various indicators can be listed and evaluated on the basis of Table 1.

Traditional media availability can be measured by such indicators like 'daily newspaper circulation', 'radio receivers' and 'television receivers' which still reflect the most common 'traditional' media used in different life spheres and for different purposes. In comparison with the new media (e.g. Internet, mobile phones), traditional media is available to almost the whole population of the developed world since skill requirements and financial restrictions are lower, while the level of familiarity is extraordinarily high due to an experienced use over decades. Japan reaches the upper EU standards, mainly due to its high television rate.

ICT availability in households and Internet access, indicators provide information on enablers for the participation of individuals in the information society, including the access to the increasing number of related online services in various parts of the daily life, well-being, etc. It can be assumed that these ICT-based tools will become even more important for most of the individuals in the fulfilment of many tasks and needs in the future; consequently, they will be key tools in one's daily life in the knowledge-based society. Germany – with a rather average performance in the EU 15 – slightly ranks above Japan.

Table 1. Main indicators of knowledge-based society

	EU			Japan	USA
	range	average			
		EU-25	EU-15		
Radio, TV, daily newspaper per 1,000 inhabitants (1995)					
radio receivers	1,450 (UK) – 250 (P)			900	2100
TV receivers	600 (F) – 250 (EL)			700	800
daily newspaper circulation	470 (S) – 75 (P)			345	460
ICT & Internet access in households (2000) in %					
mobile phone subscribers	88 (L) – 9 (LT)			52	38
internet users	58 (S) – 3 (LT)			30	57
internet hosts	14 (FI) – 1 (LT)			4	29
personal computer	51 (S) – 1 (LT)			32	59
Patterns of ICT usage (2002)					
E-mail users / 100 households	68 (NL) – 20 (P)			.	70
DSL, cable modem lines and broadband / 100 inhabitants	4.1 (S) – 0.01 (SK)			1.1	3.2
Education: pupil/teacher ratio (2000)					
pre-primary school	44 (LV) – 5.5 (DK)			31	21
primary-school	22 (IE) – 10 (DK)			21	15
secondary school	17.5 (UK) – 7.5 (E)			14	14.5
Patterns of ICT usage by 15-year-olds (2000): everyday computer availability and usage					
availability at home in %	90 (S) – 22 (LV)			.	69
availability at school in %	48 (DK) – 5 (D)			.	45
usage at home in %	61 (S) – 18 (LV)			.	48
usage at school in %	22 (DK) – 3 (CZ)			.	18
Computers connected to internet (2000)					
in schools in %	88 (LU) – 24 (I)			36	39

Spending on education per student USD					
pre-primary		4,000		3,800	7,500
primary		4,800		5,800	7,500
lower secondary		5,900		6,000	8,400
upper secondary		6,000		7,000	9,000
tertiary		9,000		11,500	20,100
Expenditure on tertiary educational institutions as % of GDP (2002)					
public		1.1		0.4	1.2
private		0.2		0,7	1.4
total		1.3		1.1	2.6
Students in tertiary education as a % of people aged 20-29 (2002/03 academic year)					
	44.6 (FI) – 5.4 (LU)	22.5	21.7	.	.
Public expenditure on education as a % of GDP (2002)					
	8.5 (DK) – 4.0 (EL)	5.2	5.2	3.6	5.4
R&D expenditure in billion EUR					
2003	54.5 (D) – 0.01 (MT)	188.2	184.7	119.7	251.6
Government budget appropriation or outlays on R&D as a % of GDP (2003)					
	1.01 (FI) – 0.18 (LV)	0.77	0.79	0.72	1.07
R&D intensity (R&D expenditure as a % of GDP)					
1999	3.65 (S) – 0.51 (LT)	1.87	1.92	2.96	2.63
2003	3.98 (S) – 0.27 (MT)	1.92	1.97	3.15	2.59
2004	3.74 (S) – 0.29 (MT)	1.90	1.95	3.25	.
R&D expenditure financed by the Business enterprise sector in %					
2000	90.7 (LU) – 17.5 (CY)	55.2	55.5	72.4	69.3
2003	80.4 (LU) – 16.7 (LT)	54.3	54.6	74.5	63.1
R&D personnel as a % of persons employed (2003)					
	0.64 (CY) – 3.1 (FI)	1.44	1.54	1.66	.

Legend: A = Austria, B = Belgium, CZ = Czech Rep., CY = Cyprus, D = Germany, DK = Denmark, E = Spain, EE = Estonia, EL = Greece, F = France, FI = Finland, HU = Hungary, I = Italy, IE = Ireland, L = Luxemburg, LT = Latvia, LV = Lithuania, LU = Luxembourg, MT = Malta, NL = the Netherlands, P = Portugal, PL = Poland, S = Sweden, SI = Slovenia, SK = Slovakia, UK = United Kingdom.

Source: Statistical Yearbook of Japan, EC Science and technology in Europe – Data 1990-2004, Advancement of the knowledge-based society Comparing Europe, the USA and Japan.

There are different ways of using ICT. Networking is a key part of the knowledge-based society, by supporting teamwork and communication processes and thereby by increasing productivity and improving work quality. It is an increasingly common phenomenon that social networks are enhanced through ICT-based communication, and that new networks are established. The possibility of using E-mail was a revolution in the world of communication and networking since it provides the fastest way to transmit large amounts of data. The number of 'e-mail users' indicates how much the e-mail, as a way of communication, has penetrated among and personal and business partners, by increasingly substituting for telephony or postal letters. European frontrunners like the Netherlands and Denmark have almost reached the USA levels of penetration, but in most of the other countries, particularly in southern European countries, this way of communication is not widespread yet. Japan's ratio is slightly higher than that of the EU's average.

DSL, cable modem and other broadband lines, which are the most advanced and fastest but also the most expensive of the Internet access technologies, are overtaking analogue and ISDN lines. Improvements in high-speed access to online data speed up networking and therefore becomes necessary in a competitive working environment. Broadband connections in private households are also used. However, the more work in office turns into work at home such as teleworking, the higher the work-related usage purposes will become. Sweden, the USA and the Netherlands have the highest rank concerning broadband connectivity, while surprisingly in Luxembourg, in Ireland and in the UK, some broadband connection lines are hardly found. Japan is lagging behind compared to the more advanced countries.

In the process of setting up a knowledge-based society, the education and its infrastructure play specific roles. Obviously, the addition of pre-primary, primary and secondary education is the foundation stone of the knowledge-based society, while enabling pupils to learn and think and while transmitting the basic accepted values. In this context, the pupil/teacher ratio indicates certain quality in education: a low ratio is supposed to stand for a better attendance and control of the pupils and thus contributes to better learning methods. The number of teaching hours, as another indicator, represents the learning input of the pupils, which merely provides a quantitative measure without drawing qualitative conclusions.

(a) In the EU, the general trend is that the younger the pupils are, the fewer teachers per pupil ratio remain. In the new member states of the EU, the pupil/teacher ratios are notably higher for the younger pupils. Denmark heads the European countries, by maintaining a maximum attendance of ten pupils per teacher, while Italy, Spain, Greece and Austria also provide a proper education infrastructure with better ratios. In pre-primary and secondary schools, the United Kingdom has the highest (worst) pupil/teacher ratio within the EU. Ireland shows the worst performance in primary schools. The ratios of Japan tended to be close to the worst European ratios. It means that Japan's infrastructure of education is not better than that of the EU. However, the level of basic education and schooling assessed by the PISA Report[6] shows that Japan and Finland have the highest ranks, whereas Germany falls behind.

(b) Concerning the number of teaching hours – as another indicator – the USA goes far beyond other countries such as the EU member states. On the other hand, Japan's education system, well known for attaining a broad middle class, is characterised by few teaching hours per year and high pupil/teacher ratio. This shows that the proper effectiveness of a school system can also be achieved by other means, such as, for example, a higher disciplinary standard which would assume that discipline and effectiveness are embedded in the cultural system of Japan.

ICT education plays an increasing role in the education. Nowadays, the young people of 15-years-old constitute the future generation of young workers in 2015. Since the use of computers and Internet access will become increasingly necessary in most of the jobs as well as in education, the required skills need to be learnt at the earliest stage possible. In this case, skills do not only refer to technical abilities (such as how to use a PC or access the Internet) but also to qualitative skills (e.g. helping the pupil to assess the quality of the web content). Widespread ICT availability in public schools also helps to avoid the development of a digital divide, allowing an access to pupils who are deprived of and cannot afford them internet access at home.

For the young generations, the school and family environment can both provide a daily ICT availability. The statistics show that school access is still generally less usual than home access. Noticeably, the USA, which registers the highest amount of personal computers per inhabitant, substantially lags behind Sweden, is the 'home availability' frontrunner, where almost every child gets computer access at home. In Japan the situation is better than the average situation in the EU.

6 PISA: OECD's Programme for International Student Assessment. It is a collaborative effort among the member countries of the OECD to measure how well young adults, at age 15 and approaching the end of compulsory schooling, are prepared to meet the challenges of today's knowledge societies. PISA measures reading, mathematical and scientific literacy on continuous scales.

In most of the countries, a huge gap can be found between the general computer availability and the daily computer availability at school. This gap obviously makes the distinction between schools providing computer lessons in closed computer rooms compared to the schools providing free access at any time or using it as an additional element for other subjects taught. Germany well illustrates the former example of school. Denmark, the USA and Sweden have reached a higher stage of provision, with general and everyday availability and as a result get closer to a similar range. Some new member states (e.g. Czech Republic, Hungary and Latvia) get close to the EU average level in terms of school ICT equipment; however, their rates about home access remain low. Germany falls behind, along with Portugal, France, Greece and Italy when we refer to the Internet connectivity of schools, whereas in Luxembourg and Finland almost all the computers in schools have web access. The situation in Japan is similar to Germany's. Slightly more than a third of computers at school were connected to internet.

In order to achieve positive economic performance and growth, a governmental support for R&D and technological development is required. Governments must serve as a model for private sector companies and invest an adequate percentage of GDP in R&D. The prospective but not yet competitive technologies such as the wind power or solar energy need to be fostered in order to boost the overall technological development, growth and employment. Both in the EU and Japan, governmental expenditures on R&D reveal this political concern about technological innovation: this is especially the case when the further development and trade of R&D results is difficult, problematic or still at an early stage. Within the EU, Sweden, Germany and Finland are at the top of the list. The average of the EU member states was substantially lower. The ratio of the Japanese government's expenditures on R&D to the GDP did not exceed the EU average. The relatively low share of governmental expenditures on R&D in Japan is offset by the high contribution of the private business sector for the financing of R&D activities. The share of the Japanese private business sector is the highest in the world. It was 74.5% in 2003 and even exceeded the USA's. The share of the European private business contribution to the R&D is significantly smaller.

The data of the total R&D expenditure as a % of GDP (that is R&D intensity) show substantial differences. In 2003, the ratio of Japan (3.15%) exceeded the one of the EU average (1.92%) and of the USA (2.59%). In spite of its high ratio, Japan has not broken the records. There are two EU member states (Sweden 3.98% and Finland 3.48%) where the R&D expenditures to GDP ratios were higher than Japan's.

R&D activities can also be assessed by analyzing the development of the ICT area. ICT currently constitute one of the prime focuses of R&D in industrialised nations. Close to 30% of all the R&D budgets, both public and private, are devoted to such technologies. However, the level of spending considerably varies from one country to another: the USA and Japan are strikingly ahead the European countries, whose R&D budgets, albeit disparate, remain limited[7]. Usually three indicators are used for measuring the extent to which IC technologies are applied in a nation. These three indicators combine a number of sub-indicators, especially the use of ICT, which consists of ten sub-indicators. In this case, Denmark leads, while Japan falls behind.

The total volume of ICT markets in the various countries, calibrated by GDP, gives a measure of ICT penetration of the economy and, indirectly evidences the progress made towards the knowledge-based economy. In order to evaluate the use of ICT in a nation, many sub-indicators were used. These sub-indicators appeared in Table 2. The Nordic countries are the leaders while Japan falls behind.

Table 2. ICT indicators

	Index	Home internet access	Internet use in the population	Cellular phone subscribers	Internet in schools	Workers who use computers for work
Finland	0.46	0.15	0.19	1.10	0.29	0.28
Sweden	0.21	1.01	0.67	0.96	0.16	0.88
Denmark	0.71	1.10	1.15	0.62	1.78	1.18
Netherlands	-0.16	1.10	0.35	0.35	-0.79	-0.03
Germany	-0.41	-0.71	-1.58	-0.40	-0.92	-1.38
UK	-0.57	-0.62	-0.77	0.21	-0.52	-0.93
Japan	-1.39	-1.57	n/a	-1.22	n/a	n/a
USA	0.05	-0.45	n/a	-1.63	n/a	n/a

	Internet dial-up access costs		ADSL prices	Home ADSL access	Availability of government services online
	residential	business			
Finland	1.66	0.62	-0.23	-0.59	1.14
Sweden	-0.90	-1.34	-0.02	0.00	0.71
Denmark	-0.43	-0.02	0.67	0.48	0.63
Netherlands	-1.13	-1.34	0.19	1.07	-1.34
Germany	-0.20	0.25	1.16	0.71	-1.00
UK	0.03	0.51	-1.76	-1.66	-0.14
Japan	n/a	n/a	n/a	n/a	n/a
USA	0.96	1.31	n/a	n/a	n/a

Source: Knowledge-based society barometer (2002).

[7] Pouillot and Puissochet, 2002.

The indicator for eCommerce comprises four sub-indicators: 1) Internet users who have purchased online; 2) percentage of companies selling online; 3) percentage of companies buying online; and 4) the number of secure servers.

The issue of S&T productivity is getting increasingly important. The process of commercialisation and increasing competitiveness is reflected in the emergence of new activities and new products for the domestic and export markets. This new situation induces restructuring of the existing activities through strong structural changes towards high tech and knowledge intensive activities, and through the modernisation of the old economy by the spread of new technologies. The competencies to commercialise the knowledge and the additional assets to knowledge are also required for competitiveness in the knowledge-based economy. Although the measure of the workforce's productivity in science and technology is a difficult task, several indicators have been developed. With this indicator, the USA and Sweden are the leaders while Japan, Denmark and the UK fall behind.

The variation in entrepreneurial attitudes can be examined by considering for example that, nowadays, in the USA many of the largest companies are very young while in Europe, all of the biggest companies have the same size in 1998 as in 1960. This point can be evidenced by the measure of entrepreneurship and venturing, where the USA together with the Netherlands are the leaders whereas Germany and Japan fall behind.

4. Summary of the Comparison

The performance of some sample of countries can be compared in terms of information society, knowledge-based society, knowledge-value society and sustainable development measures[8]. Whatever the measures in use, Sweden is ahead. In the measure of information society, Japan and Finland are the first; but then do not prevail any longer; Japan is falling quite steeply. Germany and the United Kingdom are poorly performers. The Netherlands, Denmark and the USA fall behind in the measure of information society but improve their performance when we move onto the knowledge-value society measure. The results are given in Table 3.

The information society measure consists of three components. These components first evaluate the level of basic education and schooling together with the skills and competencies of the general public; it

[8] This part draws on the Knowledge society barometer (2002).

focuses then on investments in science and technology. Finland and Sweden are the leaders in terms of investment in human resources while Germany falls behind (section (A) of Table 3).

A country's development towards a knowledge-based society is assessed on three measures: pool of human resources in science and technology, applications of ICT technologies, and the impact of R&D on national economic competitiveness and employment. In this case, Sweden and the USA are ahead, while the Netherlands falls behind (section (B) of Table 3).

The three measures used to evaluate the knowledge-value features of a society include the adaptation of innovative procedures, the level of entrepreneurship and venturing, and the role played by the innovation networks in the society. The results show that, the Netherlands is the first, followed by Sweden, whereas Japan falls behind (section (C) of Table 3).

Sustainable development is an important aspect. In order to evaluate a nation's performance with respect to sustainable development, measures were used in relation with the conception of a society which is more prosperous and fairer, and which promises a cleaner, safer, and healthier environment. In this matter, Sweden is the leader, while the USA falls behind.

Innovative society measures have particular importance. The knowledge-based society barometer can also be examined according to human, organisational and economy-wide dimensions. First, measures focus on an individual's capabilities and attitudes. Then, an organisation's investments are evaluated – be they are related to research, development, adaptation of ICT, the establishment of innovative procedures in the firm, or the setting up of environmentally friendly processes.

Table 3. Knowledge-based society performance measures

(A) Information society measures				
	Index	Basic education and schooling	General skills and knowledge	Investment in R&D
Finland	0.78	1.08	0.25	1.01
Sweden	0.77	-0.10	1.37	1.03
Denmark	-0.24	-0.74	0.38	-0.36
Netherlands	-0.25	n/a	-0.01	-0.49
Germany	-0.63	-1.22	-0.57	-0.09
UK	-0.41	0.53	-0.76	-1.00
Japan	0.33	1.13	n/a	-0.46
USA	-0.42	-0.69	-0.89	0.32

(B) Knowledge-based society measures				
	Index	S&T capabilities	Applications of ICT	Impact of R&D
Finland	0.24	0.95	-0.32	0.09
Sweden	0.53	0.58	0.54	0.47
Denmark	-0.25	-0.35	0.01	-0.41
Netherlands	-0.36	-1.05	-0.25	0.22
Germany	-0.29	-0.37	-0.50	-0.02
UK	-0.10	-0.01	0.13	-0.41
Japan	-0.26	-0.05	-0.30	-0.42
USA	0.52	0.26	0.75	0.56
(C) Scores on knowledge-value society measures				
	Index	Adaptation of innovative procedures	Entrepreneurship and venturing	Innovation networks
Finland	-0.14	-0.03	0.04	-0.43
Sweden	0.41	0.27	0.55	0.41
Denmark	0.37	1.29	-0.13	-0.05
Netherlands	0.60	-0.07	0.83	1.04
Germany	-0.33	-0.13	-0.69	-0.17
UK	-0.15	-0.72	-0.23	0.51
Japan	-0.80	n/a	-0.67	-0.93
USA	0.26	n/a	0.81	-0.29
(D) Scores in sustainable development				
	Index	Societal values	Environmental responsibility	Environmental systems
Finland	0.24	-0.26	0.09	0.89
Sweden	0.94	0.77	1.31	0.74
Denmark	0.32	0.31	0.48	0.19
Netherlands	-0.22	0.16	-0.37	-0.45
Germany	-0.19	-0.34	-0.20	-0.04
UK	-0.45	-0.65	-0.12	-0.58
Japan	-0.36	n/a	0.12	-0.83
USA	-0.62	n/a	-1.30	0.05
(E) Scores on innovative society				
	Index	Impact of R&D	Entrepreneurship and venturing	Innovation networks
Finland	-0.10	0.09	0.04	-0.43
Sweden	0.48	0.47	0.55	0.41
Denmark	-0.19	-0.41	-0.13	-0.05
Netherlands	0.70	0.22	0.83	1.04
Germany	-0.29	-0.02	-0.69	-0.17
UK	-0.04	-0.41	-0.23	0.51
Japan	-0.67	-0.42	-0.67	-0.93
USA	0.36	0.56	0.81	-0.29

Source: Knowledge-based society barometer (2002).

5. Conclusion

The assessment of the key patterns of the Japanese and European knowledge-based society – foresight projects – has evidenced basic differences. Obviously, both the European Union (EU) and Japan have to tackle the prerequisites so that a thorough and fair knowledge-based society can be set up. The EU's knowledge-based society project is viewed in terms of development and intends to be simultaneously: a) integrative; b) explorative; c) experimental; d) developmental; e) forward looking. The project should consider life as a mixture of living conditions, working conditions and industrial relations, and analyze these strands through experimental, developmental and future-oriented methods. The outcome should provide paths towards a positive transformation. The European project is also narrowly linked with policy strategy goals set out in the Lisbon European Council meeting. The main goal of the strategy consists in making Europe 'the most competitive and dynamic knowledge-based economy, capable of providing a sustained economic growth with more and better jobs in addition to a greater social cohesion'.

The education sector plays the most important role, because the basis of a knowledge-based society has to be built up. This work starts in schools. The development of human capital has been and will carry on being one of the key driving forces for the creation of a knowledge-based society in the future. Special attention needs to be paid to the following crucial aspects:

a) ICT Provision and Education

ICT lessons and free access to ICT for pupils at school and in other public places, at any time will ensure digital literacy, irrespective of social and financial aspects.

b) English as a Common Language

A good level in English is necessary to guarantee an access to the amount of information available on the Internet, as well as to facilitate communication in a globalised world.

c) Pupil/Teacher Ratios

A low pupil/teacher ratio, i.e. a small number of pupils per teacher, can be viewed as an indicator of high levels of attention paid to the pupil, and turns into an efficient learning support. It helps to facilitate the training and development of the human and social skills of individuals. These skills are a key factor for the participation in a knowledge-based society that encompasses all the private and work-related spheres:

it includes the ability for teamwork, the development of better work-family balances as well as job and life satisfaction in general. However, there are other factors (e.g. the education system structure) which also need to be considered and which are pretty relevant to ensure a maximum and active participation in the knowledge-based society.

d) Flexibility, Sense of Responsibility and Self-management

The development of relevant and logical reasoning, together with the ability to take responsibility, are essential requirements and help individuals with developing the appropriate skills to survive and actively participate in a knowledge-based society. These skills include the ability to engage in self-directed learning, in independent job searches, and flexibility in all the spheres of life (e.g. arranging official affairs per eGovernment, private and professional correspondence per e-mail, searching information in internet, etc.).

The restrictive budgetary policies of the government and the search for teachers could raise some problems due to the shortage of vocations for the teaching profession in most of European countries. Lot of work remain to be done for the member states, including huge spendings, to catch up with the levels of the frontrunners among others Denmark. It has turned to be absolutely required to reach such a standard. Without a relevant education system, people's abilities to think, to get knowledge and to respect the values of society will not be sufficiently developed and will significantly suffer. An active participation in a knowledge-based society would be unlikely. Japan experiences similar problems but differences also exist.

The ability to compete in the global knowledge-based economy – for both Japan and the EU member states – will depend on whether the higher education institutions can meet the increasing demand for high-level skills. In return, it will depend on substantial improvements in the quality of schooling and equity in learning opportunities. It is quite clear that basic education only is unlikely to meet the increasing and ongoing changes in demands for skills. The promotion of higher education has become one of the priorities within education policies.

The changes in the production sector play another key role. As far as workers are concerned, excellent skills in this field will foster digital literacy, global teamworking and flexibility, and will constitute the basis of employment, wealth and well-being. Concerning the company, regulations still need to be less rigid in a few European countries to provide more flexibility for both companies and workers. The openness to innovation becomes fundamental. This implies the willingness and readiness to practice new forms of working, including various forms of teleworking, lifelong learning and greater autonomy for workers. The same can be mentioned in the case of Japan.

Regarding competition and innovation, the EU is able to find its own way, which is likely to differ from its competitors, the USA and Japan. For the time being, Europe lags behind the USA and has to bridge the gap in terms of ICT use and other knowledge-based society prerequisites. The EU has got several such features which may be turned to the advantage of the Europeans. These features include the existence of 'tacit' knowledge[9], cultural and social traditions, well-established models of social partnership and the existence of further regulatory institutional entities which support a balanced and socially acceptable development together with the spread of innovations.

The third very important area deals with the social impact and the adjustability of the European and Japanese societies to the new and fastly changing conditions. The population's ability to think and act, independently and responsibly, its cultural diversity together with tolerance and social sensitivity may result in a better working environment and innovation; finally, such an environment is likely to turn into a competitive advantage. In Japan and throughout the European countries, the DIDIX (digital divide index) showed a divide in terms of education and income. Concerning age, the gap will disappear, as young people in today's Europe and Japan are generally much more digitally aware than the elderly generations. This fact implies various social implications.

To some extent, this situation is already reflected in labour productivity and patent applications. In addition, governments can improve innovation ability, not only by setting up a proper education system but also by investing in R&D and thereby pushing technological advances and other innovations forward much faster. In the EU, there are already some striking examples of successful member states in this field but some European countries lag behind other EU member states and other countries of the world, particularly Japan. The slow technological advances and slow progress in innovation in these EU countries certainly hamper a faster economic development.

The enlargement has deteriorated the general position of the EU due to the less developed acceding countries; as a result, the EU became more heterogeneous. Despite all, the new member states and the EU

9 Tacit knowledge consists often of habits and culture that we do not recognise in ourselves. Knowledge that enters into the production of behaviours and/or the constitution of mental states but is not ordinarily accessible to consciousness. In the field of knowledge management the concept of tacit knowledge refers to a knowledge which is only known to you and hard to share with someone else, which is the opposite from the concept of explicit knowledge.

candidate countries match the EU member states in terms of traditional education measures. However, a considerable gap exists about the penetration of ICT, vocational training and other knowledge-based society indicators. In order to make those countries meet the EU requirements, some positive trends – some of which are already apparent such as good computer availability at school or good training evaluation – need to be sustained. An increase in the knowledge and human capital transfer could be another way to improve the education system and foster innovation. These activities should be seen as additional to financial help, and likely to have a direct impact on the development of a knowledge-based society in the different states.

E-mail is already usual in Europe, although broadband access technology is still something new. The development of both will carry on spreading in workplaces and enhance further flexible working opportunities from various places – including home – as well as productivity and competitiveness. Countries where broadband access is provided at competitive prices will first reap the benefits. In addition, broadband connections at home will pave the way for teleworking as well as new entertainment and communication applications which require huge and fast data transmission, such as video-conferencing and media-on-demand services.

Comparisons between Japan and the EU or other international comparisons show the challenges EU and Japan will face. These comparisons indicate that these challenges, which also emerge in other parts of the world, can be successfully coped with. We can draw some lessons from the analysis of the efforts of countries. Education and skill will be some keys for the EU to reach its ambitious Lisbon goals; concerning Japan, these keys will enable it to improve its international competitiveness. The current world departs from the traditions and the fame of the past: it does not tolerate weakness and ignorance of the basic needs. The individuals and countries which are likely to succeed will be able to adapt themselves and operate any changes as well as overcome any resistance. The crucial task is to ensure that societies are prepared to face these challenges.

Literature

Bohlin, E. (2003), "Telecommunications Policy Research in Information Society Discourse," *World Telecommunications Markets*, Vol.III of the *International Handbook on Telecommunication Economics*, edited by Gary Madden, Edward Elgar Publication.

Empirica (2003), ICTs and the adaptability of work arrangements in the European Union 2000-2002. Results from the ECATT and SIBIS Projects, Bonn.

Eurostat (2005), Science and technology in Europe – Data 1990-2004.

Hall, B. (2000), "The assessment: Technology policy," *Oxford Review of Economic Policy*, 18, 1, 2002, p. 1-9.

Hamel, G. (2000), *Leading the Revolution*, Cambridge, MA, Harvard Business School Press.

Knowledge Society Barometer (2002), European Foundation for the Improvement of Living and Working Conditions.

Lundvall, B.-Å. (2002), "User-producer relationships, national systems of innovation and internationalisation," in Malerba, F., *Sectoral Systems of Innovations and Production, Research Policy* 31, p. 247-264.

OECD (2002), *Access to and use of information technologies. Information and communication technologies*, Paris (www.oecd.org).

—— (2002), *Education at a glance 2002*. Online education database, Paris (www.oecd.org).

Pouillot, D. and Puissochet, A. (2002), "R&D Spending on ICT," *Communications & Strategies*, No.48. p. 33-51.

—— (2002), "R&D Spending on ICT Overall Evolution in the Major Industrial Countries, and Close-up on Telecom Operators' New Organization IDATE," *Montpellier Communications & Strategies*, No.48, 4th quarter 2002, p. 33.

Sakaiya, T. (1991), *The Knowledge-Value Revolution or a History of the Future*, New York, Amazon.

—— (2000), "The knowledge value revolution and Internet fair 2001 Japan." Speech at OECD Forum, 27 June 2000.

SIBIS (2002), Statistical indicators benchmarking the information society. IST-Programme project No.IST 2001-38219 led byempirica, Bonn (www.sibis-eu.org).

Simai, M. (ed.) (2003), "Practical guide for active national policy makers – what science and technology policy can and cannot do?," in *VATT Research Report,* No.103.

UN Economic Commission for Europe (2002), "Towards a knowledge-based economy," Regional assessment report.

UNESCO (2002), Institute for Statistics, Global and internationally comparable statistics on education, science, technology, culture and communication, Montreal.

United Nations Statistics Division (2002), Millennium indicators database, New York, http://millenniumindicators.un.org/unsd/mi/mi_goals.asp 20.

EU Social Model Viewed from Japan

Proposal for Japan-EU Social Security Agreement

Prof. Dr. Shinichi Emile OKA

Department of Social Welfare, Meiji Gakuin University, Tokyo

Introduction

What distinguishes the most Europe from other societies in the world is the sacro sanct principle of the Welfare State. Europe has been the spearhead of the world in theorising and putting into practice the welfare state concept and has greatly influenced the spread of such a concept in the rest of the world. Japan too has learned a lot from the European welfare state, in terms of introduction or reform of the welfare schemes. The basic role of the European welfare state should be maintained and even emphasised in the context of European integration. Japan, USA and other advanced countries will never substitute Europe in this role.

1. EU Social Security Policy

Without beyond any doubt, the EU has been initially created for an economic purpose. The essential mission of the European Economic Community (EEC) social security policy has been to ensure the free movement of workers between the member states. As a result, workers were mainly targeted by this policy and the poverty-stricken minorities without any job were excluded from the EEC policy. The individuals who were excluded generally never tried to go abroad in order to get a job.

A recent EU program intends to pass regulations in order to protect the socially excluded persons; in our opinion, this initiative is a positive step forward. However the social policy which matters still remains at the discretion of the member states. Moreover, the inclusion of excluded persons aims at giving them employment opportunities.

EU only plays the role of a coordinator of the different socials security schemes managed by each member state. The EU itself has not put in place any social security scheme, so EU is unlikely to help directly people at risks, socially speaking. The EU can only negotiate with the government of the member state concerned and offer advices on the way a person can be helped and who is likely to provide this help. It has already been thought that EU must establish its own social security scheme for specific people who are excluded from national schemes. However such an idea has never been put into practice[1].

EEC was initially created to form 'The United States of Europe'. While some aspects of EEC are quite similar to those of the USA, with regard to the central government, they are radically different. The field of social policy remains at the discretion of member states and EU can not directly intervene into the domestic policies without being allowed to do so by a specific legislation. This EU legislation should give EU specific competence to influence directly the member states. Otherwise EU can not interfere into the national policies of the member states.

EU is nothing more than a coordinator: The European community can negotiate with the governments of member states but cannot do so with the European citizen. EU only plays an advisory role but cannot protect anyone directly. This basic structure has never been modified up to now, which apparently shows the limits of EU social policy.

2. Recent Action of EU

General Remarks

It is not the first time that EU social policy gives us the impression that the projects and the agenda for the future are promising altogether; however, no one can deny that policy effects, in practice, are very modest and hardly achieved. For instance, while the New Social Agenda mentions many projects in various fields, the concrete proposals prepared are not necessarily realistic.

The legislation is carefully drafted. However it seems unlikely that fruitful results will be achieved within 2010.

In a word, the basic strategy of the consists of setting up a convergence policy through which EU tries to promote voluntary actions from the member states in the direction suggested by EU. If the policy matter

---

1 Pieters, D., *Thirteenth State*, Leuven, Acco, 2003.

fits all of the member states, they can all agree with it. But whether the member states really give effect to the legislation or not, is another matter.

In our opinion, the EU social policy deriving from Lisbon seems quite relevant given the recent context. The policy orientations mentioned in the Social Agenda can be viewed as perfectly relevant. However, many issues are to be coped with, as illustrated below.

New Social Agenda

EU reflected the period after Lisbon Strategy and regarded as success of the Strategy. Then EU revamped the Lisbon strategy by introducing the Social Agenda in 2005. Undoubtedly, the statistic data show improvements in the economic indicators between 2000 and 2005. But nothing evidences whether this success is due to the Lisbon Strategy or not. Many other factors might have contributed to the economic improvement of this period.

The assessment of EU policy's effectiveness has never been undoubted because EU basically plays a role of coordinator and has never been an actor. First, we must examine the effectiveness of national policy. Thereafter, the analysis of EU policy can be done. Every state tries to recover from the economic recession while promoting an economic growth on the basis of its own economic policy irrespective of the EU strategy. Another aspect needs to be dealt with: To what extent each member state follows the EU Guideline.

The EU explained that the economically advanced countries are countries endowed with the strongest social protection. That is to say "social policy is working as a productive factor. Good social policies strengthen growth and jobs."[2] Social progress might be one of the consequences of the economic success but it is far from being one of the causes. The development of social welfare tends to create new jobs. However, the kinds of jobs created in this way, are mostly related to welfare and health services, which are typically female jobs, and may not contribute directly to the active economic growth in general.

Generally, economically advanced countries may fulfil the following conditions: high productivity, high technology standard, high education level and high motivation, etc., they can enjoy then high standard of social welfare. In the case of countries with low level of productivity, low standard of technology, low level of education and low motivation,

[2] European Commission, *The Social Agenda 2005-2010*, 2005, p. 10.

they do develop social welfare, without any guarantee of economic growth.

Since the 1970s oil shocks, the European Community (EC) often insisted on the importance of social dimension. But the EC social policy had never been drastically improved. Now, EU puts again the emphasis on social protection mainly to cope with growing fears of poverty. The Social Agenda 2005-2010 looks like Action Program for Social Space in the 1970s.

"The 2005-2010"[3] targeted two goals: full employment and a more social cohesion. While the policy was economically oriented from the very beginning of EEC, this new Agenda follows and even strengthens this line. But the importance of the social dimension remains secondary. First, a higher economic performance should be achieved, which fosters the creation of jobs. Thereafter more resources should be devoted to the social matters. However, if the member states follow this line of conduct, they will never be integrated on an equal footing: as long as the countries do not achieve an economic growth, they will never improve the welfare of the society.

Regarding the increase in social cohesion which means "equal opportunities for everybody," it is necessary to carry out the four following measures:

– Modernising social protection

– Struggling against poverty and promoting social inclusion

– Promoting diversity and non-discrimination

– Social services of general interest.

'The modernisation of social protection' has been a key component since 2000 and has improved the policy contents. The Open Method of Coordination has widened the scope of application from poverty to pension, health and long-term care, as mentioned later. We have some doubt about the significance and the reality of 'modernisation'. The Communication of the Commission provides an excellent analysis but does not refer to any real proposal for further legislation[4].

While talking about 'Social Inclusion', the EU policy tends to focus on poverty eradication. The idea suggested by 'social inclusion' does not only include poverty-stricken people but the whole categories of socially excluded individuals. The EU social security policy has mainly targeted "workers," which will not even change in the future. However

---

3 *Ibid.*, p. 22.

4 European Commission, *Modernising and Improving Social Protection in the European Union: Communication from the Commission*, 2005.

EU has made a step forward by including in its policy all kinds of individuals comprising the poverty-stricken people.

Policy for All

Historically, as mentioned above, EEC and the subsequent EC focused on specific categories of persons such as active workers. As a result, from the Treaty of Rome (1957) onwards, the elderly people, the children, the housewives, the disabled people, the poor were not priorities. Basically, social security policy means in practice, social insurance policy so that the areas of public aid, social welfare services and so on are excluded from the main policy's target.

EU recently stresses on the inclusion of all the people in their policy. Under the title of 'modernisation', EU tends to extend its policy to all kinds of persons including homeless, the older and younger generation, etc. The new agenda puts the stress on full employment, equal opportunities and social protection for everyone[5]. Those general principles may be approved of by all the member states.

However new aspects are emerging. EU carries on enlargement and consequently, the number of states and European citizens are increasing. We think that widening the policy's targets in the context of geographic enlargement will trigger new risks together with the possibility of slowing down the EU policy effectiveness in the near future. At least, it will take much more time to prepare a new legislation and carry out new policy.

Knowledge-based Society

Lisbon European Council insisted on "the most competitive and dynamic knowledge-based economy in the world, capable of providing a sustainable economic growth, a better and greater social cohesion"[6] in 2000. EU expects prosperous years thanks to the information and communication technology (ICT), which can induce, in turn, the economic growth and finally the high standard of social welfare.

However ICT can shape a new world not only for Europe but also for many other countries. Japan, United States and many other countries think the same. On the other hand, ICT can give the developing countries a huge opportunity to develop their economy and catch up with the industrialised countries. While thinking about the economic competition

---

5 Communication from the Commission on the Social Agenda, COM (2005), IP/05/152.

6 Strategic Goal for 2010, Lisbon European Council, March 2000.

at global scale in the future, Europe is really unlikely to create the competitive potentials.

Japan also considers that ICT are tools to stimulate the new industry, to create new jobs and widen the market. Japan is still under the economic depression and carries out many drastic reforms. Obviously, social security is not the exception. Japanese government also gives much more importance to ICT with potentials to create new types of employment. The unemployment ratio in Japan remains high currently from 4% to 5% and many economists expect the economic recovery leaded by ICT.

Open Method of Coordination

Lisbon Summit introduced the Open Method of Coordination (OMC), which was inspired from European employment strategy and also from the areas of social exclusion and pension. Then this method became effective in other social policy areas including health and long term care. We can consider it as a step forward.

However, given the limits of the European Social Fund, the effectiveness of the OMC is restricted as well. It may be more effective in employment policy but less effective in social protection policy which requires more funds to organise and coordinate the different schemes with a complex structure.

OMC is only a method to promote convergence which does not necessarily bring successful results. It also happens that even the best method produces nothing in practice. 'Convergence' originally means voluntary action and needs some time to reach the goals. Nobody knows which new results can be achieved in this way.

The experiences of the member states do not show any noticeable results about the convergence of social security schemes. On the contrary, the national reports often mentioned the difficulties and problems which appear in putting into practice the OMC[7]. The adoption of an EU common policy is differently experienced in each member state. Some states can easily implement the EU policy whereas others have some problems to make it comply with its domestic system. For instance in the field of social security, it is easy to imagine that states adopting the Beveridge model work better than those with the Bismarck model.

---

7 See the National Papers in the following work. Zeitlin, J. & Pochet, P. (eds.), *The Open Method of Co-ordination in Action*, Brussels, P.I.E. Peter Lang, 2005.

Poverty and Social Inclusion

Poverty is becoming one of the bigger social risks in Europe. The enlargement of EU means the inclusion of poverty-stricken countries into EU. Therefore social inclusion strategy is getting more important in the EU as a whole. Over the years, it has been suggested several times[8] the introduction of minimum standards of protection at the European level. However such interesting proposals had never been convincing, because EU mainly targets the workers who are already protected by the minimum wages and do not need any help from the community.

The general behaviour of the EU regarding poverty must be analyzed and acknowledged. However, some remarks might be made. The idea of 'inclusion' is considerably focused on employment. The disabled and elderly people are not among the targets of this strategy.

The Agenda only starts with the reasons why the existing national schemes against poverty are insufficient. Once again, EU plays the roles of adviser and coordinator but it is never the spearhead. EU is entitled to say whatever to the member states but has no say regarding the situation in each country of the poor. This matter is at the discretion of the member states.

Pension Portability and Pension Reform

As far as pension scheme is concerned, the Directive on the portability of pensions is currently only a proposal. The well known EEC Regulation was enacted in 1971 and made possible for all the legal social security schemes to be coordinated with the national schemes. This new Directive only targets the private pension schemes, which means the application of the same treatment to the cross-border movements[9].

Most of the European countries still carry out drastic reforms over pension schemes. Pension is the most important social security scheme and the most contentious between the generations. It is easier to prepare legislation on private pension than on social security pension. The EU enacted the Directive on supplementary pension schemes[10]. However the policy effects are still uncertain.

---

8 For instance, see Deleeck, H., "Social security and 1992," in Pijpers, A. (ed.), *The European Community at the Crossroad*, The Hague, Martinus Nijhoff, 1992, p. 91-117.

9 Communiqués de presse, 20 October 2005.

10 Official Journal of the European Communities, L 235/10, 23 September 2003.

3. The Significance of the European Social Model

European Social Model

The EU social security policy mainly aims at renewing the European social model and facing globalisation by modernising the existing social security schemes in each member state. Under the European social model, "all national systems of EU countries are marked by the consistency between economic efficiency and social progress."[11] This assertion is quite sensible and logical.

However, this way of thinking is not specifically European. Many other advanced countries including Japan are more or less getting the same way. If there is not any wealth, the subsequent distribution and welfare are non existent. Originally, economic performance and social welfare should not be on sides apart. Basically, Europe faces problems by trying to maintain a high standard of welfare even after the economic crisis. Therefore, there is nothing surprising with the concept of "European social model." Globalisation is not only a European concern but a worldwide concern as well.

However, we are doubtful whether "all the national systems of EU member states are marked by the consistency between economic efficiency and social progress." The degree of consistency between economic efficiency and social progress varies from one country to another. For instance, we can easily think about the usual division between Sweden and Denmark. The degree of consistency in Sweden has been traditionally quite high, whereas in Denmark it is rather low.

Again, the New European social model is expecting to make the economic efficiency consistent with the social progress. This idea suggests that EU wants social progress to derive from economic growth as it occurred in the 1960s. On the other hand, if economic prosperity can not be achieved, it means that social progress will move backwards. However, in practice, it is complex to curb the social security expenditure for social and political reasons. Therefore, the European social model will face a crisis if EU fails in reaching an economic growth. Currently, the EU thinks that economic growth could be boosted by the information technology, but they should also consider the possibility of a failure in the economic policy.

---

11 European Commission, *Report of the High Level Group on the Future of Social Policy in an Enlarged European Union*, 2004, p. 27.

The Report stated that "globalisation puts the European social model under pressure and leads to the need to adapt it."[12] It goes on saying that "globalisation calls for new forms of security for the workers like lifelong learning and capital ownership." It ended up by comparing international cooperation with a model of regional integration. But, the basic attitude is very modest saying the technical cooperation focused on good governance.

European Social Model in a Global Context

The European social model has traditionally been the basis of international social security policy. For instance, the activities of the International Labour Organisation (ILO) have been designed on the basis of the European social model which derives from the Bismarck model). ILO has made efforts to diffuse the social security schemes along with the European Model as the international standard. However many international standards adopted by ILO do not always fit all of its members in the world.

Here, two aspects which have nothing to do with the European Model shall be explained. First of all, the role of the family: many Asian countries have their own culture and social structure to which belongs the family. Among the Asian families, two or three generations still live together; the younger generation deeply respects the older one. Even in Japan, most of the elderly persons are cared for by their families who are financially helped by the long-term care insurance introduced in 2000. In some Asian countries, people out of relatives are not allowed, culturally speaking, to visit and look after the grand parents.

The second aspect deals with the tripartite structure of ILO comprising labour unions, employers' organisations and government. Historically, European countries were the precursors to promoting social security through the labour movements. As many developing countries are deprived of well-organised labour unions, ILO tries to set up labour unions in every country, which does not make any sense for us. Regarding Japan, labour union does not necessarily plays a key role in determining social security schemes. Sometimes, it is argued that the influence of the government was stronger on the introduction of social security. Japanese experts in social security notice that Europe has a bottom up process for social security in contrast with the Japanese top down process.

Many other examples show that the European social model adopted by ILO is not universal and that ILO has consequently limited policy

---

12 *Ibid.*, p. 28.

effects. Japan can put forward an Asian social model instead of a European one. It is necessary that ILO widens the diversity of social models to head the global social security.

4. Japan as a Social Welfare Model

Japanese Social Model

In addition to both aspects already mentioned, another distinction separates Japan from the European welfare model. Japanese companies play a key role in increasing the social welfare. Japanese companies can provide, among others, housing facility, family benefits, retirement allowance and so on[13]. The contents differ from one company to another. Even small companies and public sector companies provide some kind of welfare.

Japan is a dynamic society in comparison with the European countries. From the very beginning, Japan might meet the requirements of the new European social model proposed by EU. However, Japanese social security schemes are in general modest[14], because Japanese people do not want to depend upon the others and prefer to implement private protection schemes such as private insurance, saving scheme, company welfare and so on. In Japan, it is crystal clear that the introduction of too much social welfare discourages people from working.

EU said that "making social protection more employment-friendly" was a striking issue for the modernisation of social security. Obviously, the pending question is what employment-friendly social security is about. It merely means that lower social protection and lower tax are key conditions to make the employment-friendly social protection possible. Japanese policy decision makers have mainly created incentives for workers. At least, they want to avoid discentives to work by increasing the social security standards.

Japanese social security tends to strike a balance between the various economic cycles. For instance, when the ratio of unemployment si high, unemployment benefits are more quickly delivered due to a reduction of income[15]. In Japan, the subsidies from the national budget are scarce.

---

13 Oka, S., "Function of Complementary Social Schemes: Japan," in Cousy, H. *et al.* (eds.), *Complementary Social Insurance*, Brugge/Brussels, Die Keure/La Charte, 2004, p. 127-158.

14 See the datail, Oka, S., "Social security Law: Japan," in *Encyclopaedia of Laws*, New York, Kluwer, 1995.

15 Oka, S., "Employment Insurance in Japan: relief or prevention," *Canadian Review of Social Policy*, No.38, 1996, p. 19-29.

Most of the Japanese complain about a decrease in their benefits when they need them and an increase when there is no need to. In contrast, many governments in Europe, take special measures in case of employment crisis, such as increasing more the unemployment benefits and extending the period of payment

Japan is likely to adjust properly the economic conditions in the field of social security but in many other areas as well. Another typical example is wage. The international trade unions have often criticised the Japanese trade unions for their weak movements and modest negotiations. Japanese unions are company-based and collective negotiation is carried out at the company level. Trade unions have never required pay rises to the employers of a company in the period of managerial trouble. It means that wage is socially linked to the economic performance of a company and more generally of the whole society.

Basically, Japanese people like working. Since the primary school, Japanese are taught that working is a virtue and they are strongly encouraged to work along their entire life. Japanese people depend much less on social security than the European. Even the elderly people try to work as long as possible. Given the small amount of their further pensions, they prefer to work longer[16]. In practice, legislation has been passed in 2004 to promote employment among the elderly people.

For 60 years following the World War II, Japan has been trying to catch up with the European Welfare State. However Europe is now approaching to Japan or United States in the welfare state models. Modernisation in EU policy means that social policy should be adjusted to the economic policy.

5. Globalisation and Social Security in Japan

Immigration in Japan

Since the Middle Age up to 19th century, Japan had closed its doors to foreign countries. Geographically, Japan is located in the Far East and is isolated from the rest of the international community. In the Modern Age, Japan tends to work differently from the international movements in many fields. Japan has not any striking history of immigration. Japan seems to be the sole country in the world to maintain a single race with a single language within its borders.

16 See Oka, S., "Politique de l'emploi en faveur des personnes âgées au Japon," *Revue Française des Affaires Sociales*, No.4, 1990, p. 127-141.

In terms of immigration, Japan has adopted a closed-door policy. In the 1980s, the immigration mainly from Asia was a source of tensions during periods of economic prosperity in Japan. The employers' organisations insisted on the need for foreign workers in the domestic labour market due to a serious shortage of workers. However, the further economic recession put an end to the open-doors policy. While Japan economy still remains in recession, the recent trade agreements put Japan under more pressure to accept foreign workers.

Japan in Asia

EU social security policy is certainly endowed with the most advanced mechanism in the world. Japan must also learn from the European experiences. While some experts of social security stress on the need for Asian social security agreements such as those existing within EU, such proposals are unlikely to be put into practice.

The situation is radically different between EU and Japan. Many countries suffer from the overpopulation and high levels of poverty in Asia. Japan is not only geographically isolated from Asia but also economically, politically and socially. On the one hand, the Japanese average income is getting extremely high in comparison with other Asian countries. Therefore Japan can not easily open the labour market to foreign countries. Free movements of workers will never be realistic in Japan. Even with a restricted immigration policy, the illegal immigration is gaining pace. As a result, this immigration is out of governmental control.

On the other hand, Japan was the only country in Asia which ratified the ILO Convention 102 on the social security[17]. Most of the Asian countries have not incorporated yet in their national legal order the international social security schemes. Even South Korea and China have not done it yet. Therefore, there is no way the social security schemes will be coordinated between Asian countries. First, Japan has to support the neighbouring countries to set up their own social security schemes. The adoption of the ILO Social security convention will be the next step.

International Agreements on Social Security

Concerning the globalisation of social security in Japan, it is necessary to mention two new trends: the first one is the bilateral social security agreements signed with other advanced countries. The second trend is the negotiation of trade agreements with developing countries,

17 C102 social security (Minimum Standards) Convention, 1952.

under which Japan must accept a number of foreign workers coming from those countries.

In 1999, Japan signed the agreement on Pension Scheme with Germany, which was the first bilateral agreement on social security of Japan. Thereafter, Japan has concluded quite similar agreements with Great Britain, United States, France, South Korea and Belgium; for now, Japan is negotiating with some other countries.

The globalisation of social security has just started in Japan. However, many problems are already likely to occur. If Japan carries on signing those kinds of bilateral agreements with different countries and in various fields, the public administration for the social security schemes of foreigners will get very complex; and the number of foreigners coming from everywhere is likely to increase in the next years.

The content of international social security agreements that Japan concluded with advanced countries are described in Table 1. The agreements with Germany, UK, South Korea and USA only deal with pension schemes, while those concluded with France and Belgium not only regulate pension but also medical insurance, unemployment insurance and industrial accident insurance. Then the agreements with UK and South Korea only regulate the exemption of obligatory application of social security in one country to avoid double application but the other agreements also include the regulations on the aggregation of insured period.

The European Commission said: "if there are ten countries, there are ten social security models." Therefore, there might be ten different agreements with ten partner countries. Obviously, as Japan is concluding bilateral agreements with each member state, it might get a diversity of legal documents. Dealing with foreigners differently in social security schemes might cause many problems.

Trade Agreements and Japanese Social Welfare

On the other hand, Japan has concluded Free Trade Agreements (FTA) and other Trade related agreements. Most of them are concluded with Asian developing countries. FTAs are apparently based on different areas linked to social security but they are in fact, closely related with social security. Japan demands from its partner countries a fair trade and positive impacts for the Japanese industry. In turn, many partner countries want Japan to accept immigration. For these economic motives, Japan has gradually opened its door to foreign workers.

Recently, a dispute occurred on whether the foreign workers should still be accepted in the sectors of medical care and social welfare where there is usually a shortage of personnel. Such professions require hard work but are badly paid and not really popular among the young Japanese. More precisely, nurses from the Philippines are targeted. Obviously, the organisations concerned are opposed to an increase in the number of foreign workers. However, without any doubt, the number of foreign workers will keep on rising in the near future.

Another problem which is raised is that social security regulations extremely discriminate against foreigners in Japan. The number of illegal immigrants is increasing. Their situation is not taken into account by the Japanese social security schemes. In most of the cases, foreigners cannot benefit from public aids.

Legal immigrants themselves experience quite many problems in getting access to social security. The Japanese labour law allows temporary working contracts. Legally, the foreign workers are required to apply for all the social insurance schemes and alternatively, have to pay the contributions. Regarding pension scheme, the Japanese government introduced the lump sum pay back scheme for foreign workers who must go back to their native countries. And, they are paying less than what they are likely to pay for a contribution. If a foreigner is 40 years old or over, he or she also has to pay contributions for long-term care insurance. While usually there is no way that they will get long-term care after 65 in Japan, they are compelled to pay the contribution out of their wages.

Obviously, they will lose money if they apply it to their social insurance. Therefore, many foreign workers in Japan try to not apply for social security, which induce the employers to exclude them from the social security in order to reduce the social costs. If foreign workers refuse to apply for social insurance, they fall into illegality. Under the current legislation, the number of illegal foreigners and foreigners' complaints has increased.

6. Future Cooperation between EU and Japan

Many countries belong to Europe and they influence each other in different ways. People have also moved across the borders for a long time. Then, Europe has long experienced the international coordination of social security schemes since the agreement between France and Italy in 1904. The enactment of an EEC Regulation in 1974 made possible the coordination among all the social security schemes from each member state. Thereafter, the EU goes on coordinating the social security schemes among the member states for those workers who move across the borders. In the era of globalisation, all of the countries in the world must draw lessons from the European experience.

However, the Japanese situation really differs from the European one. Japan is an isolated island in the Far East and has been little influenced by the neighbouring countries; that is the reason why Japan had built its own style of social security. Now, in turn Japan must adjust itself to the international movements as one of the leading country in Asia and even in the worldwide economy. The movements of workers beyond the frontiers are an international tendency and cannot only be stopped by Japan. Therefore Japan must manage to coordinate properly.

As mentioned above, Japan started to conclude bilateral agreements with advanced countries. If Japan follows this way, it will take a few decades or more to sign agreements with many countries in the world including the European member states; and the contents of the legal texts might differ from one country to another. Workloading and confusion are expectable in the state administration in the future. It is enough to imagine the case of a Japanese company which has to apply the legislation in force according to the nationality of the worker and the field concerned: this procedure will be the same for each individual.

Finally, I personally suggest the negotiation of an agreement between EU and Japan about the enforcement of the European social security legislation, which is much better than negotiating various agreements between Japan and each European member state. It is not necessarily difficult to do so. Because EU has already achieved the coordination of social security schemes through the enforcement of both EEC Regulation 1408/71 and EEC Regulation 571/72; now, the scope of application of these Regulations only needs to be extended to Japan. If Japan accepts and participates in the contents of both of these Regulations, the EU-Japan agreements of social security can easily be carried out. Japan does not belong to the EU but can conclude an agreement in specific areas.

Even though my proposal is unrealistic, Japan would make better use of these Regulations than conclude agreements with the European member states. It seems to be much easier for each member state to follow up the Regulations on social security with Japan. If Japan can participate in the adoption of these Regulations as all the member states, the management of the coordination of social security schemes among European countries and Japan will get easier and best fitted.

In economic matters, the national interests differ and sometimes member states compete against each other. However in social matters, many member states are sharing common interests and none of them can be damaged by some specific agreements such as a Japan-EU agreement.

The agreement on social security between EU and Japan can greatly contribute to reduce the costs of a double application of the social security schemes and to promote the economic activities. None of the European countries may be disadvantaged by the legislation and companies together with workers can benefit from it. This is a proposal of my own, a dream which can come true.

With a wider application of the EEC Regulations about the social security schemes to Japan and other countries, the mechanism of coordination of the social security schemes can be spread into the world. Japan-EU agreement can be the first step of such a process. In a globalised economy, the most advanced aspects of the European Regulations can be applied to the world, which will greatly contribute to improve free movement of workers all over the world.

References

Adnett, N. & Hardy, S. (2005), *The European social model*, Edward Elgar, Cheltenham.

Bourrinet, J. & Nazet-Allouche, D. (2002), *Union européenne et protection sociale*, La Documentation Française, Paris.

Brine, J. (2002), *The European Social Fund and the EU*, Sheffield Academic Press, Sheffield.

Council of Europe (2005), *Social Security: A Factor of Social Cohesion*, Strasbourg.

De Burca, G. (ed.) (2005), *EU Law and the Welfare State: In Search of Solidarity*, Oxford Univ. Press, Oxford.

Johnson, A. (2005), *European Welfare States and Supranational Governance of Social Policy*, Palgrave, Hampshire.

Jorens, Y. (ed.) (2003), *Open Method of Coordination*, Baden-Baden, Nomos Verlagsgesellshaft.

Oka, S. (2005), *Theory of International social security* (Japanese), Gakubunsya, Tokyo.

Pestieau, P., (2006), *The Welfare State in the European Union*, Oxford Univ. Press, Oxford.

de la Porte, C. & Pochet, P. (ed.) (2002), *Building Social Europe through the Open Method of Co-ordination*, P.I.E. Peter Lang, Brussels.

Van Berkel, R. & Moller, I.H. (2002), *Active Social Policies in the EU*, The Policy Press, Bristol.

Vaughan-Whitehead, D.C. (2003), *EU Enlargement versus Social Europe?*," Edward Elgar, Cheltenham.

Zeitin, J. & Pochet, P. (eds.) (2005), *The Open Method of Co-ordination in Action*, P.I.E. Peter Lang, Brussels.

Table 1. International social security agreements concluded by Japan

	Germany	*UK*	*S. Korea*	*USA*	*Belgium*	*France*
Japanese Residents (persons)	22,286	40,895	19,630	225,589	5,848	26,799
Japanese Companies	999	1,492	896	6,725	252	624
Total Double Payment (billion Yen/year)	8.1	25.6	0.7	83.4	4.1	14.6
Premium ratio (%)	20.3	20	9	15.3	37.94	37.66
Workers of double payment (persons)	5,893	7,780	2,195	5,4982	1,667	4,045
Their family (persons)	6,923	10,890	970	74,751	2,494	4,586
Double payment per capita (million Yen)	1.45	2.94	0.385	1.73	2.45	3.6

Source: Toyokazu ONO, "Sekai no Roudou," April 2005, p. 45 (Japanese).

R&D Intensity

An Insight into the Japanese Success and the Lisbon Failure[1]

Azèle MATHIEU &
Bruno VAN POTTELSBERGHE DE LA POTTERIE[2]

Université libre de Bruxelles (ULB), Solvay Business School, Centre Émile Bernheim

1. Introduction

According to its recently released Innovation Scoreboard, the European Union (EU) suffers from a worrying gap in terms of innovation compared to the USA and Japan[3]. It is a matter of concern because innovation is the starting point of a long term economic growth and employment creation. It is even more worrying in the context of the well known Lisbon Agenda.

In 2000, European decision makers decided to cope with poor economic performances by establishing the Lisbon agenda. The Lisbon agenda stated that EU had to turn into by 2010 "the most dynamic and

---

1 This chapter is based on the paper presented at the EU-Japan conference "The implications of the EU Constitution and Enlargement on EU-Japan Relations," 22-23 November 2004, Brussels, Université libre de Bruxelles (ULB), Conference organised by TEPSA in cooperation with The Social Science Research Institute and the COE Programme of the International Christian University of Tokyo and the Université libre de Bruxelles (ULB) (Institute for European Studies and Solvay Business School); with the support of the Japan Foundation.

2 This paper was mainly written when Bruno van Pottelsberghe was Professor at the Université libre de Bruxelles (ULB) before he became Chief Economist at the European Patent Office. The views expressed in this article are purely those of the authors and may not in any circumstances be regarded as stating an official position of the EPO or of the ULB.

3 Cf. *The Financial Times*, 13 January 2006, "EU is 50 years behind the US for innovation."

competitive knowledge-based economy in the world capable of sustainable economic growth with more and better jobs and greater social cohesion, and respect for the environment."

This failure results from, amongst other things, the difficult external conditions from 2000 onwards, an overloaded agenda, a poor coordination within the EU, conflicting priorities and a lack of determined political action, as pointed out by the High Level Group chaired by Wim Kok.

The Lisbon agenda covers five broad priority areas of policy (the knowledge-based society, the internal market, the business climate, the labour market, and environmental sustainability). Amongst them, the establishment of a knowledge-based society implies: "increasing Europe's attractiveness for researchers and scientists, making research and development (R&D) a top priority and promoting the use of information and communication technologies (ICTs)."[4]

Two years after the presentation of the Lisbon agenda, the Barcelona European Council, reviewed the progress made towards the Lisbon goals. Then it was agreed that investment in R&D should reach 3% of the EU GDP by 2010 and that the amount of business funding should cover two-thirds of the whole R&D expenses. This agenda was set when relative R&D expenses were much higher in the USA and Japan (respectively 2.7% and 3% of GDP in 2000) than in the EU (about 1.9%).

This chapter aims at understand better the drivers of R&D expenses across the Triad countries. More particularly, my purpose is to provide an explanation of the role of the EU market integration, of the science and technology policies, of country and sector-specific factors. The next section illustrates the 'Lisbon failure', and puts forward that the poor R&D performances of the EU – compared with the USA and Japan – are probably due to low expected returns to R&D and a relatively small specialisation in high-tech industries. The following sections subsequently attempt to explain why the perceived return to R&D is smaller in Europe than in Japan or the USA. Section 3 deals with four witnesses of the high fragmentation of the European market that cause a lower expected return to R&D. Section 4 analyzes the S&T policies that aim at reducing the spending on R&D, and hence improving its expected return. Section 5 presents a simple quantitative model which aims at testing whether the relative R&D performances are more driven by country-specific factor or sector-specific factor. Section 6 draws the conclusions.

---

4 See "Facing the Challenge: The Lisbon Strategy for Growth and Employment," Report from the High Level Group chaired by Wim Kok, November 2004.

2. An Interpretation of the Lisbon Agenda

Six years after its release, the Lisbon agenda failed in reaching its goals. Both statistical evidence and the head of the EU acknowledge it: "In contrast to the success of the single market and the euro, the Lisbon agenda has not brought about a reform spree. Although it has contributed to initiating a discussion on subjects traditionally considered as the domain of national governments, five years down the line the reform record is still largely disappointing."[5]

Figure 1 clearly shows two striking differences between the EU on the one hand and Japan, the USA on the other hand. Firstly, the R&D intensity has always been significantly lower in the EU than in Japan or the USA. Secondly, over the past thirteen years, the gap between the fifteen European countries and Japan or the USA has substantially widened. However, there is a strong heterogeneity within the EU-15 area.

Figure 1. Evolution of the R&D intensity (DIRD/GDP) in Japan, in the USA and in Europe, 1981-2003

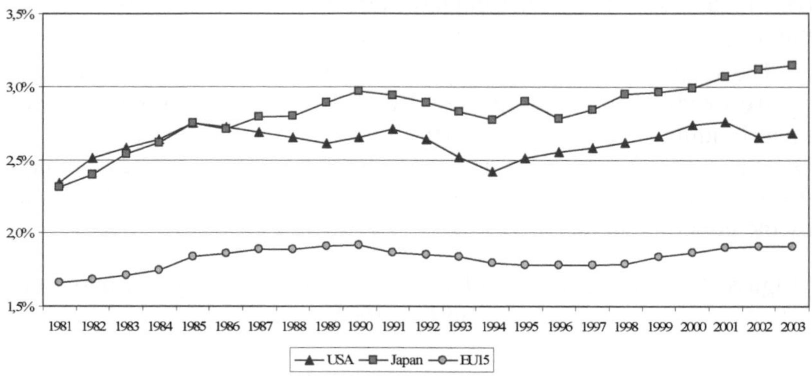

Source: OECD, MSTI (2005).

Figure 2 illustrates the discrepancies in R&D intensities between countries in 2003. While the Scandinavian countries pull the European average upwards, the Mediterranean countries like Italy, Spain and Greece push it downwards. In 2003, Japan – with a R&D intensity of 3.1% – and the USA, with a R&D intensity of 2.7% – are far ahead of the EU 15 with a 1.9% R&D intensity.

5 José Manuel Barroso, *Achieving Lisbon*, Global Agenda Magazine, Edition 2005.

Figure 2. R&D Intensity (DIRD/GDP) of the EU countries, the USA and Japan, 1981 & 2003

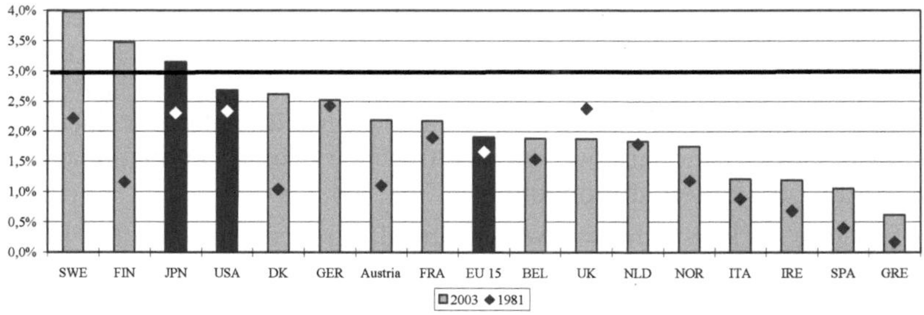

Source: OECD, MSTI (2005).

The comparison of the 2003 national R&D intensities with these of 1981 shows that the United Kingdom was the sole country with a higher R&D intensity in 1981 than in 2003. Over the period, the R&D intensity of Germany increased a little, ranging from 2.4% to 2.5%. The strongest increase in R&D intensity has been registered in Finland with a 2.3% rise. In Sweden, Finland, Denmark and Austria, the increase in R&D intensity has gone beyond 1% between 1981 and 2003.

The Lisbon Objective aims at making the level of business funding of two-thirds of the total business R&D expenses (or similarly government funding should secure one-third of total R&D expenses). In 2003, Denmark, Finland, Sweden and Japan were the only countries, amongst the studied countries, to have a share of R&D lower than 30% funded by the government (see Figure 3).

Figure 3. Share of the total R&D expenses funded by government, 1981 & 2003

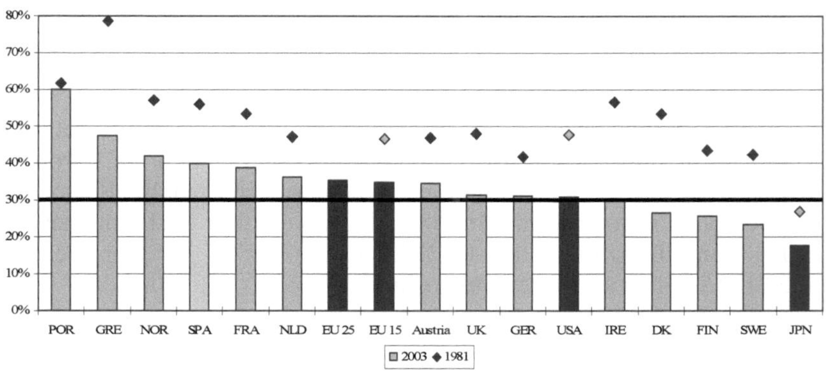

Source: OECD, MSTI (2005).

Figure 3 shows that all the countries have substantially reduced the contribution of government funding in the total R&D expenses. Between 1981 and 2003 the role of government funding has dropped by about 50% of the total R&D to about 30%. The strongest decrease in government funding have been illustrated by Greece (-31.2%), Denmark (-27%), Ireland (-26.1%) and, to a lower extent, by Sweden (-18.8%), Finland (-17.7%) and the United States (-17%). It is interesting to notice that the countries with the highest levels of R&D intensity are the countries with lowest share of government R&D funding (see Japan, Sweden, Finland and Denmark, for instance).

Over the whole period studied, Japan had the lowest ratio of government R&D funding to GDP in contrast with the EU 15 and the USA (see Figure 4). In the USA, the early 1980s were characterised by a noticeable increase in the government funding of R&D (from 1.1% to GDP in 1981 to 1.3% in 1987). The following 15 years have shown a sharp decrease in the American public spending on R&D, mainly caused by the end of the Cold War, and consequently reduced defence-related fundings. From 2000 onwards, a revival seems to occur in government R&D funding, probably due to a change in the broad socio-economic objectives of the USA. There has been a clear cut convergence between the three pillars of the Triad. The EU 15 is found between the USA and Japan in terms of share of the total R&D expenses funded by government on GDP. This share slightly decreased between 1981 and 2003 from 0.8% to 0.7%.

Figure 4. Evolution of the ratio of government funded R&D to GDP, 1981-2003

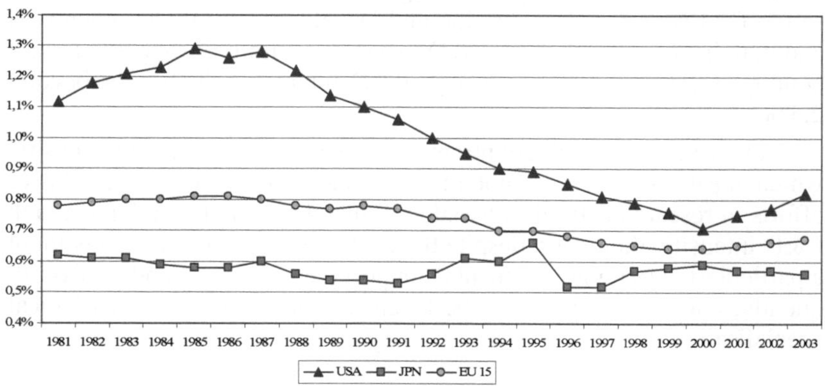

Source: OECD, MSTI (2005).

The Drivers of Business R&D Expenses…

The Lisbon agenda – which turns the EU into the most competitive knowledge-based economy in the world – can be interpreted as follows: the *actual return* to R&D must increase. Indeed, an increase in competitiveness requires an improvement in the level of labour productivity, induced by an accelerated rate of technical change. At a given level of R&D expenses, an improved level of competitiveness can be reached only through a higher return to R&D expenses.

The second part of the Lisbon Objective, which states that R&D expenses should reach 3% of GDP, means that the amount of R&D expenses must increase, and therefore, that the *expected rate of return* to R&D must increase: a higher expected return to R&D induces more investment in R&D activities.

In other words, the Lisbon agenda can be interpreted as the willingness to improve both the expected and the effective rate of return to R&D. This can be reached either through wider potential sales and benefits associated with new products and processes, or through a lower cost of R&D. The market size for goods and for technology is one indicator of the potential returns to R&D, whereas Science and Technology policies basically aim at reducing the spending on R&D.

If one keeps on doing a country-level analysis, the R&D intensity would therefore depends on the size of the country and on the science and technology policies whose purpose is the reduction of spendings on R&D. The size of a country is an indicator which helps to predict, at least partly, the relative efforts made in R&D. The USA and Japan, for instance, are by far the largest homogenous market amongst the Organisation for Economic Co-operation and Development (OECD) countries, and both have relatively high R&D expenses. Within Europe, the largest country, Germany, also has a high R&D intensity which goes beyond 2.5%.

However, some small countries also have a very high R&D intensity, which means that size is not the only factor underlying the relative efforts in research activities. Sweden, Finland and Denmark have a high R&D intensity altogether, despite their relatively small size, and without a particularly strong governmental support (see Figures 2 and 3). Consequently, another factor has to be taken into account: the technological specialisation.

Table 1. Top 3 R&D intensive sectors[6] by country, 2001

Business R&D Intensity (2001)	Countries	***Top 1 Sector***	***Top 2 Sector***	***Top 3 Sector***
3.7%	Sweden	Sub total electrical-electronical (22%)	Services sector (22%)	Motor vehicles (18.5%)
2.7%	Finland	Sub total electrical-electronical (47%)	Services sector (19%)	Non-Electrical Machinery (9%)
2.2%	Japan	Sub total electrical-electronical (34%)	Motor vehicles (13%)	Office & Computing Machinery (13%)
2.0%	USA	Services sector (38%)	Motor vehicles (8%)	Professional Goods (6.5%)
1.9%	Germany	Motor vehicles (29%)	Sub total electrical-electronical (14%)	Non-Electrical Machinery (10%)
1.5%	France	Sub total electrical-electronical (16%)	Motor vehicles (15%)	Services sector (12%)
1.4%	United Kingdom	Drugs & Medicine (25%)	Services sector (18.5%)	Sub total electrical-electronical (12%)
1.0%	Norway	Services sector (45%)	Sub total electrical-electronical (14.5%)	Non-Electrical Machinery (6%)
0.6%	Italy	Services sector (22%)	Sub total electrical-electronical (18%)	Motor vehicles (12%)
0.5%	Spain	Services sector (38%)	Drugs & Medicine (10%)	Sub total electrical-electronical (9%)

Source: OECD (2005, 2006a, b).

Table 1 shows the Top 3 R&D sectors and the broad business R&D intensity of several countries in 2001. The Top 3 business R&D intensive countries were then Sweden (3.7%), Finland (2.7%) and Japan (2.2%). In each of these countries, the most important business sector performing R&D is the *Sub total electrical-electronical.* This sector represents 22% of the total business R&D expenditure for Sweden, 47% for Finland and 34% for Japan. As this sector is highly intensive in R&D, it is not surprising to notice high macro-level R&D intensities for these countries. Finland for instance spends nearly half of its business R&D in one sector, which probably reflects the role of Nokia in the Finish economy. In the countries with a low business R&D intensity, the sector of services, which is far from being the most intensive in R&D, remains the most important sector performing R&D.

In a nutshell, three main factors apparently contribute to the R&D intensity: market size, S&T policies, and technological specialisation. As far as market size is concerned, one could wonder why Europe,

6 The sectors are classified according to the share of business R&D expenses they represent in total business R&D expenses.

which is by far a larger market than USA or Japan, has not a higher R&D intensity. It might be justified by the non existence of an integrated market in Europe. The next section presents four witnesses of a lack of integration in the 'European' market.

3. Fragmented Markets: Four Witnesses

Despite the liberalisation of the European market ten years ago and the introduction of a single currency in 2002; the European market is still highly fragmented. According to the European Commission, the creation of the Internal Market allowed "boosting EU economic growth by at least 1.8%, adding nearly 900 billion euro to the EU's collective prosperity and helping create 2.5 million extra jobs."[7] However, despite this substantial evolution towards a single market, it seems that the unified market is still far reaching. Below, we will briefly present four broad indicators of market fragmentation in Europe:

Product and Service Markets

As a matter of example, we focus on a firm producing goods in Amsterdam and selling them in Belgium: It is still called an export activity. At the opposite, if we have got a firm producing goods in New York City and selling them in Los Angeles, we call this process 'distribution'. Fragmented markets generate obstacles to trade; hamper innovation and productivity growth and creates differences in prices in the fields of technology, goods, services and labour forces. More particularly, fragmented markets reduce both the effective and expected return to R&D.

The creation of a European Internal Market in 1992 generated a positive impact on the economy as measured – amongst others – by the consumer price convergence (decrease in the price divergence from 4% between 1992 and 1998), the growth of intra-EU trade flows in goods and the foreign direct investment across European countries. However, ten years later, a status quo of these indicators appeared. For example, the price dispersion which is measured by the coefficient of variation was 14.5% in 1998 and increased to 15.3% in 2000 (see Figure 5).

In the mid-1990s, some categories of goods (clothing, sports-related goods and household appliances) experienced a price convergence, whereas nowadays there is not any significant evolution towards convergence. The price of some other categories of products (fuel, power, motor cars, tobacco and floor coverings) even diverged (CEC, 2002). According to the European Commission (CEC, 2002), "the observed

7 See European Commission (2004b).

slowdown in price convergence seems to result from the exhaustion of the initial shock-wave effects, from the creation of the Internal Market and from successive accessions to the EU."

Figure 5. Price dispersion in the EU for goods and services, 1995-1999 (coefficient of variation)

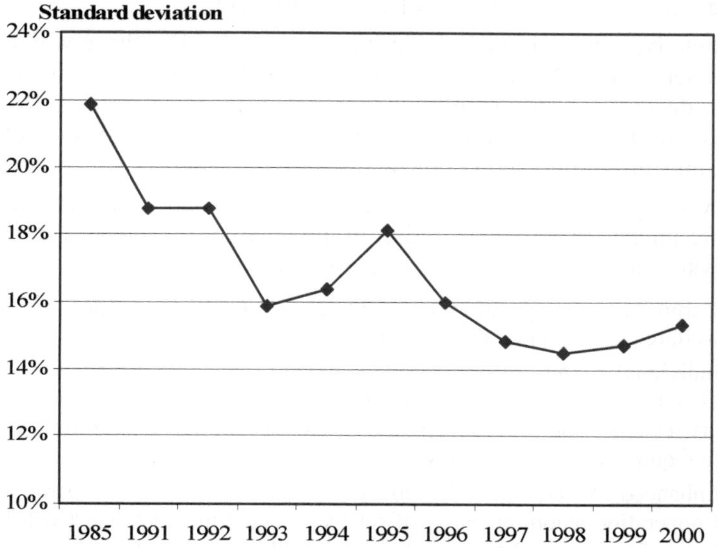

Note: The table shows the price dispersion in the EU 15 for goods and services measured by the coefficient of variation, e.g. a coefficient of 0.22 in 1985 means that the price level in the EU-15 countries varies 22% around the mean.
Source: CEC (1999, 2000, 2002).

One of the causes of the gap in competitiveness between Europe on the one hand, USA and Japan on the other hand, is the fragmentation of its market for goods but it is more crucially due to the very high fragmentation of its market for services. For example, divergence between prices of the car insurance amounted to 30% about in 2001 compared to a divergence of 15% for the global market of goods and services in EU 15 (see Figure 5).

The Lack of a Harmonised Tax System

Today each of the twenty five EU countries has its own tax scheme. This heterogeneity in tax schemes affects both the business and labour mobility. Moreover, it represents an additional cost for European firms which operate in different European countries. This additional cost is often charged on the final price at the expense of the consumer. For example, "the price dispersion in the European car/spare market is significantly wider because of tax differences and a lack of competition. In Germany, 16% of Value Added Tax (VAT) is added onto the wholesale price of a Fiat Punto. In the neighbouring Denmark, 200% of VAT and registration tax are almost added. On average, 40% of car taxes are added to the wholesale prices of cars" (CEC, 2002).

Finally, concerning the fiscal incentives to R&D, "those which have been set by the OECD widely vary in their form and other features of their design"[8]. Consequently the different fiscal incentives to R&D across the European Union differently affect the spending on R&D and thus the current net value of those research projects.

A study prepared for the European Commission[9] evaluates the economic impacts of tax cooperation in the enlarged European Union. The analysis leads to the following interesting conclusions:

> Corporate tax cooperation can yield gains in GDP (a growth of 0.5%) and welfare (gains smaller than 0.5%).
>
> Individual country effects can be wide and sometimes negative. (…) Individual countries may experience significant changes in economic activity, tax revenues and government budgets. An agreement on tax reform is likely to require elaborate compensation mechanisms.
>
> Enhanced cooperation is the most likely route towards tax cooperation. (…) Cooperation among a subset of relatively equal member states will lead to less radical policy changes, but also to smaller gains. (…)
>
> The financing of tax reforms is crucial. The selection of fiscal instruments for balancing government's budgets can sometimes have a significant influence on the effects of corporate tax cooperation. This means that corporate tax harmonisation is likely to be bundled with additional tax policy reforms.

The Lack of Labour Mobility

The importance of an increased labour mobility in Europe has been recognised by European policy makers who designated the year 2006, the European Year for Workers' Mobility. As illustrated in Figure 6, some European countries have a high level of unemployment, as Poland with a 17.7% rate of unemployment, whereas other countries, like Ireland are characterised by a low level of unemployment. A higher

---

8 See OECD, 2003.

9 European Commission – DG Taxation and Customs Union (2004a), "Economic Effects of Tax Cooperation in an Enlarged European Union – Simulations of Corporate Tax Harmonisation and Savings Tax Coordination," report prepared by Copenhagen Economics, p. 6-7.

mobile market for employees will permit to reach a better fit between regions or sectors with a shortage of employees and those with an oversupply of work.

Figure 6. Total unemployment rate (%) in 2005

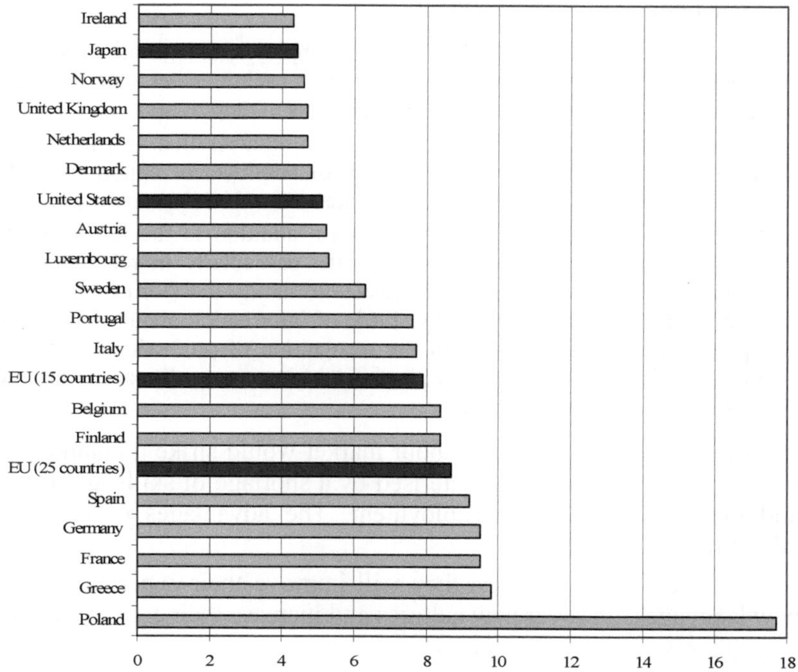

Source: Eurostat. "Unemployment rates represent unemployed persons as a percentage of the labour force. The labour force is the total number of people employed and unemployed" (Eurostat).

Japan and the USA have by definition a highly mobile workforce, which explains, at least to some extent, the lower rate of unemployment at the aggregate level. The aggregate rate of unemployment in Europe (EU 25) is nearly twice as high as the unemployment rates of the USA and Japan. Europe does not register good performances in both job-to-job mobility and geographical mobility. Regarding the *job-to-job mobility*, while "EU workers stay in the same job for an average period of 10.6 years, US workers keep the same job during, on average 6.7 years."[10] Concerning the *geographical job mobility*, "every year on

[10] See website dedicated to the European Year for Workers' Mobility: http://europa.eu.int/comm/employment_social/workersmobility2006.

average, 7.2% of EU citizens change their place of residence, among which 15% refer to a change in job as the main reason for the move. In contrast with 16.2% of US citizens who move home each year, among which 17% are doing it for occupational reasons."[11]

This lack of labour mobility in Europe is due to many factors such as those mentioned by EAS (2006):

> "The lack of an integrated European-wide employment legislation, with different taxes and benefit systems according to each member state, immigration issues (...) and variation in the legal status of employees (...)."
>
> "Companies also consider that differences in remuneration, linguistic skills amongst employees and the availability of employment opportunities for spouses, set significant obstacles to the international labour mobility (...)"
>
> "(...) other social and cultural barriers (in addition to the language) are viewed as more important by individuals, particularly in relation to the treatment of spouses and elements related to family ties (for example, children's education) and to housing. Lack of information about employment opportunities and worries about the recognition of professional qualifications are also significant negative factors." Moreover, qualifications may not be recognised in the host country.

A more mobile European labour market would strike a balance between regions or sectors characterised by a shortage of skills and labour and those facing high unemployment. The advantages of a mobile labour market would be:

– Concerning employees, they will improve their experience, learn new languages, discover new cultures and increase their employability;

– As far as companies are concerned, they will access a larger and more diversified pool of workers;

– In general, the demand and the supply of work will better fit each other and the competitiveness of Europe will increase.

The Lack of a European Technology Market

On 16 January 2006, the Directorate General Internal Market and Services of the European Commission announced a consultation process on the future patent policy in Europe. This public hearing focuses on three major issues: the community patent, how the current patent system in Europe could be improved; and the possible areas of harmonisation:

> The Commission is seeking views on what action could be taken while work on the Community patent is continuing, in particular within the framework of the existing patent system, or by bringing national patent systems more

11 *Ibid.*

closely in line with each other through either approximation of laws or mutual recognition of national patents[12].

This consultation process can be considered as the cutting hedge of an escalating and long winded debate on the way Europe should put in place a properly harmonised patent system. The past few years have seen an intensified politicisation of intellectual property (IP) issues. One of the most sensitive and long winded bones of contention about the European patent system is linked with the high cost of patenting, which is partly due to the failure at implementing effectively the European community patent or the more recent London Protocol[13]. The high opportunity cost of this failure, for firms and society at large, is viewed as one important factor hindering innovation in Europe, which explains why the European Union' commissioner of Directorate General Internal Market, Mr. McCreevy, wants to make "one final effort" to solve the issue[14].

François and van Pottelsberghe (2006) make an in-depth analysis of the cost factor in patent systems. They suggest that the total cost of a patent (from the application date at the EPO until its acceptance and maintenance in several European countries) can be divided into the following four categories:

Process costs are composed of procedural fees (filing fees, search, examination, country designation, etc.).

Translation costs consist in translation services often provided by patent attorneys. (…) The higher the number of countries in which the patent is protected is, the higher the cost induced by translation services is. (…)

External expenses include costs of services associated with the drafting of the patent and the filing of the patent office. (…) The costs of these services include expenses linked with all the actions implemented

12 Press Releases, IP/06/38; the questionnaire can be downloaded on http://europa.eu.int/comm/internal_market/ indprop/index_en.htm.

13 Cf. Patent World (February 2006, Issue 179, p. 7) the declaration by Professor Alain Pompidou, President of the EPO, who urges action to be taken on the London Protocol, the EPLA (European Patent Litigation Agreement, designed to improve the enforcement of European patents, enhance legal certainty and promote the uniform application and interpretation of European patent law) and the Community Patent: "The Protocol must be ratified by eight countries, of which England, France and Germany must be three, before it can come into force. If it comes into force it would mean that the claims of a patent would only be translated into English, French or German."

14 See the *Financial Times*, 16 January 2006, "One final effort to create a low-cost EU patent."

for a patent: filings, payment of fees, monitoring translations and procedural actions.

Maintaining costs consists in renewing fees to keep the patent valid during a maximum period of twenty years. They are due each year at the JPO and at the national patent offices of the EPC member countries or after a certain period at the USPTO; they are generally gradually increasing over the time. Once a patent is granted by the EPO, it must be validated and put in force in each national patent office of the EPC member countries. The renewal fees significantly vary according to each country.

Figure 7. Comparative cost structure of patent application and maintenance, 2003 (EURO)

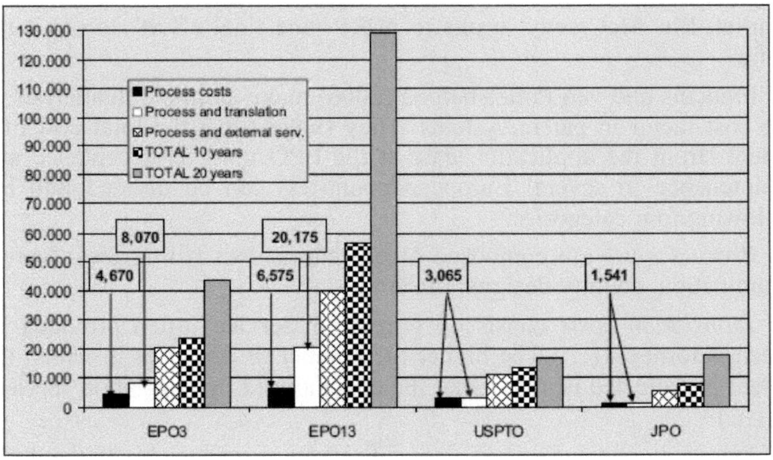

Source: van Pottelsberghe de la Potterie and François (2006).

Figure 7 shows the patenting costs induced by the processes carried out by the European Patent Office (EPO), the USA Patent and Trademark Office (USPTO) and the Japan Patent Office (JPO). For the EPO the cost of an average patent has been calculated for two types of patents. The first one designates the three largest countries (EPO-3: Germany, France and the UK) and the second one refers to 13 countries[15].

The patenting cost in Europe is much higher than in the USA or in Japan. The higher the number of designated states applying for protec-

[15] According to the EPO annual report of 2003, 13 countries are effectively designated for protection by more than 60% of the patent applications: Germany, Great Britain, France, Italy, Spain, The Netherlands, Sweden, Switzerland, Belgium, Austria, Denmark, Finland and Ireland.

tion is, the higher the cost of patenting will be. For instance, the renewal of a patent for 20 years, granted by the EPO, in 13 European countries, would cost about EUR 129,000; compared to EUR 16,000 in the US patent system and EUR 21,000 in the Japanese patent system. The European patent system is far more expensive than the patent systems in Japan or in the USA: this mainly results from a distinct process: once a patent is granted by the EPO, it must be validated and translated into each state applying for protection. Van Pottelsberghe and François investigate then on what extent the market size would compensate for the relative differences in terms of cost.

Their results show first that the US technology market is three times more attractive (in terms of number of filings) than the European technology market. Secondly, the cost of a patent (claim) which designates 13 EPO Member countries is 4 to 8 (5 to 10) times more expensive than in the US, dependent on the length of protection. Thirdly, when the number of claims is taken into account instead of the number of patents, and when the market size is accounted for through the 3C-index (cost per claim per capita), a clear negative relationship emerges between the cost of patenting and the demand for patents, witnessing a strong patent applications elasticity on prices.

Cost is not the sole issue. As shown by Jaffe and Lerner (2004) and Quillen and Webster (2001), quality, or rigor, also matters. Several indicators lead van Pottelsberghe and François (2006) to conclude that the EPO is more selective in its granting process (longer time of examination and smaller granting rate). The USPTO grants more patents, and faster than the EPO, which witnesses a lower quality: the substantive examination is much faster and the grant rate is substantially higher. If the patents granted by the EPO are indeed of a higher quality, then one would obviously expect a higher cost, and fewer applications. However, what makes a European patent more expensive is not the higher quality of its examination process, but rather the cost of translation which follows the granting process, and the complexity of its validation and maintenance in each national patent office (see Figure 7).

The European market, which is nowadays composed of 25 countries, is more than twice as large as the US market in terms of consumers. If the cost per claim per capita index is taken into account, it would clearly justify the higher nominal examination fees at the EPO, which would ensure a rigorous granting process thanks to significant economies of scale. The current high quality process of the EPO takes place in the frame of a complex, expensive and fragmented European market for intellectual property. These costs do not reflect the effectiveness of a patent system, but rather a selection mechanism strongly based on the financial resources of the inventors.

Several attempts to reach a more integrated market are currently tackled by European policy makers. A first, although incremental, possibility for improvement would be to harmonise the validation and renewal fees across the EPO member states. A second, and significant, potential improvement of the system lies in the current proposals of the European Patent Litigation Agreement (EPLA) and/or the London Protocol. While the former would simplify the complexity and the cost of litigation in Europe (through a centralised court), the latter would substantially reduce the translation requirements, and hence the cost of patenting. Finally, the most important advance in reducing the complexity and the cost of patenting in Europe would be reached through the Community Patent – i.e., a unique gateway for patenting, while automatically targeting the whole European market, one fee structure and lower translation costs.

4. Science and Technology Policies

Various policy tools aim either at reducing the spending on R&D (subsidies and tax incentives), or at providing the business sector with "ideas" (public laboratories, academic research). Guellec and Van Pottelsberghe (2003 and 2004) have measured the impact of government funding, fiscal incentives, and direct performance of research in public laboratories or universities on the level of business R&D expenses and on economic growth. The main findings they get are the following:

- tax incentives and government funding have a positive impact on business R&D; however they are substitutes (if the intensity of one of the government instrument increases, the impact of the other is reduced);
- the effect of government funding varies according to its generosity: it reaches a certain threshold and then decreases beyond the optimal funding rate which ranges from 10 to 20% of business R&D;
- direct funding and tax breaks are more effective when they remain stable over the time;
- however, civilian research performed by public labs and universities has not any effect on business R&D, but defence-related public research crowds out business R&D.

Table 2. Evolution of the subsidisation rate, the fiscal generosity and the business R&D intensity

	*Subsidization rate (%)**			*Fiscal generosity***			*R&D intensity (%)****		
	1981	2001	Growth	1981	2001	Growth	1981	2001	Growth
Finland	9	3.4	↓	-0.02	-0.01	↑	0.7	2.7	↑
France	24.6	8.4	↓	-0.01	0.07	↑	1.2	1.5	↑
Germany	16.9	6.7	↓	-0.05	-0.025	↑	1.9****	1.9	↑
Norway	24.9	10.3	↓	-0.04	-0.02	↑	0.7	1	↑
Sweden	13.6	5.9	↓	0.08	-0.01	↓	0.4	3.7	↑
United Kingdom	30	8.9	↓	0.00	0.10	↑	1.7	1.4	↓
Japan	1.9	0.8	↓	-0.02	0.01	↑	1.4	2.2	↑
USA	31.6	9.4	↓	0.18	0.07	↓	1.7	2	↑
Italy	8.8	14.9	↑	-0.03	-0.03	↓	0.5	0.6	↑
Spain	4.1	9.5	↑	0.14	0.38	↑	0.2	0.5	↑

*The subsidization rate is equal to R&D funded by government and performed by business on total business R&D expenses.

** The fiscal generosity is measured by 1-B-index (see Annex for more details about the B-index).

*** The R&D intensity is equal to total business R&D expenses on total business added value.

**** The added value for Germany being available only since 1991, the R&D intensity of Germany is this of 1991 and not of 1981.

Source: OECD (2005, 2006a, b, c, d).

Table 2 presents the subsidisation rate and the level of fiscal generosity in several countries, for both years 1981 and 2001. Four main observations can be drawn from the table. First, subsidies have been strongly substituted by fiscal incentives. Over the past twenty years, most of the countries have substantially reduced the level of subsidies and increased the level of fiscal advantages towards business R&D. Secondly, the European countries are highly heterogeneous: some countries have a strong level of subsidisation, such as Italy or Norway, whereas others present high levels of fiscal incentives (like Spain and France). Thirdly, the countries with the lower level of business R&D intensity have a high level of financial support (through subsidies or fiscal incentives) to business R&D. This latter observation puts forward that the countries with a relatively low level of R&D intensity rely more on S&T policies to stimulate R&D expenses. Japan, Sweden and Finland have high levels of R&D intensity and very low levels of subsidisation.

5. Quantitative Evidence

In this section, we empirically investigate whether R&D intensity is more driven by country-specific or sector-specific factors. The first empirical analysis relies on three simple economic estimates (Ordinary Least Squares) based on a cross section database in 2001. The twenty-one industries are indexed by i (= 1,...,21), and the whole ten countries are indexed by j (= 1,...,10) and t stands for the year 2001. There are 210 observations.

$RI_{i,j,t} = \beta_j J_t$ (1)

$RI_{i,j,t} = \beta_i I_t$ (2)

$RI_{i,j,t} = \beta_j J_t + \beta_i I_t$ (3)

Regarding the variables themselves, *RI*, *J*, and *I* are respectively business R&D intensity, country and industry-specific vectors of dummies. β_i and β_j are the vectors of parameters to be estimated. The results are provided in Table 3.

The first estimates a regression of R&D intensity on the ten studied countries fixed effects. Do national differences justify the diversified levels of R&D intensities across the countries? Regarding the results of this first regression (Table 3, column 1), 8 out of 10 countries have a significant impact on R&D intensity. The adjusted R-squared suggests that national differences explain 9% of the variation in R&D intensity across the studied countries. The impacts of Spain and Italy on the R&D intensity are not significantly different from zero. The countries that are associated with the highest impact are Sweden (17%), Japan (13%), the UK (10%) and the USA (10%). Interestingly, Finland stands in an intermediate position, with a 7% impact, whereas it is the second highest level of R&D intensity in Figure 2.

The second regression measures the sector-specific impact on the R&D intensity (Table 3, column 2). These industrial differences explain much more the various levels of private R&D intensities than the national differences. The adjusted R-squared suggests that sector-specific factors explain 38% of the variance in the level of R&D intensity across countries and industries. The traditional R&D intensive sectors have the highest impact on R&D intensity (Office and computing machinery, electrical and electronical, Drugs and medicines, and aircraft)[16].

[16] The high-technology industries are: *Chemicals excl. Drugs, Drugs & Medicines, Non-Electrical Machinery, Office & Computing Machinery, Professional Goods, Sub-total electrical-electronical, Aircraft, Shipbuilding & Repairing, Motor vehicles, Other Transport Equipment.*

Table 3. Results of the three regressions of R&D intensity on country- and industry-specific effects, 2001

Dependent variable is RIt

Regression #		1
	0.126***	(4.56)
Japan	0.067**	(2.26)
	0.075***	(2.73)
Finland	0.036**	(2.16)
France	0.035	(1.30)
Germany	0.069**	(2.39)
Italy	0.037	(1.34)
Norway	0.169***	(5.67)
Spain	0.099***	(2.77)
Sweden	0.099***	(2.94)
United		
Kingdom		
USA		
Adjusted R-squ		0.092
F-statistic		1.987
Prob(F-statisti		0

		2
Food, Beverage &	0.012	(0.36)
Tobacco	0.013	(0.4)
Textiles, Apparel &	0.055	(1.51)
Leather	0.077**	(2.13)
Rubber & Plastic	0.233***	(6.43)
Products		
Chemical excl. Drugs	0.023	(0.58)
Drugs & Medicines	0.023	(0.68)
Petroleum Refineries	0.029	(0.85)
& Product	0.01	(0.32)
Iron & Steel	0.063*	(1.94)
Non-Ferrous Metals		
Metal Products	0.279***	(7.72)
Non-Electrical	0.163***	(5.04)
Machinery		
Office & Computing	0.274***	(8.03)
Machinery	0.168***	(4.93)
Professional Goods	0.052	(1.43)
Sub-total electrical-	0.135***	(4.18)
electronical	0.089**	(2.29)
Aircraft		
Shipbuilding &	0.025	(0.7)
Repairing	0.008	(0.23)
Motor Vehicles		
Other Transport	0.017	(0.52)
Equipment	0.005	(0.17)
Woods Products,		
Furniture,		
Other Manufacturing,		
nec		
Paper, Paper Prod. &		
Printing		
Non-Metallic Mineral		
Products		
Services sector		
Adjusted R-squared		0.380
F-statistic		6.669
Prob(F-statistic)		0

		3
	0.055	(1.47)
Japan		
	0.015	(0.39)
	0.004	(0.12)
Finland		
	0.01	(0.26)
France		
	-0.035	(-
Germany		
	-0.005	0.93)
Italy		
	-0.034	(-
Norway		
	0.102***	0.12)
Spain		
	-0.001	(-
Sweden		
	0.025	0.89)
United *Kingdom*		
	0.001	(2.64)
USA		
	0.041	(-
Textiles, Apparel &		
	0.061	0.03)
Leather		
	0.219***	(0.58)
Rubber & Plastic		
		(0.02)
Products		
	0.017	(0.87)
Chemical excl. Drugs		
	0.008	(1.31)
Drugs & Medicines		
	0.014	(4.66)
Petroleum Refineries		
	-0.003	
& Product		
	0.049	(0.34)
Iron & Steel		
		(0.18)
Non-Ferrous Metals		
	0.266***	(0.3)
Metal Products		
	0.15***	(-
Non-Electrical		
		0.07)
Machinery		
	0.262***	(1.11)
Office & Computing		
	0.165***	
Machinery		
	0.034	(5.65)
Professional Goods		
	0.122***	(3.38)
Sub-total electrical-		
electronical		
	0.087*	(5.77)
Aircraft		
		(3.61)
Shipbuilding &		
	0.011	(0.81)
Repairing		
	-0.007	(2.75)
Motor Vehicles		
	0.003	
Other Transport		
	-0.008	(1.79)
Equipment		
Woods Products,		
		(0.24)
Furniture,		
		(-
Other Manufactur-		
		0.16)
ing, nec		
		(0.07)
Paper, Paper Prod.		
		(-
& Printing		
		0.19)
Non-Metallic		
Mineral Products		
Services sector		
Adjusted R-squared		0.450
F-statistic		6.270
Prob(F-statistic)		0

Note: The estimates cover 21 industries in 10 different countries in 2001. *RI*, the dependent variable denotes R&D intensity. All regressions are estimated with the OLS method and a cross section dataset. T-statistic are shown between parentheses; *** indicates the parameters that are significantly different from zero at a 1% probability threshold; ** at 5%; and * at 10%.

The third regression investigates on what extent the differences in the level of R&D intensities are explained by the industrial – and/ or national – differences. The national and the industrial differences explain 45% of the variance in R&D intensity, which is higher that the percentage of variances explained by the national effects taken alone or by the sole industrial effects (Table 3, column 3). Sweden is the only country to have a significant impact on the R&D intensity, which means that Sweden has built a specific national environment favourable to research and development. Several sectors still have a high and significant impact on R&D intensity. In other words, these results suggest that the international differences in R&D intensity observed in Figure 2 are mainly driven by the technological specialisation of countries and not by a country specific environment more favourable to R&D, except for Sweden.

The second part of the empirical analysis is made of four regressions. The first one is a regression of R&D intensity on the *fiscal generosity*, measured by the B-index at the national level (see the appendix for a definition of the B-index). The second one is a regression of the R&D intensity on the national *subsidisation rate* (business R&D expenses funded by government on the total business R&D expenses). The third one is a regression of the R&D intensity on *the share of publicly performed R&D in total R&D*. These three regressions allow a measurement of the relationship between the direct or indirect national support to business R&D and the total business R&D intensity. The fourth regression measures the impact of the *technological specialisation* (measured by the share of business R&D expenses in high-technology industries on the total business R&D expenses). The models are presented as follows:

$$RI_{i,j,t} = \beta_b B_{j,t} + \beta_i I_t \quad (4)$$

$$RI_{i,j,t} = \beta_{sub} SUB_{j,t} + \beta_i I_t \quad (5)$$

$$RI_{i,j,t} = \beta_{gov} GOV_{j,t} + \beta_i I_t \quad (6)$$

$$RI_{i,j,t} = \beta_{ht} HT_{j,t} + \beta_i I_t \quad (7)$$

The 21 industries are indexed by i (= 1,…,21), and the 10 countries are indexed by j (= 1,…,10). Concerning the variables themselves, *RI*, *B*, *SUB*, *GOV* and *HT are* respectively business R&D intensity, the *B*-index[17], government R&D funding implemented in business, the share of publicly performed R&D on total R&D and the share of business R&D expenses in high-tech industries on total business R&D expenses. $\beta_i I_t$ takes into account the industry-fixed effects. Country-specific effects are implicitly taken into account by the four S&T policies variables. β_b, β_{sub}, β_{gov} and β_{ht}, are the parameters representing the impact of the four exogenous variables.

---

[17] The smaller (more negative) the *B*-index, the better the fiscal treatment of a country.

The results are presented in Table 4. Direct and indirect national supports have a negative and significant relationship with the level of R&D intensity (columns 4, 5 and 6). As these results reflect a cross section of countries and industries for a given year, they cannot be used to represent the impact of a policy tool on business R&D intensity, but rather as some kind of correlation. For a proper estimation of the impact these policy tools have on business R&D, a time dimension is required, as pointed out by Guellec and van Pottelsberghe (2003). The negative relationships suggest that S&T policies are stronger in the countries which necessarily need them, i.e. the countries with relatively low business R&D intensity. Countries like Spain, Norway and France where the share of government funding is higher than one-third have relatively low R&D intensity.

Table 4. Results of the regression of R&D intensity on the B-Index, the subsidisation rate and the technological specialisation, 2001

Dependent variable is RIt							
Regression #	*4*		*5*		*6*		*7*
B	0.132** (2.16)	***SUB***	-0.7*** (-3.71)	***GOV***	- 0.821*** (-5.06)	***HT***	0.093** (2.15)
Adjusted R-squared	0.39		0.42		0.46		0.39
F-statistic	6.716		7.502		8.527		6.712
Prob(F-statistic)	0		0		0		0
Total panel (balanced) observations							185

Note: The estimates cover 21 industries in 10 different countries in 2001. *RI*, the dependent variable denotes R&D intensity, *B* the B-Index, *SUB* the national subsidization rate, *GOV* the share of publicly performed R&D on total R&D and HT the share of business R&D performed in high-tech. industries on total business R&D. All regressions are estimated with the OLS method, and a cross section dataset. The regression include industry-specific effects. T-statistics are shown between parentheses; *** indicates the parameters that are significantly different from zero at a 1% probability threshold; ** at 5%; and * at 10%.

Source: OECD (2005, 2006a, b, c, d).

The technological specialisation of a country (measured through the share of private R&D expenses in high-technology industries on the total private R&D expenses) has a positive and significant impact in explaining the level of R&D intensity across countries and industries (see Table 4, column 7). This result means that the higher the technological specialisation of a country is, the higher its R&D intensity will be.

6. Final Notes

The Lisbon Agenda, launched in 2000 by the European policy decision makers, was extremely ambitious. Europe had to become the most knowledge-based competitive economy in the world, and its R&D intensity had to reach a level of 3% by the year 2010. Nowadays, at less than five years to the deadline, the Lisbon agenda has rather turned into a '*Lisbon failure*'. There is no sign of a particularly improvement in the European competitiveness, and its R&D intensity has barely increased; however, the total R&D expenses remain under a low threshold of 2% of GDP. In Japan and the USA, the R&D intensities were quite high, well above the thresholds of 3 and 2.5% of GDP, respectively.

This chapter aimed at gaining a better understanding of the drivers of R&D intensity, and the reasons underlying the poor performance of Europe in comparison with the USA and Japan. To start with, we have first translated the Lisbon agenda into its basic implications. The improvement of the European competitiveness and R&D intensity mean that both the effective return to R&D and its expected return have to get better. We argue that the relatively low R&D intensity of Europe is mainly due to a relative low expected return to R&D. We have then investigated on the reason why the expected return is low. Two major drivers can consequently be identified. Either the potential market has to increase, or the spending on R&D has to decrease. Whereas the former is implicitly related to the European single market, the latter refer to science and technology policies (i.e. reducing the cost of doing R&D).

The market size is one determinant of business R&D expenses. If Japan and the USA have such high levels of R&D expenses, it is at least partly due to their market size. Germany, albeit to a lesser extent, also has a relatively high R&D intensity. However, the aggregate EU level of R&D intensity remains relatively low, despite representing a larger market than the USA and Japan. We argue that the relatively poor performance of Europe mainly results from the lack of an integrated market. It is reflected by the lack of a single market for product and services, the lack of an homogeneous tax scheme within Europe, the lack of labour mobility across countries, and last but not least, the lack of a European technology market. This latter argument points out both a real issue for the European innovation system and a symbolic representation of the failure at creating an integrated market for product and services. How can the EU improve the expected return to R&D if the inventions performed by its SMEs cannot be directly protected, at an affordable cost, in the whole European area. The European patent system is so far much more expensive than the patent systems in Japan or in the USA, which is mainly due to the fact that once a patent is granted by the EPO, it must be validated and translated into each state willing to get protection. In this respect, the currently highly debated London Protocol – whose purpose is to reduce translation costs – and EPLA (European Patent Litigation Agreement) – aiming at establishing a centralised Court for patent litigation in Europe – would drastically improve the perception of a European technology market.

Another way for stimulating R&D expenses consists in decreasing the spendings on R&D. This is one of the major goal of the S&T policies, and especially of R&D subsidies and fiscal incentives towards R&D. Guellec and van Pottelsberghe (2003) show that R&D subsidies and fiscal incentives stimulate business-funded R&D, provided certain conditions are fulfiled. Our statistical analysis has shown that across the various countries studied in this chapter, those with the lowest level of R&D intensity have the strongest government support to business R&D. In other words, government support is higher in countries which necessarily need business R&D. Regarding the countries with a high R&D intensity, like Japan or Sweden, the government funding of business R&D is quite limited.

Finally, there are still some countries with a relatively small size, but with a very high R&D intensity, like Sweden, Finland and Denmark for instance. Here, such high levels of R&D intensity are justified by their technological specialisation. Finland is a good example, with nearly half of its business R&D expenses which is concentrated on one broad sector (electrical and electronical products). Our quantitative analysis of 21 industrial sectors amongst 10 countries clearly show that the most important driver of R&D intensity is much more industry related than country related. The econometric analysis does confirm that the countries with a high level of specialisation in high-tech industries benefit from particularly high levels of R&D intensity. Sweden, Finland and Japan are indeed highly specialised in high-tech industries, and therefore enjoy a high R&D intensity. When sector specific effects are taken into account, the only country that keeps a particular high (above than normal) R&D intensity is Sweden.

References

EAS (Euro Attractions Show) (2006), "Labour Mobility and Flexibility: Staffing Attractions from both within and beyond the European Union or Educated Entertainers and Mobility," Austria. (https://www.iaapaimis.org/intproject/HandOuts/eas06LabourMobility.pdf).

Commission of the European Communities (CEC) – DG Taxation and Customs Union (2004a), "Economic Effects of Tax Cooperation in an Enlarged European Union – Simulations of Corporate Tax Harmonisation and Savings Tax

Coordination," report prepared by Copenhagen Economics. (http://europa.eu.int/comm/taxation_customs/resources/documents/taxation/gen_info/economic_analysis/economic_studies/economic_effects_enlargedEU.pdf).

CEC (2004b), "First Implementation Report on the Internal Market Strategy (2003-2006)." (http://europa.eu.int/comm/internal_market//strategy/index_en.htm).

CEC (2002), "Report from the Commission – Economic Reform: Report on the Functioning of Community Product and Capital Markets".

CEC (2001), "Report from the Commission – Economic Reform: Report on the Functioning of Community Product and Capital Markets".

CEC (2000), "Report from the Commission – Economic Reform: Report on the Functioning of Community Product and Capital Markets".

François D. and B. Van Pottelsberghe de la Potterie (2006), "The Cost Factor in Patent Systems," *Working Papers CEB from Université libre de Bruxelles, Solvay Business School, Centre Émile Bernheim (CEB)*, Working Paper No.06-002, 32 p.

Jaffe A. and J. Lerner (2004), *Innovation and Its Discontents – How Our Broken Patent System is Endangering Innovation and Progress, and What to Do about It*, Princeton University Press, Princeton and Oxford, 236 p.

Guellec D. and B. Van Pottelsberghe de la Potterie (2003), "The Impact of Public R&D Expenditure on Business R&D," *Economics of Innovation and New Technologies*, 12(3), p. 225-244.

Guellec D. and B. Van Pottelsberghe de la Potterie (2004), "From R&D to productivity growth: do the institutional settings and the sources of funds of R&D matter?," *Oxford Bulletin of Economics and Statistics*, 66(3), p. 353-376.

José Manuel Barroso, "Achieving Lisbon," *Global Agenda Magazine*, Edition 2005.

OECD (Organisation for Economic Co-operation and Development) (2006a), *Research & Development Statistics – Total Business Expenditure on Research and Development (BERD) by Industry (Table 13) ISIC Rev.2*, Vol. 2006 release 01, Source OECD Science and Technology Statistics, Paris. (http://thesius.sourceocde.org/vl=2160301/cl=16/nw=1/rpsv/ij/oecdstats/16081242/v209n1/s30/p1).

OECD (Organisation for Economic Co-operation and Development) (2006b), Research & Development Statistics – Total Business Expenditure on Research and Development (BERD) by Industry (Table 13) ISIC Rev.3, Vol. 2006 release 01, Source OECD Science and Technology Statistics, Paris. (http://thesius.sourceocde.org/vl=2160301/cl=16/nw=1/rpsv/ij/oecdstats/16081242/v209n1/s31/p1).

OECD (Organisation for Economic Co-operation and Development) (2006c), *Research & Development Statistics – Business Expenditure on Research and Development by Industry and Source of Funds (Table 14) ISIC Rev.2*,

Vol. 2006 release 01, Source OECD Science and Technology Statistics, Paris. (http://thesius.sourceocde.org/vl=2160301/cl=16/nw=1/rpsv/ij/oecdstats/16081242/v209n1/s32/p1).

OECD (Organisation for Economic Co-operation and Development) (2006d), Research & Development Statistics – Business Expenditure on Research and Development by Industry and Source of Funds (Table 14) ISIC Rev.3, Vol. 2006 release 01, Source OECD Science and Technology Statistics, Paris. (http://thesius.sourceocde.org/vl=2160301/cl=16/nw=1/rpsv/ij/oecdstats/16081242/v209n1/s33/p1).

OECD (Organisation for Economic Co-operation and Development) (2005a), STAN Industry, Vol.2005 release 05, Source OECD STAN Structural Analysis Database, Paris. (http://thesius.sourceocde.org/vl=2160301/cl=16/nw=1/rpsv/ij/oecdstats/16081307/v265n1/s1/p1).

OECD (Organisation for Economic Co-operation and Development) (2005b), Main Science and Technology Indicators, Vol.2005 release 02, Source OECD Science and Technology Statistics, Paris. (http://thesius.sourceocde.org/vl=2160301/cl=16/nw=1/rpsv/cw/vhosts/oecdstats/16081242/v207n1/contp1-1.htm).

OECD (2003), "Tax Incentives for Research and Development: Trends and Issues," http://www.oecd.org/dataoecd/12/27/2498389.pdf.

Quillen, C. and O. Webster (2001), "Continuing patent applications and performance of the US Patent Office," *Federal Circuit Bar Journal*, 11(1), 1-21.

Report from the High Level Group chaired by Wim Kok (2004), "Facing the Challenge: The Lisbon Strategy for Growth and Employment."

Warda, J. (2001), "Measuring the Value of R&D Tax Provision in OECD Countries," *OECD STI Review*, 27.

Warda, J. (2002), "A 2001-2002 Update of R&D Tax Treatment in OECD Countries," Report prepared for the OECD Directorate for Science, Technology and Industry.

Appendix 1. The B-Index formula

The first step in calculating the B-index is to determine the numerator – the present value of the after-tax cost (ATC) of a one dollar (USD 1) expenditure on R&D. The next step is to determine the present value of the before-tax income required to cover the present value of a one dollar outlay on R&D expenditures and to pay the applicable taxes. Thus, the generic formula for the B-index is as follows:

$B = (1 - uz)/(1 - u)$

Where:

$(1 - uz)$ = after-tax cost per dollar of R&D expenditure
z = present value of d
u = corporate income tax rate.

The B-index is calculated with 90% current expenditures and 10% capital expenditures for all countries. In Figures 2 and 3, the comparisons, which estimate the generosity of R&D tax provisions, are presented as one minus the B-index.

In a world in which there are no taxes ($u = 0$), the value of the B-index will be 1. A firm would never find it profitable to undertake a project for which the present value of project related income was less than the present value of project costs. No project with a benefit-cost ratio of less than 1 would be undertaken. In a world where taxes exist, however, the value of the B-index can still be 1, provided that all R& D expenditures are fully deductible in a current year ($z = 1$) and are taxed at the same rate. For example, if $u = 50\%$ then $B = (1 - 0.5)/(1 - 0.5) = 1$. The B-index will vary from 1 only when R&D expenditures are not fully deductible ($z<1$) or are more than fully deductible ($z > 1$), and/or where there exist allowances or tax credits for R&D that reduce the after-tax cost of an R&D project (that is, the after-tax cost of one dollar of expenditure on R&D).

Source: Warda, 2001.

AMU Deviation Indicator for Coordinated Exchange Rate Policies in East Asia

Eiji OGAWA

1. Introduction

The monetary authorities of East Asian countries have been strengthening their regional monetary cooperation since the Asian Currency Crisis in 1997 through the Chiang Mai Initiative (CMI): the ASEAN+3 (Japan, China, and Korea) established it as a network of bilateral and multilateral swap arrangements for managing a currency crisis in the member countries. Under the CMI, the monetary authorities should conduct a surveillance process for preventing a currency crisis in the future. However, the monetary authorities have not any standing institution for carrying out any surveillance process in East Asia. Instead, they regularly meet as the Economic Review and Policy Dialogue in the ASEAN+3 Finance Deputy Ministers Meeting for surveillance over their macroeconomic performance.

By taking into account recent movements of intra-regional exchange rates in a context of US dollar depreciation against major currencies, we found asymmetric responses among East Asian currencies to the US dollar depreciation and in turn, misalignments among them. Ogawa (2004) found that East Asian currencies were classified at least into two groups; one group of currencies has been appreciated against the US dollar while the other group of currencies has been pegged to the US dollar. We can identify that monetary authorities face a coordination failure[1] in conducting exchange rate policies among East Asian countries that causes a biased change in intra-regional exchange rates. The Malaysian government, especially, has followed the Chinese government by shifting the exchange rate system from a dollar peg system to a currency basket system. It evidences the coordination failure.

---

1 Ogawa and Ito (2002).

In this paper, we introduce a proposal of deviation measurements for coordinated exchange rate policies in East Asia to improve the monetary authorities' surveillance process in terms of regional coordination of exchange rate policies (Ogawa and Shimizu, 2005; RIETI, 2005). The deviation measurements are based on an Asian Monetary Unit (AMU), which is a weighted average of intra-regional currencies according to the calculation method in the case of the European Currency Unit (ECU)[2]. An AMU Deviation Indicator is measured as a deviation from the estimated AMU based on the GDP measured at PPP weight and trade weight for each of the thirteen East Asian countries (ASEAN10+3).

The reminder of this paper consists of the following sections. Section 2 shows asymmetric responses of East Asian currencies to the US dollar depreciation under a variety of exchange rate systems of East Asian countries. Section 3 points out the need for regional monetary coordination to solve coordination failure among East Asian countries in selecting their exchange rate system. Section 4 describes our method of estimating the AMU in case of four different patterns of weights and selecting two of them from a viewpoint of stability of the AMU value in terms of currency basket – composed of the US dollar and the euro. Section 5 calculates deviation indicators for each of the East Asian currencies from the AMU. The final section draws some conclusion.

2. Asymmetric Responses of East Asian Currencies to the US Dollar Depreciation

In recent years, the United States has increased the current account deficits and depreciated the US dollar in a situation where decelerated huge capital inflows to the United States. The depreciation of the US dollar has led to the appreciation of other currencies which includes the euro and the Japanese yen. However, we can find asymmetric responses to the US dollar depreciation among East Asian currencies, which results from different choices of exchange rate systems: floating exchange rate system, managed floating exchange rate system, and dollar pegging system. The asymmetric responses of East Asian countries should bias the relative prices of products made in East Asian countries and misallocate resources among the East Asian countries.

---

2 Tanaka and Jin (2003) used the similar method to calculate the exchange rates of East Asian currencies against a weighted average of East Asian currencies. Their sampled currencies are ASEAN4 (excluding Indonesia) plus Japan, China, Korea, Taiwan and Hong Kong. They used nominal GDP and nominal GDP measured at PPP for their weights.

Firstly, we focus on the International Monetary Fund (IMF)'s classification for exchange rate systems in East Asian countries because movements in exchange rates depend on the kind of exchange rate system the monetary authorities are adopting. According to the IMF's classification in 2003, Japan, Korea, and the Philippines are using a floating exchange rate system. Indonesia, Singapore, Thailand, Cambodia, Myanmar, Lao, and Vietnam are adopting a managed floating exchange rate system. China and Malaysia preferred to adopt a fixed exchange rate system, especially by pegging their domestic currencies to the US dollar; however, both countries announced to change their exchange rate systems into a managed floating exchange rate system with reference to a currency basket on 21 July 2005. Hong Kong and Brunei are adopting a currency board system. Hong Kong is pegging its home currency to the US dollar while Brunei is pegging its home currency to the Singapore dollar. Thus, we can divide the East Asian countries' exchange rate systems into three groups: a floating group, a managed floating group, and a fixed (dollar pegging) group. The adopted exchange rate system may determine the degree of linkage of each of the currencies with the US dollar.

The rest of the world should react to the depreciation of the US dollar. When we have a look at the movements of exchange rates of the East Asian currencies, we find asymmetric reactions to the US dollar depreciation. The Japanese yen has appreciated against the US dollar since 2002. The Korean won, the Thai baht, and the Singapore dollar have also appreciated against the US dollar since 2002 together with the Japanese yen, although they have recently depreciated against the Japanese yen. The Indonesia rupiah has appreciated against the US dollar and the Japanese yen while the Philippine peso has depreciated against the US dollar and the Japanese yen. The Chinese Yuan, Hong Kong dollar, and the Malaysian ringgit have pegged to the US dollar. They have depreciated against the Japanese yen after 2002 because the US dollar depreciated against the Japanese yen.

One group of countries that adopt the floating or managed floating exchange rate system faces home currencies' appreciation against the US dollar since 2002. The group includes Japan, Korea, Thailand, and Singapore. The other group consists of countries that officially adopt or *de facto* fix their home currencies to the US dollar. The group includes Malaysia, Hong Kong, and China. Their exchange rates have been fixed against the US dollar in recent years. On one hand, they have been depreciating against the currencies of the former group of countries – Japanese yen, Korean won, Thai baht, and Singapore dollar due to the depreciation of the US dollar since 2002. Thus, all effects of the depreciation of the US dollar might be carried on the currencies under more flexible exchange rate systems.

Ogawa and Ito (2002) put forward the possibilities of coordination failure in choosing exchange rate system and exchange rate policy within a game theoretical framework as long as one country's dollar peg system has an adverse effect on others' exchange rate system through relative price effects. Ogawa (2002) carried out an empirical analysis on whether the dollar pegging currencies had adverse effects on other East Asian countries' exchange rate system and exchange rate policy. They do not choose a desirable exchange rate system but the *de facto* dollar peg system because the dollar pegging countries keep on adopting official or *de facto* dollar peg systems. In other words, the monetary authorities in East Asian countries face a coordination failure in opting for a desirable exchange rate system among East Asian countries. Accordingly, it is clear that we should make regional coordination for a desirable exchange rate regime instead of having a formal or *de facto* dollar peg system.

It is suggested that the dollar pegging countries should adopt a more flexible system such as an intermediate exchange rate system that consists of both currency basket and currency band. The most flexible system does not refer to a free floating exchange rate system but to an intermediate exchange rate system which is located between the free floating exchange rate system and the dollar peg system.

Under the currency basket system, the monetary authorities should not target the US dollar but a currency basket which is a composite of the US dollar, the Japanese yen, and the euro from the viewpoint of international trade partners and FDI. East Asian countries have strong economic relationships in terms of trade, FDI, and international finance between each other and with European countries as well as with the United States. On the one hand, under the currency band system, the monetary authorities should set a band in which the exchange rates are free floating without intervening in the foreign exchange market. The exchange rate band for central banks to conduct their own monetary policies as long as exchange rate did not reach a ceiling nor a floor of the band.

It is necessary that East Asian countries stabilise their exchange rates among the intra-regional currencies and balance their exchange rates against outside currencies such as the US dollar and the euro. The monetary authorities from East Asian countries coordinate their exchange rate policy with their exchange rates against the outside currencies in order to ensure a stability of the exchange rates at both intra-regional and international level. They should not only care about the US dollar and the euro but also about the Japanese yen because Japan has a larger portion in intra-regional economic relationships[3].

3. Regional Monetary Cooperation in East Asia

The monetary authorities of East Asian countries should prevent biased changes in the relative prices caused by the US dollar depreciation under the different exchange rate systems in East Asian countries. To do so, they have been coordinated in the choice of their exchange rate systems and exchange rate policies.

Kawai, Ogawa, and Ito (2004) suggested the following advices concerning the exchange rate policy in East Asia.

First, the monetary authorities of the ASEAN+3 should discuss the exchange rate issue as a part of the surveillance process. They should focus on the exchange rate issue as well as on domestic macroeconomic policies and on the soundness of financial sector: the exchange rates of home currencies against neighbouring countries' are indeed linked by its terms of trade and its competitive prices. Each country in the East Asia region has strong economic relationships with the other intra-regional countries as well as the United States and the European countries. Exchange rates among the intra-regional currencies should affect economic activities in each country of East Asia through intra-regional trade, investments, and finance. The monetary authorities should not only hold under account movements of the exchange rates but also their deviations from the regional averages and, in turn, their exchange rate policies *per se*.

The surveillance process, in itself, might not be sufficiently solid to preserve the regional policy coordination in the long run because the monetary authorities from each country are not committed to the policy coordination. They may make a limited contribution to the policy coordination. It is necessary to have a mechanism that will be able to preserve the regional coordination in the long run by compelling the monetary authorities to be committed to the regional policy coordination. Regarding the regional policy coordination, it is necessary that all the monetary authorities in the region agree on an arrangement to create a regional common unit of account that consists of a basket of regional currencies. They might make a commitment to follow the regional common unit of account in carrying out their exchange rate policy. It is desirable to create a regional common unit of account to which mone-

3 Ogawa and Shimizu (2006) investigated relationships between effective exchange rates and AMU Deviation Indicators.

tary authorities of East Asian countries should target in conducting their exchange rate policies in order that they should make regional policy coordination for their exchange rate policies with each other. To do so, an AMU should be introduced as a regional common unit of account into East Asia. For this purpose, a common currency basket that includes regional currencies of the ASEAN+3 countries is created.

4. AMU and AMU Deviation Indicator

A. The Purpose of AMU and AMU Deviation Indicators for East Asian Currencies

The monetary authorities of East Asian countries have been strengthening their regional monetary cooperation since the Asian currency crisis of 1997. This monetary cooperation – which resulted in the CMI after the crisis – was established by the ASEAN+3 as a network of bilateral and multilateral swap arrangements to manage a currency crisis in the member countries. Under the CMI, the monetary authorities should conduct surveillance to prevent a currency crisis in the future.

As a criterion of the new surveillance system, we put forward the creation of an AMU and AMU Deviation Indicators for East Asian currencies. These should contribute to the coordination of exchange rate policies in East Asia, thereby enhancing the monetary authorities' surveillance capabilities. We calculate the AMU as a weighted average of East Asian currencies according to the method used to calculate the ECU adopted by EU countries under the European Monetary System (EMS) prior to the introduction of the euro. The AMU Deviation Indicators for each East Asian currency are measured to show the degree of deviation from the Benchmark Rate for each of the East Asian currencies in terms of the AMU.

We provide a Nominal AMU Deviation Indicator on a daily basis and a Real AMU Deviation Indicator, which is adjusted to differences in inflation, on a monthly basis. The Real AMU Deviation Indicators are more appropriate for conducting surveillance on the effects of changes in exchange rates on the real economy, while the Nominal AMU Deviation Indicators are more useful for monitoring their day-to-day deviations from the AMU.

B. Calculating the Value of the AMU

We choose the ASEAN10+3 currencies as the component currencies of the AMU. The ASEAN10+3 comprise Brunei, Cambodia, Indonesia, Laos, Malaysia, Myanmar, the Philippines, Singapore, Thailand, Vietnam, Japan, South Korea, and China.

We calculate the AMU according to the method used to calculate the ECU under the EMS prior to the introduction of the euro in 1999. As the ECU was defined as a basket of currencies of EU member countries, the AMU is defined as a basket currency of the ASEAN10+3 countries. The weight of each currency in the basket is based on both the countries' respective shares of GDP measured at PPP, and trade volumes (the sum of exports and imports) in the total of sampled countries for the relevant country. We calculate the countries' shares of GDP measured at PPP and their trade volumes for 2001-2003 as the currency shares of the AMU. The average for the past three years on the basis of available data, is used to calculate the currency shares in order to reflect the most recent trade relationships and economic conditions of the thirteen East Asian countries for the calculation of the AMU.

We should quote the value of the AMU in terms of weighted average of the US dollar and the euro because both the United States and EU countries are important trading partners for East Asia. The weighted average of the US dollar and the euro (hereafter, US$-euro) is based on the East Asian countries' trade volumes with the United States and the euro area. The weights on the US dollar and the euro are set at 65% and 35%, respectively[4].

Then, we choose a benchmark period in order to calculate AMU Deviation Indicators. The benchmark period is defined as the following: the total trade balance of member countries, the total trade balance of member countries (excluding Japan) with Japan, and the total trade balance of member countries with the rest of world should be relatively close to zero.

Table 1 shows the trade accounts of the thirteen East Asian countries from 1990 to 2003. It indicates that the trade accounts were the closest to balance in 2001. If we assume that a one-year time lag before changes in exchange rates affect trade volumes, we should choose 2000 and 2001 as a benchmark period. For the benchmark period, the exchange rate of the AMU in terms of the US$-euro is set to be a unity. We define the exchange rate of each East Asian currency in terms of the AMU during the benchmark period as the Benchmark Exchange Rate.

---

4 We calculate the average trade volumes for 2001-2003.

Table 1. Trade Accounts (net) of ASEAN10 + Japan, South Korea and China

million of US$

	with Japan*	within ASEAN+3	with World
1990	-23,437	-1,738	35,513
1991	-33,084	-4,710	56,318
1992	-41,172	-871	87,331
1993	-54,184	-4,995	86,324
1994	-65,089	9,511	1,969,336
1995	-73,856	14,610	2,376,160
1996	-59,680	12,231	2,437,658
1997	-54,531	26,440	236,500
1998	-29,802	12,102	215,241
1999	-32,065	4,791	4,819
2000	-37,239	-6,593	-6,562
2001	-23,997	1,934	1,953
2002	-40,027	12,265	12,289
2003	-55,724	27,701	27,727

Notes: All figures are calculated by the authors. Trade data are from DOT (IMF) and GDP data are from IFS (IMF).

* The figure of trade account with Japan is the total amount of current account (net) with 12 East Asian countries.

In short, the AMU weights are calculated on the basis of the arithmetic average of both shares of trade volumes and GDP measured at PPP for the years 2001-2003. The Benchmark Exchange Rate for each currency is defined in terms of the AMU during 2000-2001. Table 2 shows the AMU weights as well as trade volume, GDP measured at PPP, arithmetic shares, and the Benchmark Exchange Rates.

We can use the AMU weights in Table 2 to calculate an exchange rate for the AMU in terms of the US$-euro as follows[5]:

(1)

$$US\$/euro/_{AMU} = 0.0069\,US\$/euro/_{BN\$} + 7.4235\,US\$/euro/_{CBR} + 2.7711\,US\$/euro/_{CNY}$$
$$+ 452.7871\,US\$/euro/_{IDR} + 30.5681\,US\$/euro/_{JPY} + 113.1459\,US\$/euro/_{KRW}$$
$$+ 5.9500\,US\$/euro/_{LOK} + 0.1953\,US\$/euro/_{MLR} + 0.0239\,US\$/euro/_{MYK}$$
$$+ 1.3347\,US\$/euro/_{PLP} + 0.1075\,US\$/euro/_{SP\$} + 2.0630\,US\$/euro/_{TLB}$$
$$+ 243.0432\,US\$/euro/_{VTD}$$

5 BN$ = Brunei dollar, CBR = Cambodia riel, CNY = Chinese yuan, IDR = Indonesian rupiah, JPY = Japanese yen, KRW = Korean won, LOK = Lao kip, MLR = Malaysian ringgit, MYK = Myanmar kyat, PLP = Philippine peso, SP$ = Singapore dollar, TLB = Thai baht, VTD = Vietnamese dong.

Table 2. AMU weights of East Asian Currencies (benchmark year=2000/2001)

	Trade volume* %	GDP measured at PPP**,%	Arithmetic shares % (a)	Benchmark exchange rate*** (b)	AMU weights (a)/(b)
Brunei	0.41	0.41	0.41	0.5912	0.0069
Cambodia	0.19	0.21	0.20	0.0003	7.4235
China	21.65	47.93	34.79	0.1256	2.7711
Indonesia	4.67	5.56	5.12	0.0001	452.7871
Japan	27.31	28.30	27.80	0.0091	30.5681
South Korea	12.86	6.65	9.76	0.0009	113.1459
Laos	0.09	0.08	0.08	0.0001	5.9500
Malaysia	8.85	1.83	5.34	0.2735	0.1953
Myanmar	0.38	0.38	0.38	0.1598	0.0239
Philippines	3.12	2.74	2.93	0.0220	1.3347
Singapore	11.90	0.81	6.36	0.5912	0.1075
Thailand	6.60	3.56	5.08	0.0246	2.0630
Vietnam	1.96	1.53	1.74	0.0001	243.0432

* Trade volume is calculated as an average of total export and import volumes for 2001-2003 from the Direction of Trade Statistics.

** GDP measured at PPP is the average of GDP measured at PPP for 2001-2003 from the World Development Report, World Bank. For Brunei and Myanmar, we use the same share of trade volume since there are no GDP data for Brunei and Myanmar.

*** Benchmark exchange rate ($-euro/Currency) is the average of daily exchange rate in terms of $-euro in 2001 and 2002.

Figure 1 shows daily movements in the nominal exchange rate of the AMU in terms of the US$-euro. As a matter of reference, we add daily movements in both of the nominal exchange rates of the AMU in terms of the US dollar and the euro. The nominal exchange rate of the AMU in terms of the US$-euro is relatively stable compared with both exchange rates of the AMU in terms of the US dollar and the euro. The stability of the AMU in terms of the US$-euro results from the portfolio effect of mixing both currencies

C. Calculating Nominal and Real AMU Deviation Indicators

We use the nominal exchange rate of each East Asian currency in terms of the AMU to calculate a Nominal AMU Deviation Indicator for each East Asian currency from the Benchmark Exchange Rate from the viewpoint of deviation from the AMU, which is a weighted average of East Asian currencies concerned according to the following formula:

(2)

$$\text{Nominal Deviation Indicator } (\%) = \frac{\text{actual exchange rate of } AMU/_{a\ currency} - \text{benchmark exchange rate of } AMU/_{a\ currency}}{\text{benchmark exchange rate of } AMU/_{a\ currency}} \times 100$$

An increase in the AMU Deviation Indicator means an overvaluation compared to the benchmark level. On the one hand, a decrease in the AMU Deviation Indicator means an undervaluation compared to the benchmark level.

Figures 2 and 3 show movements in the Nominal AMU Deviation Indicators on a daily and monthly basis, respectively. They show that the Korean won has been overvalued 15% compared with the benchmark period since May 2005. On the one hand, the Philippine peso has been depreciating over the time. It is recently undervalued of 15% compared with the benchmark period. In addition, the Lao kip has been undervalued of 30% compared with the benchmark period due to its devaluation in May 2005.

Then, we calculate an AMU Deviation Indicator in real terms by taking into account inflation rate differentials. Given that the Nominal AMU Deviation Indicator is defined as an equation (2), we calculate a Real AMU

Deviation Indicator according to the following equation:

(3)

$$\begin{aligned} &\textit{Rate of Change in Re al AMU Deviation Indicator}_i \\ &\qquad = \textit{Rate of Change in Re al AMU Deviation Indicator}_i - \left(\dot{P}_{AMU} - \dot{P}_i\right) \end{aligned}$$

where $\dot{P}_{AMU}$ is the inflation rate in the AMU area, and $\dot{P}_i$ is the inflation rate in country quoted i.

We use Consumer Price Index (CPI) data as the price index in calculating the Real AMU Deviation Indicator[6]. As the CPI data are only available on a monthly basis, we calculate the Real AMU Deviation Indicator per month. As for the inflation rates in the AMU area, we calculate a weighted average of the CPI for the AMU area by using the AMU shares, which is the combination of shares in terms of trade volumes and GDP measured at PPP.

Figure 4 shows movements in the Real AMU Deviation Indicators on a monthly basis for each of the East Asian currencies. We can find some differences between the Nominal and Real AMU Deviation Indicators. In the case of Indonesia rupiah, the Real AMU Deviation Indicator has been rather appreciating since July 2003 while the Nominal AMU Deviation Indicator has been depreciating from July 2003 onwards. The differences reflect a higher inflation rate in Indonesia.

6 We use the CPI data as a price index because there are data constraints for some of the sampled countries where we have no alternative data but to use the CPI data as a price index.

Higher inflation tends to cause the appreciation of home currency even though it is depreciating. The Lao kip has been appreciating in terms of the Real AMU Deviation Indicator although it has been depreciating in terms of Nominal AMU Deviation Indicator. In contrast, both the Korean won and the Thai baht have been appreciating in terms of Real AMU Deviation Indicators by echoing appreciation in terms of Nominal AMU Deviation Indicators.

We should monitor the Real AMU Deviation Indicators rather than the Nominal AMU Deviation Indicators in order to consider the effects of exchange rates on real economic variables such as trade volumes and real GDP. On the other hand, the Nominal AMU Deviation Indicators are more useful than the Real AMU Deviation Indicators when we consider both frequency and time lags as important for monitoring these measures. Accordingly, we should use the Nominal and Real AMU Deviation Indicators as complementary measures for scrutinising the exchange rate policies and related macroeconomic variables and, in turn, for devising coordinated exchange rate policies among the East Asian currencies.

5. Conclusion

In this paper, we have put forward deviation measurements for coordinated exchange rate policies in East Asia so as to enhance the monetary authorities' surveillance process in terms of regional coordination of exchange rate policies. The deviation measurements are based on an AMU that is a weighted average of intra-regional currencies according to the calculation method in the case of the ECU. An AMU Deviation Indicator is measured as a deviation from estimated AMU based on the GDP measured at PPP weight and trade weight for each of the thirteen East Asian countries (ASEAN10+3).

We found that only the Singapore dollar and the Brunei dollar had +/-2.5% of deviation from the benchmark rates. The East Asian currencies had almost 30% of deviations from the benchmark rates between the extreme currencies in November 2004 in comparison with the benchmark rates in 2000 and 2001. The diversity of exchange rate systems in East Asia tends to make misalignment among the East Asian currencies wider.

Regarding the deviation indicators, we have not only calculated in nominal terms but also in real terms by taking into account inflation rate differentials. From the viewpoint of data frequency, nominal deviation indicators can be watched in real time, and we are able to use them as the indicator of daily surveillance. On the other hand, considering effects of exchange rate on real economic activity, we should look at the deviation indicators in real term. Accordingly, it is necessary to focus on both the nominal and real deviation indicators as an indicator for surveillance the coordinated exchange rate policies in East Asia.

Thus, we can use the deviation indicators of actual exchange rate of East Asian currencies in terms of the AMU from the benchmark rate to identify how much each of the East Asian currencies deviates from the AMU that is equivalent to a weighted average of the East Asian currencies. We can use the measurement for active surveillance process in terms of intra-region exchange rates in order to make coordinated exchange rate policies among the ASEAN+3.

References

Jin, Ming, Hao (2003), "Stability of the Exchange Rate by the Basket of Currencies in East Asia: The Examination of the Application of the ECU Divergence Indicator Guideline Method in East Asia," *Kenkyu-nenpo Keizaigaku (Tohoku University)*, Vol. 65, p. 111-127. (in Japanese)

Kawai, Masahiro, Eiji Ogawa, and Takatoshi Ito (2004), "Developing New Regional Financial Architecture: A Proposal," mimeo.

Ogawa, Eiji (2002), "Economic interdependence and international coordination in East Asia," in Exchange Rate Regimes for Asia (Kobe Research Project) (http://www.mof.go.jp/jouhou/kokkin/tyousa/tyou042f.pdf), Ministry of Finance.

Ogawa, Eiji (2004), "Regional Monetary Cooperation in East Asia against Asymmetric Responses to the US Dollar Depreciation," *Journal of the Korean Economy*, Vol. 5, No. 2, p. 43-72.

Ogawa, Eiji and Takatoshi Ito (2002), "On the Desirability of a Regional Basket Currency Arrangement," *Journal of the Japanese and International Economies*, Vol. 16, No. 3, p. 317-334.

Ogawa, Eiji and Junko Shimizu (2005), "A Deviation Measurement for Coordinated Exchange Rate Policies in East Asia," *RIETI Discussion Paper*, No. 05-E-017.

Ogawa, Eiji and Junko Shimizu (2006), "AMU Deviation Indicator for Coordinated Exchange Rate Policies in East Asia and its Relation with Effective Exchange Rates," *RIETI Discussion Paper*, No. 06-E-002.

RIETI (2005), "AMU and AMU Deviation Indicators," RIETI's website (http://www.rieti.go.jp/users/amu/en/index.html).

Tanaka, Soko and Seiichi Fujita (2003), "*Euro to kokusai-tsuuka system (Euro and the international currency system)*," Sotensha publishing. (in Japanese)

Tanaka, Soko and Jin Ming Hao (2004), "Dollar, euro, yen no tsuka Basket niyoru higashi Asia no kawase souba kyoryoku (The foreign exchange coordination by the currency basket composed with the US dollar, the euro and the Japanese yen in East Asian countries)," *Sekaikeizai-hyoron*, 6-20 November. (in Japanese)

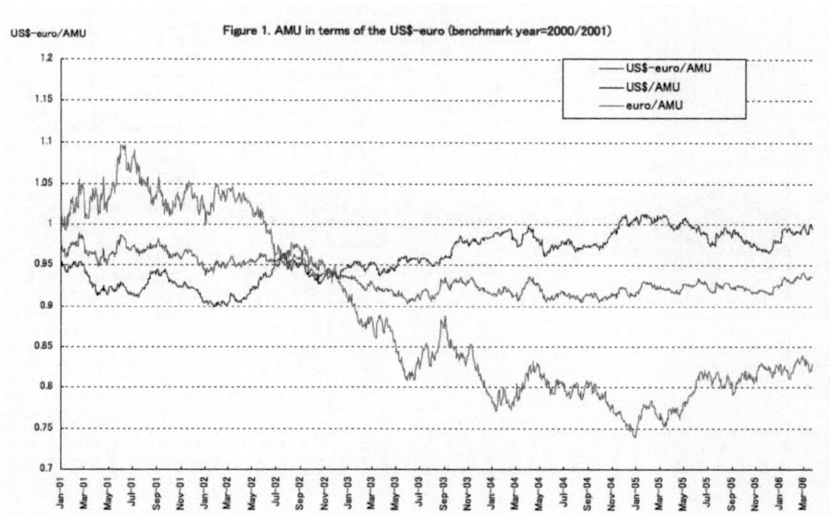
US$-euro/AMU
Figure 1. AMU in terms of the US$-euro (benchmark year=2000/2001)
US$-euro/AMU
US$/AMU
euro/AMU
1.2
1.15
1.1
1.05
1
0.95
0.9
0.85
0.8
0.75
0.7
Jan-01
Mar-01
May-01
Jul-01
Sep-01
Nov-01
Jan-02
Mar-02
May-02
Jul-02
Sep-02
Nov-02
Jan-03
Mar-03
May-03
Jul-03
Sep-03
Nov-03
Jan-04
Mar-04
May-04
Jul-04
Sep-04
Nov-04
Jan-05
Mar-05
May-05
Jul-05
Sep-05
Nov-05
Jan-06
Mar-06

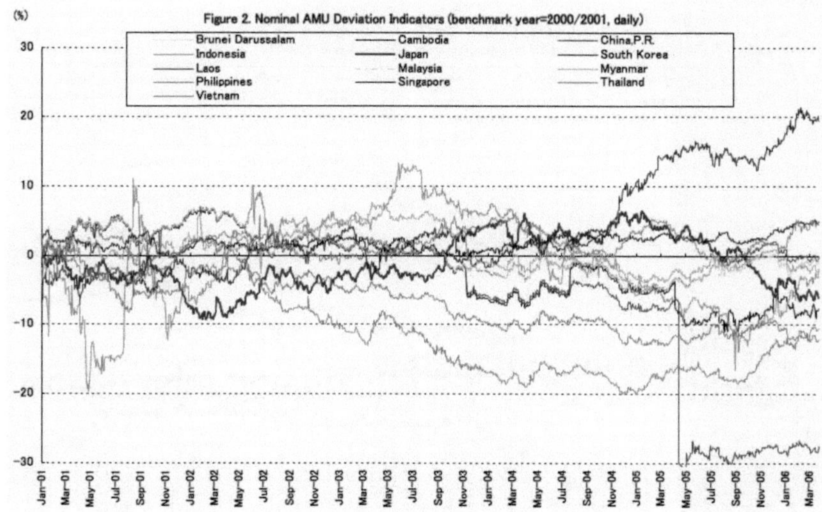
(%)
Figure 2. Nominal AMU Deviation Indicators (benchmark year=2000/2001, daily)
Brunei Darussalam
Cambodia
China,P.R.
Indonesia
Japan
South Korea
Laos
Malaysia
Myanmar
Philippines
Singapore
Thailand
Vietnam
30
20
10
0
-10
-20
-30
Jan-01
Mar-01
May-01
Jul-01
Sep-01
Nov-01
Jan-02
Mar-02
May-02
Jul-02
Sep-02
Nov-02
Jan-03
Mar-03
May-03
Jul-03
Sep-03
Nov-03
Jan-04
Mar-04
May-04
Jul-04
Sep-04
Nov-04
Jan-05
Mar-05
May-05
Jul-05
Sep-05
Nov-05
Jan-06
Mar-06

Figure 3. Nominal AMU Deviation Indicators (benchmark year=2000/2001, monthly)

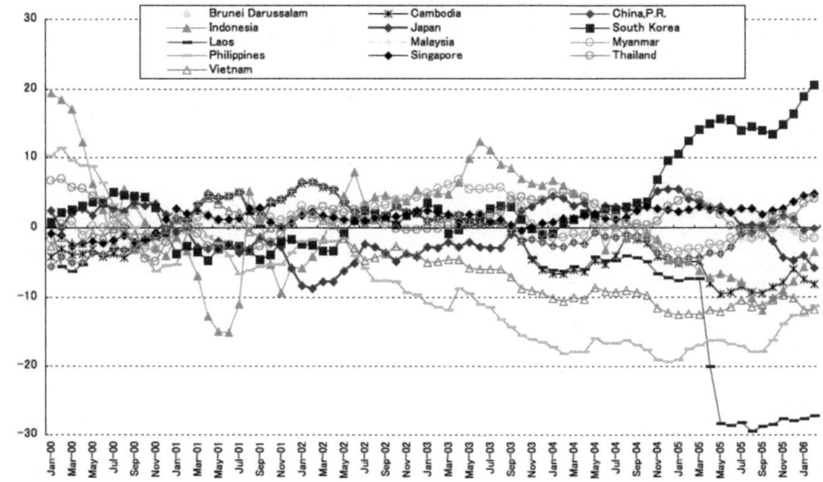

Figure 4. Real AMU Deviation Indicators (benchmark year=2000/2001, monthly)

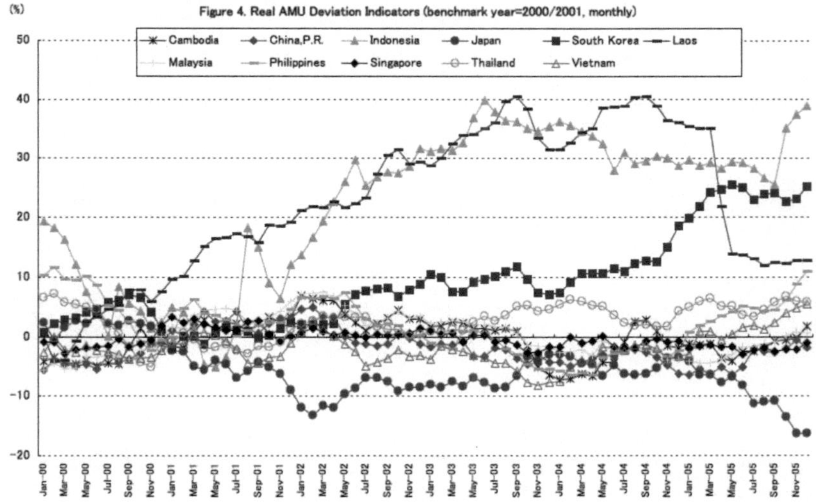

The Doha Development Agenda, a Cheap Round, Really?

Pierre DEFRAIGNE

Professor ULB, UCL & College of Europe
Director eur-IFRI[1]

What makes the Doha Round the most urgent priority of the global governance agenda is simply that there is no other global public good, with a positive impact on world growth, in the making or within reach today.

Three ingredients are needed for its success: a substantive and fair compromise between the US, the EU and the G-20 which would also carry true benefits for the G-90; an ultimate deadline in a not too far distant future, but still workable; a political momentum. The first two conditions are met: the Hong Kong package although bearing mainly on modalities and not yet on figures and dates, is very promising; the expiry of the Trade Promotion Authority granted by the US Congress to the President in June 2007 provides us with a very tight time set. What remains uncertain is the degree of political readiness within the new Triangle of trading powers. Nobody among them though would probably have the guts to say no; even the USA who, still caught in the Iraq quagmire as they are, try to reconcile themselves with multilateralism. Therefore one has just to find among the political leaders the one who will have the vision and the courage to throw his political credit in building up a coalition of the willing to wind up the Round quickly on a success. The Doha Round, although leaving many problems unresolved and despite the fact that it's only a piece in the global governance jigsaw, is worth engaging the battle.

What is really at stake? What are the alternatives? What needs to be done to turn trade liberalisation into effective development?

---

1 This chapter was completed in June 2006.

What Is at Stake? A Decisive Step towards a More Balanced, More Efficient and More Sustainable International Division of Labour

The perception according to which the Doha Round is dubbed as a cheap one stems from the change in the initial agenda. The undisputable success of the Uruguay Round which dismantled the 30-years-old MFA quota system, brought back agriculture in the loop of the negotiation, integrated intellectual property protection in the disciplines of the GATT and eventually set up the WTO on a universal membership base with a pretty effective jurisdictional branch, the DSM, unprecedented in the field of global governance, left nevertheless participating countries with deep frustrations and somewhat contradictory expectations.

On the one hand, the industrialised countries wanted to finish the business of market access through dismantling a new set of 'behind-the-border' obstacles, namely the Singapore issues – domestic policies, or the lack of them – in competition, investment, public procurement and trade facilitation – as well as to expand services liberalisation still at an embryonic level but for the most advanced countries. The Cairns group soon enough realised that their formidable victory on agriculture in the UR was mainly about extending the WTO principles and disciplines to the sector, but without much actual content with regard to effective cuts in subsidies and tariffs reduction. The developing world was also frustrated by the inclusion of intellectual property protection in the system on developed countries terms. Most developing countries were overwhelmed by the complexity of the deal and by the burden of implementing its provisions while not garnering significant additional benefits: the Agreement on agriculture was perceived as a victory on paper and the MFA dismantlement about which all ITCB members were pretty enthusiastic at the start, raised later the prospect of China reaping the whole harvest. Northern Trade Unions and civil society launched a vigorous campaign on what was described as an unfair and incomplete deal: not enough had been done for the developing countries; major issues had been left outside such as workers rights and environment – the so-called 'trade-ands' – whereas TRIPs violated the poor countries right to access to medicines. The EU therefore agreed in 1998 to push the launch of a new Round, the Millennium Round, with the view for the North of keeping the momentum of further liberalisation and for the South, of correcting the imbalances of the deal.

The EU took the lead in designing a broad and comprehensive agenda balancing liberalisation and rules setting, and based on the key principle of the single undertaking according to which there is agreement on nothing as long as there is no agreement on anything.

Alas, the agenda got slimmer along the way to launch (Doha 2001). Firstly, Seattle ministerial conference (1999), the first to fail in WTO's short history, marked the actual dropping of the core labour standards off the tentative agenda – confirmed in Doha (2001) – because of an unanimous hostility from the developing countries following a rather provocative statement of President Clinton, on the eve of the US Presidential election, linking market access and respect of ILO Conventions. Post launching, the first Ministerial, Cancun (2003), another fiasco, watered further the programme by what was perceived by some participants as a premature EU concession to the developing countries, namely the storage of three of the Singapore issues – competition, investment and transparency in government procurement – on the shelves of the WTO, leaving only Trade Facilitation on the Doha Development agenda. Yet this major cut, particularly at odds with the development needs which provide the rationale for the Round, was probably the price to pay to prevent the DDA from sinking inexorably into the abysses. The Round was then put on life support until may 2004 when, a bold move from the EU – a joint letter from Pascal Lamy and Franz Fischler, respectively then Trade and Agriculture Commissioners – provided the Five Interested Partners (FIP) for farm matters – Brazil, USA, EU, India and Australia – with the elements of a core deal on agriculture modalities. This deal was endorsed in Geneva on 31 July, unlocking the global negotiation.

At first sight the gap between the original grand design and the present 'down to earth' agenda is huge, hence the prevailing mood of disenchantment among the observers and the temptation to drop the whole exercise altogether or at least to put it off by several years under the fallacious hope that meanwhile trade liberalisation ambition would have picked up. True, the agenda has shrunk, but it is actually more substantive than commonly perceived; moreover nothing indicates where a reversal of the Doha sceptical mood could come from. The opposite is actually true: trade liberalisation is a step by step process. It compares more to Pascal Lamy's morning jogging than to Steve Fossett's global circum-navigation by balloon record. It is the Round routine which maintains the multilateral trade system in good shape. It forces Geneva negotiators and their capitals to keep alert to protectionist moves and to react quickly to an approaching threat, a bit like the Capitol's geese, while they keep busy clarifying the extraordinary complexity of a in-depth liberalisation agenda for 150 countries ranging from Vuanutu to the USA. Let us look at the state of play of the negotiation.

What Is on the Offer? What Can We Expect in Terms of Sustainable Development?

On agriculture which was from the start the maker or breaker of the deal, the progress is staggering. But it would be wrong to put it exclusively to the credit of the Round since the dynamics of change were essentially domestic, particularly in Europe. There are indeed on both sides of the Atlantic, and it is probably true everywhere, although maybe to a lesser extent in Korea and in Japan despite their higher protection level, very good domestic reasons to bring down subsidies and open up both domestic and foreign markets in the agricultural sector. The ongoing reform of a costly, unfair and environment unfriendly CAP in the EU was badly needed; the reform of an outdated, costly and inefficient Farm bill in the USA has still to take place in America. Yet it is the Round and only the Round that can lock in change where it is already underway, like in EU, and that can trigger it off where the reform process must still begin like in the USA.

Let us come back to the content of a possible agricultural deal.

Firstly there is a commitment to eliminate farm export subsidies by 2013, with a substantial part of them gone already by 2010, and parallel treatment of all other forms of export subsidies including abusive forms of export credits, state trading enterprises and food aid. Secondly, there will be effective cuts of domestic subsidies when they actually distort trade, with higher reductions for countries with the highest subsidies as well with the capping on specific products and even for the "blue box" aids, i.e. not linked to production. Thirdly, the Doha round should put an upper limit to the overall farm spending in such a way than the final cuts could be higher than the sum of the individual reductions. What remains very sensitive is the level of market access. The EU is still officially offering 39% cuts with 8% of tariff lines to be treated as sensitive products subject to more modest cuts but access by means of tariff quotas whereas the G-20 request 54% cuts and a 1% of sensitive products and the USA 66% with a 1% sensitive products. Recently EU has indicated its flexibility to move towards G-20's position. Even, under the most conservative of these proposals, agricultural tariffs would be closer to a one digit level, something that we only achieved on industrial tariffs after 50 years of trade opening.

It is important to realise that the effective level of cuts is far above the level of the UR where there was enough water under the bridge – namely the existing gap between applied and binding tariffs – to allow for non-biting reductions, i.e. cuts on paper. This time, cuts of subsidies and tariffs will bring about real changes in trade flows. In other words we are here, for the first time after the elimination of textiles quotas, dismantling one of the major North-South distortions inherited from the colonial era and the post colonial age. Moreover we are substituting extensive agriculture – for example in the Mercosur – for intensive agriculture in Europe which is a major step towards sustainability; the final impact on environment though will have to include the additional transportation costs which the deal will entail as well as possible encroachments on primary tropical forests and soil erosion in the exporting countries. But changing to a multilateral regime from a preferential one such as Cotonou which was aimed at sharing, with a few developing countries, part of the protection rent granted to EU farmers in key products such as meat, sugar and rice, brings about also major losses for those countries. Less competitive DCs fear suffering from an erosion of their preferences as a result of the progress made towards multilateral liberalisation of farm trade although FTAs are a bigger threat and, but for bananas, erosion bites the most in clothing and fisheries, and for few countries. Nevertheless transition costs must be shared and compensations granted to those poor countries, both by advanced countries and by emerging economies.

With regard to industrial products, three major advances are possible. The first one would be the engineering of a so-called Swiss formula which would bring average tariffs down through higher reductions on peak tariffs and on escalation tariffs, both again a remnant of the colonial age. The second would require high tariff countries such India and Brazil to bring down their protection level to the China one with all due transitions and flexibility. Both governments might be well aware that in many cases high tariffs hamper their industrialisation by generating cosy rents for inefficient producers as well by endangering their exports competitiveness because of the high cost of their imported intermediary goods and components or by making their equipment investments too expensive, entailing a waste of scarce savings. But resistances in both camps are strong although the situation differs among them. Brazil's offensive interests in agriculture give some leverage to the government for challenging the defensive interests of part of the Brazilian industry. India's situation is in some respects not very dissimilar to the USA one during its phase of rapid industrialisation by the end of the 19th century: it can relay on a huge and growing domestic market; contrary to China which has paid its adhesion to WTO by lowering its protection, India still enjoys high tariffs like the USA one century ago; moreover and provided it improves its business environment, it can attract technology-intensive FDI which might allow India to leapfrog in some industrial sectors with an impact on agriculture as well. Therefore India is more on the defensive on both Nama and agriculture and for that reason, it is, along with the USA the country that holds the key of the DDA. It is only the pressure from outside which will allow Brazilia and New-Delhi to cope with their domestic protectionist lobbies so as to work out the right mix of protection and openness consistent with their development needs. Thirdly, the growing number of anti dumping cases, in particular from and among emerging economies, although a horizontal problem, bears mainly on industrial products: they recreate a new line of protection often in a very unfair and costly way both for the foreign exporter and the local consumer. A streamlining of the national anti-dumping and anti subsidies legislations based on best practices would pre-empt the development of one of the most insidious and effective protection tactics. Such an updating of WTO antidumping legislation is also on the Doha round agenda.

NAMA liberalisation in particular in the large emerging economies is often presented by Peter Mandelson and Rob Portman the trade negotiators from the countries which have to bear the burden of sacrifices in farm trade, as the indispensable counterpart for their politically sensitive concessions. And indeed the old mercantilist tit for tat, for all its conceptual irrelevance, remains a very effective negotiating tool without which no deal is possible. The problem for EU and US is that, but for agriculture, their pockets are empty: they have already brought down their average MFN tariffs significantly and made preferential concessions which leave them dry of cash for the give and take game.

Here again though, the benefits of a substantive NAMA are obvious from a sustainable development standpoint: developing countries will gain in terms of market access for their industrial exports to rich countries since the latter will have to dismantle tariff peaks on products such as textiles or footwear (presently at two digits rates) and thanks to cheaper imports, they will strengthen their competitiveness and improve the standards of living of their consumers. Yet three pitfalls will have to be avoided: the concentration of the benefits in some advanced and emerging economies; the preferences erosion which derives arithmetically, for the beneficiary countries, from the lowering of MFN industrial tariffs; and last but not least, nobody can overlook the formidable adjustment costs further globalisation will impose on the advanced countries labour sector, as well as the enormous difficulty for developing countries to cope with the pressure from more advanced competitors. Although these costs are mainly transitional and will fade away in the long term, they must be addressed now because in the long term we are all dead and certainly politicians running for re-election every four years.

The issue of distribution of the welfare gains generated by trade and investment liberalisation is taking new proportions with sluggish growth in Europe and Japan and explosive inequalities in the USA. For some developing countries, such as witnessed by the clothing sector collapse in Mauritius following the final stage of MFA dismantlement or by the relocation of part of the 20-years old Mexican maquiladora industry towards China, "winner takes all" scenarios, linked to the new forms of globalisation are getting a serious possibility.

The fishing sector will see some key developments in the critical and sensitive area of subsidies which have an impact not only on competition but on the depletion of the fishing resources as well.

A new area will be added to the WTO edifice: trade facilitation. Behind this esoteric name lies a set of rules to reduce the cost of business by simplifying customs and border procedures, to the benefit of many SMEs, in particular in developing countries, but also to cut down on corruption stemming from lax customs administrations.

The most difficult liberalisation area remains the services sector despite its growing importance in trade and its critical impact on the development of the South. Services are very diverse and pose many specific problems which vary from one country to another not only on the ground of the differences in development level and therefore of impact on competitiveness, but also with regard to the institutional and regulatory setting which reflect huge differences in collective preferences. This is all too obvious in Europe for the audiovisual sector and for the general interest services such as health, education, water distribution and sometimes energy. Moreover, developing countries' main offensive interests usually lie in mode 4 of services delivery, namely temporary stay in the importing country, which resonates with the sensitive issue of clandestine immigration in USA and in EU. There is no doubt that the modernisation of the services sector, particularly in the field of business to business services, construction, distribution, finance and telecommunications services, is critical for the diversification of the export base and in general for a successful industrialisation in the developing world. There is strong evidence that some competition from outside in the services sector can stimulate critical productivity gains which percolate in the whole economic structure. Yet the high labour content of most services and their sometimes strategic impact – think of finance and telecommunications – on the overall economy make them still a very special case: on the one hand, there is a reluctance to see them fall prey to foreign investors up to a too large extent in the host country; on the other hand, in the exporting countries the lobbies might be very active, but the constituencies are rather narrow if only because most of the benefits actually accrue to the shareholders whereas, contrary to goods exports, few jobs are created a home. The finance and distribution sectors offer a typical example of this skewed sharing of benefits between business and labour. This makes it difficult to put those sectors on the top of industrialised countries offensive interests' agenda. For these reasons, the plurilateral and the bilateral routes will probably remain the most effective fashion to make headway in the area of services although valuable horizontal results can be reaped from the DDA.

A Development Round? Whose Development?

The developmental dimension of the Round is very complex to assess although, since Doha, development provides the DDA with its main political rationale. The link between trade and development is indeed a very tricky one, contrary to the simplistic assertions dear to the sect of free-trade old believers. But for the obvious case of autarky which indeed never worked, the degree of opening-up to imports, the sequencing of liberalisation, the quality of flanking policies – from a social safety net to the supply of key public infrastructures and services – confront policy-makers with difficult choices. The size of the country, its geography, its history, and the strength of its institutions orientate the liberalisation strategy along one path or another: just look at the contrasting policies of successful countries such as Hong Kong and Korea, Malaysia and Thailand with regard to the link between trade and development strategy. Countries that have the institutional and political capacity to interact with global markets – exports and FDI – have a lot to gain from a successful Round because of the so-called trickle down effect: wherever growth originates, they will benefit. Unfit countries have a lot to lose unless they engage in very demanding reforms agendas, which sometimes take one generation. Moreover, their own success is often linked to the success of their close neighbours because of the importance of regional market and policy spillovers: it is difficult for an African country, particularly a landlocked country, to benefit from trade liberalisation if its neighbours do not proceed along the same path.

The breaking up in Cancun of the developing countries block into the G-20 – the emerging economies – and the G-90 – the left behind developing countries – was therefore not a surprise and, in a way, is a very good thing from a development perspective: it clarifies indeed, at least in conceptual terms, the key question of the differentiation among developing countries, but the G-20 must here take their responsibilities. Moreover the emergence of the G-20 has rekindled a dynamics in the negotiation. Brazil can take credit for this success: theirs was a very clever and very timely move.

The G-20 will be one of the big winner in the deal, and therefore G-20 Members should be made bigger contributors than they used to be in the past. The time of free riding is indeed over: "agriculture benefits against NAMA and services concessions" is the mantra of both US and EU. Here is the key of Celso Amorin's "basic triangle": EU and G-20 get US agri subsidies cut; G-20 and US get EU tariffs down; EU and US should therefore get more access to goods and services in developing countries such as India, Brazil and South-Africa, being suggested that China high-cost ticket of entry in the WTO (2001) dispenses it now from additional concessions beyond the general reduction formula. But this Triangle has to be extended into a Quadrangle since the G-90's legitimate demands for compensating their preferences erosion must be taken into account.

A first answer lies in the usual facilities offered by the "special and differential treatment" which is the recurrent item across the whole Doha agenda (transitions, exemptions, flexibility): it amounts to a "round for free" for the small and vulnerable developing countries, a very strange expression in a mercantilist world, not very reassuring in a way. A more substantive attempt to meet the interests of the G-90 consists of extending, from all industrialised countries to the 50 least developed countries, the so called "quota free, tariff free" regime already offered by the EU under the codename "Everything but arms." Yet the most significant compensation might come from G-90 preferential market access to the emerging economies themselves whose market characteristics and perspectives might prove particularly adapted to LDC's supply. Most emerging economics have indeed been maintaining high tariffs, during the previous Rounds, as a result of the free-riding mechanism, embodied in the MFN clause. Such tariffs represent a real obstacle for industrialised countries; but they became an absolute one for the poor countries. Hence the growing request for more market access addressed by least developed and less competitive countries to the larger or/and more competitive ones, both in agriculture and in NAMA.

Then comes a package of technical and financial assistance geared towards helping developing countries to build up more institutional capacity in the area of trade as well as to upgrade their supply capacity through infrastructure investments. Such a linkage between aid and trade makes sense. Yet it also raises two questions: firstly, can dedicated aid in the area of trade prove more effective than traditional development aid, so far a mixed success to say the least? In other words aren't we offering a fake compensation for the lack of real benefits to countries entangled in poor governance, shortage of energy and infrastructures, debt and lack of entrepreneurial skills? Can they really absorb, in an efficient way, rather sophisticated aid for trade programmes whereas they are still coping with basic domestic priorities in the field of food crops health, education and basic infrastructure? Secondly, isn't there a serious risk to find ourselves, by the end of the Round, in a position where money will make the difference for wrapping up the deal? Will these be "additional and new resources" or just a reshuffling of existing programmes or of cancellation a "paper debt"? Does it make sense to buy off the nuisance power of marginal countries in the trade area by taking the risk to divert aid from more effective development achievements or necessities?

Such questions will not receive an appropriate answer in the short span of time until the DDA closure. Yet they should be looked into in the aftermath of the Round closure.

What Alternatives to the Doha Round, If Any?

Trade liberalisation takes many routes. Multilateralism is the most effective one because it gathers more participants and liberalisation benefits increase indeed with their number. But multilateral negotiation leads also to more evenly distributed benefits among participants: on the one hand, differences in size and in market power partly cancel out in the course of a negotiation which is subject to consensus on a single undertaking; on the other hand, the MFN clause has the "mechanical virtue" to which extend concessions to all Members whether they have offered concessions themselves or not. The problem here is rather about free riding i.e. the quality of the offers from each individual country.

Regionalism has its merits too: they are very high when it brings together neighbouring countries in a deep integration scheme whereas the adjustments costs are limited by the proximity of development levels! Moreover political benefits, namely peace and increased bargaining power, come on top of the economic ones. The EU's own experience epitomises the virtuous circle of deep integration among neighbours who are also peers in development. In that respect EU is a bit of a mythical benchmark, generally out of reach for the many countries, practically all WTO membership, involved today in one RTA or another. RTAs vary indeed according to the relative size of participants, the distance among them, the degree of real convergence – north-north, north-south or south-south deals – and last but not least, the depth of integration: from shallow integration limited to the elimination "at-the-border" of obstacles to deep integration coping with "behind-the-border" obstacles and covering more ground than WTO. "WTO plus" regional deals allow indeed for the possibility to explore new areas such services, investment, intellectual property, regulatory transparency and even sensitive issues such as labour standards and environment.

The dynamics of regional integration is such that "eviction costs" can become very high for non-participating countries: they are then tempted either to join the scheme or to negotiate rival schemes with the same countries. The example of Mexico sucked into NAFTA and then engaged in FTAs with EU first and now with Japan is a good illustration of what could be called "a domino effect." Whereas preferences, significant as they can be at the start, may cancel out as the result of the multiplication of schemes with a mix of the same and of new Members, the red tape costs can be on the increase as the result of the growing complexity of conflicting rules of origin. This is Baghwati's "spaghetti bowl" which undermines the attractiveness of those schemes. They have also a hidden cost: they divert political attention and negotiation expertise from the multilateral stage towards side-deals.

Most of regional schemes are only in a starting phase and the question of their final impact on partners' economies remains unknown: what is the value of the welfare gains? Do they outweigh those of a comparable multilateral deal? How are they distributed among and within participating countries? The variety of RTAs does not allow definitive conclusions. Just compare EU North-South RTAs such as the one negotiated with the Mercosur or with subgroups of ACP countries with US North-South RTAs in the Western Hemisphere or in the Mediterranean region: the former are mainly region-to-region deals, with "asymmetric" reciprocity in market access and compensatory financial transfers whereas the latter correspond to a 'hub-and-spokes' approach, with higher reciprocity and no financial transfers. Japan's FTAs are focused on investment protection and on services liberalisation.

Yet, it is undeniable that the criss-cross pattern of RTAs influences both the allocation of resources world-wide and the quality of competition among countries and among multinational companies located in those regional groupings. Even a temporary preference might prove sufficient to provide the prime mover with a competitive edge which will suffice to bar the route to late comers for a certain time. This can be particularly true in areas such as services, investment and government procurements. In the fierce battle for market shares among large companies, national trade policies can become instrumentalised by powerful special interests. This is often the main rational behind the initial move towards a new North-South RTA, but for the case of geopolitical considerations.

The present rush towards RTAs is often interpreted by observers like a lack of interest for the DDA and as the search for an alternative route: this would be especially true for the USA who ponders the political costs of farm reform against the limited but certain benefits of bilateral trade deals or against the grand vision of AFTA, the free trade area of the western hemisphere in which US would play the hub and the other countries the spokes. One also notices a DDA fatigue in Japan and in Korea. EU itself, though firmly committed to the multilateral priority, is eager not to miss the boat, for example in Asia where it is being left behind by USA, Japan, Korea, Thailand and Singapore in the race towards FTAs, not to talk of the future China-Asean RTA.

Most of these RTAs though are shallow integration schemes; few go beyond tariffs whereas exemptions of tariff lines are many. In some cases though, involving Japan and the USA, the focus on investment and intellectual property protection as well as on services, reflects the new trade interests raised by the specific needs of global firms anxious to proceed safely along the road of allocating stages of the value added chain to different national production sites according to the local comparative advantages. Increasingly few if any of those deals address the sensitive question of environmental and labour standards – although the US inserts labour provisions in all its FTAs – whereas competition and public procurements provisions appear in some of them. Nor do they address systemic issues such as farm subsidies, anti-dumping or fishery subsidies.

A clear picture doesn't emerge yet from the number and the diversity of RTAs. They reflect indeed so many different things: specific and genuine trade interests, the natural activism of trade negotiators, an anxiety about being evicted from future deals, political signals of good neighbourhood or of strategic alliance. In this respect there are resistances as well: Brazil does not want to be isolated in a US dominated AFTA. Despite strenuous EU efforts, Mediterranean countries encounter enormous difficulties to clinch trade deals among themselves while being engaged in bilateral FTAs with EU. The South-South dimension of the Euro Med FTA remains therefore to be built up.

What is certain is that the current RTA activism presents probably more benefits than inconveniences or threats as long as multilateral liberalisation moves forward. They make up a myriad of streams that all flow towards the sea of free trade. They instill a spirit of entrepreneurship and competition because they bring about new market structures which force rents out. By doing so, they stimulate world growth through a process of North-South convergence. But preferential deals, because of their sheer number tend gradually to cancel out in such a way that multilateralism appears as a major streamlining and simplification opportunity for local and global business. At least, those deals feed the dynamics of liberalisation.

Would regionalism prevail over multilateralism – which would appear as a real possibility in the case of a DDA failure – one should seriously assess the risk of drifting towards the formation of continental trading blocks made up of the Western Hemisphere, East Asia (Asean+3), and Europe with its Mediterranean periphery and Russia. Such a perspective might look at odds with the present trend of globalisation, and indeed it would represent a serious breach of global culture, making the world a less safe place. But the propensity of the USA to exert its hegemony on the American continent and the *de facto* integration which has been taking place for three decades in East Asia, first according to the "flying geese pattern" initiated by Japanese companies and today through China's role as the regional powerhouse supplied by its more advanced neighbours, make this worrying scenario a possibility. We can't simply dismiss a continental blocks trade war as a European phantasm.

This is where the Doha Round matters. The DDA is about integrating the world economy in such a way that the old mould of imperial rivalry would never be reconstituted again, contributing to the convergence among countries across continental borders and promoting common disciplines based on common values. In other words, supplying global governance for a government-free world! So the sound byte should go: the more regionalism, the more multilateralism! But multilateralism should proceed first: sequencing is crucial both in political and in practical terms.

Yet trade liberalisation is not enough: it should be matched by other headways in the other segment of global economic governance.

What Else Can Be Done for Improving the Sustainable Development?

Development is above all a domestic matter: there is little trade and aid can do if the political will is not there. Is it exaggerated to say that precisely the will to develop is the scarcest resource for development? But is such a lack of will just a matter for the country, or isn't encouraged, directly or indirectly, by the international community or at least by the leading powers US, EU and now China, who are providing their strategic support to governments despite the fact that they are at the same time inefficient, corrupt and despotic? What can global governance do about it? Are we willing to put the interests of the local populations first, ahead of our supposed strategic and commercial interests? This is of course the key question, not an easy one to answer for the *realpolitik* practitioners. Yet the growing differentiation among winners and losers, which the current globalisation as nurtured by free trade, is bringing about, makes the question more relevant than ever. The social divide in Latin America, the corrupt and inefficient despotism across the Middle East and the dramatic institutional weakness of Africa are challenges that call for an answer. Piling up development aid would make no difference since no developing country has ever taken off thanks to aid programs. Genuine success stories, all concentrated in East Asia, have relied on manufactured goods exports, foreign direct investment and effective domestic policies aiming at promoting stable growth and at containing inequalities; ODA has played only a marginal role in the outcome.

What would make a difference could be, once the local elites have consistently proved their commitment to develop their countries, to give them enough policy space to achieve their objectives. What is indeed striking is how the West can be intrusive with regard to the way a country is supposed to develop, and short on the prerequisite of the political will. Yet this is the crux of the matter: each country has to find in itself the genius to explore its own path towards modernity. This is particularly true of Africa. Textbooks are here of little use since each case is specific: beyond some basic macroeconomic discipline principles and the strict respect of the rule of law so as to generate trust on the part of the investors, the key issue is the right balance between the role of the market and the role of the State. Pragmatism should prevail here over ideology and lessons should be drawn from East-Asia success stories. We should for example not shy away from supporting interventionist policies as long as the public sector ethos embodies high standards of professionalism and moral integrity.

Supporting effective domestic policies with respect to sustainable development should be done only on a performance basis. Performance should be the key benchmark for all financial multilateral instruments and their intervention should be made perfectly consistent with the multilateral norms and conventions covering sustainable development: environmental agreements, core-labour standards, health regulations, fight against financial crime and tax evasion.

Conclusion

Multilateral trade liberalisation is on the defensive nowadays which is rather weird since there is a broad consensus on trade contribution to world growth over the last half century.

Explanations are many although not all very convincing. Firstly, the anti- or alter-globalisation movements have raised real questions about how market globalisation has been used to undermine the political capacity to cope with its distributional consequences widely overlooked in the course of liberalisation by the negotiators. From a valid and constructive criticism, the debate has often drifted into generalised suspicion about globalisation without offering any credible alternative.

Secondly, global firms are proving very apt at circumventing the remaining obstacles to trade, be they "at-the-border" or "behind-the-borders" and in doing so they use official obstacles to trade as barriers of entry for their competitors. Moreover many, particularly in the consumer products sectors, would be reluctant to champion the cause of further liberalisation for fear of antagonising the civil society. Small and medium enterprises who are the most likely to benefit from multilateral liberalisation don't have the same lobbying capacity and keep quiet. To part of the business community, bilateral deals look sexier than the DDA: they give them a false – because temporary – sense of preferential access to foreign markets, strengthening their relative competitiveness or offering them – temporary again-captive markets. RTAs soak up business interest and pressure for MFN based negotiations.

Thirdly, as pointed out above, governments might feel that RTAs provide them with better deals: the powerful partners see a possibility to exploit to the full their bargaining power which is kept under restraint in the multilateral arena whereas junior partners are often prompt to sell their birthright for a mess of pottage, i.e. a soup, of preferential access to a huge market.

The truth is that trade liberalisation might be approaching its phase of diminishing returns because the two other pillars of multilateral governance, the financial pillar and the norms-setting pillar do not keep a pace with market opening. We are entering in a phase of imbalance in the structure of global governance as illustrated by three examples of non-governance which impacts negatively trade liberalisation: the US structural external deficit and the building up of a huge debt in the hands of foreign investors; the deterioration of labour rights in emerging economies dramatically exemplified by the harsh conditions imposed on migrant workers in the Jordan clothing industry set up in the framework of the FTA with the US; capital flight towards tax havens which allow globalisation winners to escape from the sharing of benefits with the losers.

Unless there is progress on all fronts of global governance, the trade pillar will bear too much of the brunt of the globalisation and, as a result, WTO will be overexposed to criticisms and to demands which it is not designed for addressing.

Meanwhile, among the good reasons to finish the Round swiftly on a success, one stands out as the most obvious: the credibility of new-born WTO is at stake, and with it, the credibility of a generation of World leaders.

PART 2

UNIVERSAL AND REGIONAL SECURITY AND DEVELOPMENT CHALLENGES

Japan and the United Nations

Ryo OSHIBA

Hitotsubashi University

In 2005, the Japanese government seriously tried to get a permanent seat in the United Nations (UN) Security Council, but it failed in doing so. However, the year 2006 marks the 50th anniversary of Japan's membership to the UN. "When life gives you lemons, make lemonade," as the saying goes; in other words, it is necessary to strive for a new kind of UN diplomacy by putting forward new ideas. In order to find out what kind of UN diplomacy we should opt for, I would like first to look back on Japan's history of UN diplomacy.

I. History of Japanese UN Diplomacy

A. The Cold War Era

Although Japan applied for membership to the United Nations a bit after its recovery of independence in 1952, the application was blocked by the Soviet Union's veto power. Diplomatic relations between Japan and the Soviet Union were finally resumed in 1956, and Japan was allowed to join the UN in December of that same year. At last, Japan had managed to reappear on the international stage, after its withdrawal from the League of Nations and its defeat in war. When joining the UN, Foreign Minister Mamoru Shigemitsu, at the United Nations General Assembly, declared in his address that Japan would work as a bridge between the East and the West.

In its diplomatic Blue Paper of 1957, the Japanese government announced that three principles would guide its diplomatic relationships: UN centrism, diplomacy as a member of Asia, and cooperation with the free world. Why has Japan referred to the UN centrism? Some justify it as follows: (1) the United Nation's idealisation by Japan as a result of the hardships this country had experienced for becoming a member, or (2) the principles of cooperation with the free world and the UN centrism were likely to coexist because western countries, headed by the United States, were mainly democracies. Another interpretation is the following: (3) in response to criticisms from its own opposition party whose efforts to get closer to the socialist countries were insufficient, Japan, by adopting a policy of UN centrism, attempted to show that it is not exclusively devoted to the free world.

Afterwards, the Japanese government devoted itself to the development of a UN centred diplomatic policy which aims at improving its position within the United Nations. In the meantime, Japan has worked hard to become an elected member, and has been successful in this endeavour a total of nine times as of 2005. In addition, as assessed contributions are generally decided on the basis of economic power, Japan has reached such an outstanding economic growth – while being the second one behind the USA – that it pays as much in dues as the latter in the UN. Japan has also increased its voluntary contributions and managed to increase the Japanese staff members in the UN. Despite its ongoing under-representation compared to the amount of its contributions to the budget, Japan has tried to reach higher positions. On the other hand, in its efforts to strengthen the Permanent Mission to the UN, it has appointed the pioneering UN staff member Yasushi Akashi representative of the Japanese government, and Sadako Ogata Minister of the permanent mission of Japan to the UN.

B. Post-Cold War

After the cold war, the Japanese government had an aspiration: Japan expected that conflicts between countries would greatly decrease, economy and technology would increasingly gain importance, the military capabilities will improve in the future, and Japan would lead the international politics, instead of heading a military superpower.

The words "global civilian power" of the German political scientist Hanns Maull result from various theories: first, Taichi Sakaiya advocated the "tradesman state" theory; secondly, Richard Rosecrance, an international political scientist at Cornell University has suggested theories about the "rise of the trading state" in an eponymous book[1]. These are theories about a super powerful entity based on political strengths and not military ones. In contrast, Ichiro Ozawa has stressed on the need for maintaining military forces in an "ordinary" powerful entity.

---

1 Yoichi Funabashi, *Nihon no Taigai Koso (Japan's World Vision)*, Tokyo, Iwanami, 1993, Richard Rosecrance, *The Rise of the Trading State*, New York, Basic Books, 1987.

It was in such a context that the Gulf Crisis occurred in August 1990 followed by the Gulf War in the next January, which became a major turning point in the UN diplomacy of Japan: basically, it evidenced that military forces still might be significant diplomatic tools even after the Cold War.

Moreover, contributions to conflicts in terms of human supplies emerged as a key issue. As a result, not only the G-7 but the UN Security Council actively worked on making policy decisions, while Japan was unable to do something; however, it followed its "check book diplomacy" by providing financial help. This was needless and caused a deep frustration. Consequently, the Japanese government was convinced of the need for gaining a permanent seat in the UN Security Council. This would enable Japan to yield a political leadership; its participation in conflict resolution activities carried out by the UN turned out to be a prerequisite for reaching this position.

Given the situation, the Japanese government was to put more emphasis on its United Nations policy. The scenario was the following: (1) the government introduced the International Peace Cooperation Bill – which was passed and became effective in June, 1992 – which enables the Self Defense Forces to participate in UN peace-keeping activities; (2) it dispatched SDF personnel, civilian police, etc. to the United Nations Transitional Authority in Cambodia (UNTAC) in compliance with the International Peace Cooperation Law; (3) the Japanese government made an official speech in January 1992 to confirm that it was longing for a seat in the Security Council, while the International Peace Cooperation Bill was being debated in the Diet. Then, Japan put forward additional permanent members which would be deprived of veto power as a reform proposal to the Security Council at the United Nations General Assembly in the autumn of 1992. Thus, the Japanese government attempted to modify its conventional and passive United Nations policy.

It is necessary to point out that pressure from the United States strongly influenced Japanese attempts to strengthen its UN policy for several motives. First, Japan did increase its amount of voluntary contributions under its "contribution" policy to the international society from the 1980s to the early 1990s. Furthermore, in addition to its willingness to lead the UN from a Japanese perspective, it was essential to preserve good relationships with the USA.

The UN-centred diplomacy of Japan from the cold war onwards had strongly influenced the public opinion[2]. To begin with, when the controversy over the International Peace Cooperation Law was ignited, is, it was asked whether Japanese attitudes should be "active" or "passive" in terms of diplomatic stance and whether measures of "international contribution" should be "military" or "non-military." The proponents of the International Peace Cooperation Law criticised opponents as "one-nation pacifists," and steered the debate to the "active" or "passive" issue. In contrast, those who were opposed to the bill emphasised the importance of the "military" or "non-military" dimension, arguing that they were against the bill because it would have dispatched the troops abroad.

After the enforcement of the International Peace Cooperation Law, the Self Defense Forces were sent to Cambodia as part of UNTAC. Afterwards, support for the International Peace Cooperation Law has rapidly risen as well as opportunities to participate in the UN peacekeeping activities have increased. The "active or passive" debate has been settled on the "active" side. Concerning the dispute on "military or non-military," many people still feel that Japan should adopt non-military means of international contribution.

How does Japan react to the fact that it is unsuitable for gaining permanent membership in the Security Council, which handles security disputes, because it is not a military power but an economic one? The Japanese government fought back with logic. To put it in a nutshell, it was to make human security the ideological foundation stone of Japanese diplomacy. In the human security theory, it is necessary to secure both freedom from fear and freedom from willingness. Following this way of thinking, even though Japan cannot play a key role in the military sphere, it terms of pushing for freedom from poverty, Japan's ODA role is quite large, that is the reason why Japan could become a candidate for permanent membership in the UN Security Council.

I do not intend to deny the human security approach. Human security is a key idea, which overturns our conventional conception of security as *state* security. Initially, "human security" comes as a policy parlance that emerged from the UNDP (United Nations Development Programme), but it took on systematic content through the Commission on Human Security, co-chaired by Sadako Ogata and Amartya Kumar Sen[3].

---

2 Ryo Oshiba, "Japan's UN Policy in the 1990s," *Pacific Focus*, Vol.14, Spring 1999, p. 5-26.

3 Commission on Human Security, *Human Security Now: Protecting and Empowering People*, 2003.

However, for the Japanese government, this principle became an extremely convenient rhetorical tool. This is how the Japanese government has actively developed its UN diplomacy after the Cold War.

Regarding the mode of UN diplomacy after the Cold War, even among those who aggressively support it, there has been a readily apparent generation gap. Generally speaking, the older generations are highly aware of their historical experiences, in which Japan achieved independence and was finally able to join the United Nations despite the opposition of the Soviet Union, and the strong economic orientation of the diplomacy. For example, Yasushi Akashi warns that Japan should not try to be involved too aggressively in UN peacekeeping; otherwise, it will raise the anxiety of the neighbouring countries. Akashi had worked for the United Nations Secretariat since Japan joined the United Nations, and played a powerful leadership role when Japan was actively involved in UN peacekeeping in the 1990s[4].

In contrast, the younger generation (the fifties or over) is trying to develop UN diplomacy while focusing on the economic power of Japan. They strongly tend to view the United Nations reform as a Security Council reform: they more specifically tend to put it on equal footing with the issue of Japan's permanent membership in the Council, by stressing on the Japanese "achievements" after the 1990s and its financial power.

C. Security Council Reform: Agenda Setting

After the Cold War, ethnic conflicts more frequently occurred and UN peacekeeping rapidly expanded. In 1992, UN Secretary-General Boutros Boutros-Ghali, set up a department of peacekeeping structure. Secretary-General Boutros-Ghali held a Security Council summit in 1992 and worked on making the Security Council suitable to international relationships after the Cold War. The draft for the Security Council reform was presented in 1997.

However, the permanent members of the UN Security Council did not want the changes as they were nor the way they were working at this time: according to them, an increase in the number of members would decrease the importance of their positions on the whole. Britain and France were worried about the obtention by Germany of a permanent seat; this would mean that three European states would be in the Council, consequently Europe would gain more power, and movements within the EU to join the three European seats into a single one would get stronger. Concerning the Security Council reform, the discussion did

4 Yasushi Akashi, *Kokusai Rengo (The United Nations)*, Tokyo, Iwanami, 1985.

not make any progress and was deadlocked after the peak period in 1997. Hisashi Owada, the UN ambassador of this time stated that the Security Council reform would not probably been carried out in the short run.

The same year, Kofi Annan assumed the position of Secretary-General. He also worked on the United Nations reform and set up the post of Deputy Secretary-General, but this did not go beyond improvement in efficiency, the functional reinforcement – and so on – of the office. Reform of the United Nations' system itself, including the amendments to the UN Charter, was mothballed. However, the 9/11 attacks strengthened movements to carry out drastic reforms within the UN. It made people strongly aware of new forms of war, and the way to deal with such wars became an urgent issue in international politics. The unstable situation following the invasion of Iraq would, later on, also provide an opportunity for the United Nations reform.

Considering this opportunity, Secretary-General Annan emphasised the need for a UN reform in the context of the further celebration of the 60th anniversary of the creation of the United Nations in 2005; as a result, he organised a high-level reform panel. Annan managed to carry out a fundamental reform of the UN, which is a reform suitable to the 60th anniversary of the organisation, on the agenda.

The UN high-level panel report was made public in December 2004, Annan's report was released in March 2005, and the time for UN reform finally began to ripen[5]. Obviously, UN reform is a key reform, so Annan cannot merely focus on Security Council reform. He has also advocated the creation of a peacebuilding commission and has put forward the setting up of a Human Rights Council in the long run. However, Annan and others have mainly made considerable efforts into the Security Council reform. He tried to set a timeframe for the debate about Security Council reform, and tried to hush up the issue by the end of 2005. Despite the strong opposition in this field, Secretary-General Annan showed his unwavering willingness to go through the key reforms on his own, which included the amendment of the Charter. The Japanese government expected a lot from his leadership.

2. The Failure of Japan in Getting a Permanent Seat

The so-called Group of Four (G-4) draft was set up by Japan, Germany, Brazil, and India, and they expected African Union (AU) nations to support this resolution. However, AU nations were unable to agree

5 Report of the High-level Panel on Threats, Challenges and Change, "A More Secure World: Our Shared Responsibility," 2004.

internally on whether they should support or not the G-4 draft, whose purpose was the obtention of a permanent seat without veto power; in fact, they had asked for two seats with veto power for two permanent memberships representing Africa. Therefore, the submission of the G-4 draft was postponed, and Japan's UN diplomacy failed.

A. The Meaning of Failure

The failure of Japan in obtaining a permanent seat means the failure of making Japan a politically powerful country, something for which the Japanese government has sought since the 1990s. Some time ago, a "small nation" ideology – albeit from a short-term perspective – was put forward by Tanzan Ishibashi, who served as the Prime Minister of Japan after its defeat in World War II. This philosophy derived from the weight of defeat. However, later on, when Japan managed to get an economic growth, its image of "economic superpower" has won out. Behind that image, two different aspects are found: firstly, Japan as an *economic* superpower does not appear to strive to become a political superpower, and secondly Japan that rose up from ashes once again to become an economic *superpower*.

In the 1990s, the motives for shaping a political power started to get an overwhelming support. After debates on the way to cooperate in the Gulf War, PKO Cooperation Law, etc. the domestic opinion was divided on a diplomatic issue, for the first time since the conflict over the Japan-USA Security Treaty. However, the main issues of the discussion were whether Japan should aim at becoming an "ordinary" superpower, endowed with enhanced military capabilities, or whether it should turn into a non-military superpower. However, both arguments were justifying the need for becoming a political superpower. Scepticism about the true idea of being a political entity was brushed off by "one-nation pacifism." This plan aimed at putting Japan in a suitable position for being a political superpower, which implies the obtention of a permanent membership in the UN Security Council. And it failed to do so.

B. The Cause of the Failure

I am not saying that I am in favour of "one-nation pacifism" as amore suitable way of running diplomacy. As a matter of fact, I think that there was an insufficient for achieving the goal of becoming a political superpower. Concerning the reasons of the Japanese failure, I think there were tactical and strategic factors. I will start with the tactical element. The Japanese government aims to be a political entity and to gain a position which fits that; however, in power politics, tactics and negotiation methods themselves are used in issues concerning positions that the world is concerned with[6]. Such positions are not only gained because a state has the capability or qualifications for those positions. When a position is desired in international politics, it is acquired as a result of a competition with other countries. The question that needs to be asked first in the negotiations over the position of a permanent membership is the following: "is there any likelihood that Japan gets this position": it is not asked whether Japan *should* be a permanent member or has the qualifications for it.

Even if Japan has the ability or qualifications for it, the problem is whether the other states will accept it. In the world of power politics, it is not that easy to go through issues. If the obtention of a permanent seat is set on the agenda and if Japan puts itself forward as a candidate, we should start considering whether the possibility of nomination is likely or not, and whether this country can become – through proper procedures – a permanent member.

A reform of the Security Council needs for more than two-thirds of the votes at the UN General Assembly and for the ratification by all the five permanent members. In short, the permanent members have substantial veto power over Security Council reform. Even with a two-thirds majority, the reform of the United Nations is very unlikely to be ratified by every permanent member; consequently, there are quite a few chances to make the United Nations reform come true.

I believe that the likelihood that China ratifies the draft for the reforms – to enable Japan to be a permanent member – is rather low. The gap in terms of historical backgrounds between Japan and China is a major obstacle, but it is not the only one. This is justified by the willingness of China to not offer to Japan a privileged position by ratifying the reform proposal given their rivalry in East Asia. In addition, other permanent members, the United States, Britain, France, and Russia have also always wished, whether it is vocalised or not, to maintain the status quo. Even if the draft of the Security Council reform is approved in the United Nations General Assembly, the other permanent members will not put any serious pressure on China to ratify it.

The Japanese government is also probably and painfully aware of this. This could infer that Japan announced the G-4 draft in 2005 while being fully aware of it. Japanese tactics consist of getting the two-thirds majority support at the UN General Assembly and crossing over the most outlying bridge leading to the Security Council reform by setting aside the possibility of ratification. Actually, it was difficult to predict

6 Joseph M. Grieco, "Anarchy and the Limits of Cooperation," *International Organization*, Vol.42, No.3, 1988.

whether Japan would win the two-thirds plus majority at the General Assembly. So, when efforts for providing Japan with a permanent seat were made in earnest in the spring of 2005, anti-Japanese demonstrations broke immediately out across China.

While the Japanese government expected opposition from China, in the meantime it was wishing African nations' support. In a way, Japan made efforts to strengthen relationships with African nations, by holding the Tokyo International Conference on Africa's Development (TICAD) in 1993, 1998, and 2003, as a preliminary measure of its purpose.

It is true that the exchange of votes against financial aid of Japan have been effective in becoming an elected member; however, concerning fundamental reforms, such as the Security Council reform, the Japanese government forgot that African countries also behaved on the basis of power politics: on the international stage, nations desperately pursue "position."

Although I think the Japanese government has made great efforts in making achievements and building upon principles, I ask whether their expectations were sufficiently high. When chances of success cannot be accurately read, it is natural to take risks. But how did the Japanese government estimate the cost of failure? If it is the first time that Japan becomes a candidate for a permanent seat, puts forward a resolution, and finally fails, would the Japan be allowed without any doubt to a second round?

The failure in Japanese diplomacy lies more in strategic factors. Namely, despite the Secretary-General Annan's exercise of leadership and success in setting reform on the agenda, the Japanese government failed in using this opportunity to have its say in fundamental UN reform.

After 60 years of existence, the Charter of the United Nations reflects the gap between its wording and the current situation where international relations are being globalised. There is not any state which can deny the need for reform. The Japanese government has exclusively devoted itself to the obtention of a permanent seat, and has missed this opportunity. Concerning the Security Council, it should have put forward a proposal on how the structure of the permanent members should be reformed in the future; the proposal should have asked whether other major changes are necessary in the distribution of power among states.

Furthermore, if we pay attention to the fact that South Korea and other Southeast Asian nations are gaining "middle-power" positions, should not be the addition of non-permanent members a more serious proposal to put forward?[7] Japan has been criticised for not clarifying what it wants to do after getting a permanent seat. The discussion about UN reform was a good opportunity for Japan to make its plan further, but Japan missed it.

Although Secretary-General Annan showed great enthusiasm for UN reform, his influence weakened because of Japan's failure in carrying out the Security Council reform; moreover due to the recent accusations of corruption related to the Oil-for-Food Programme, he has lost much of his power as a leader. After this loss, instead of the drastic UN reform, such as the Security Council reform and other issues that would entail revisions of the Charter, focus has shifted more to the issue of ensuring accountability in the UN Secretariat. Although reform of the United Nations emerged as an international political issue on how United Nations should react to the changes in the distribution of power and changes in ideologies in international society that have occurred in the 60 years since its inception, as a movement it has fizzled out and turned into a mere UN administrative reform.

3. Issues in UN Diplomacy in the 21st Century

First of all, rethinking the objectives of the UN diplomacy in the 21st century is one of the major issues that Japan must deal with. The objectives of UN diplomacy obviously do not only include the protection of globally public goods through the UN, but also the use of UN diplomacy as the driving force for Japanese diplomacy itself. In Japan's UN diplomacy in 2005, in the rush to become a permanent member in the Security Council, Japan managed to exacerbate the mistrust of Japan with South Korea, without mentioning China. To put it in a simple way, Japan's UN diplomacy has only worsened Japan's diplomatic relations with Northeast Asia. Given these results, we have to ask what is the purpose of UN diplomacy.

Japan's foreign policy has various problems to overcome, such as the lack of partnerships, the lack of a multilateral framework in Asia, and the contentious historical background. It is also necessary to think about the way we should use the United Nations in order to solve these

7 Yoshihide Soeya, *Nihon no Midoru Pawa Gaiko (Japan as a Middle Power)*, Tokyo, Chikuma, 2005.

problems. For instance, it is necessary to question the way the United Nations should be structured to use in founding an Asian community[8].

Firstly, UN diplomacy is not just a matter the Ministry of Foreign Affairs, and the Foreign Policy Bureau especially, is in charge of. This issue had to be considered when the United Nations Bureau was part of the Foreign Policy Bureau, but it seems that the reality of the situation has not really changed.

Secondly, it is necessary to give more power to the parties who should be in charge of Japan's UN diplomacy. The United Nations has changed in character over the last sixty years. It is turning into an organisation in charge of a society of global citizens, with changes in corporate activities and policy making, such as the gradual transformation from inter-governmental organisations to global organisations.

A new generation that can give an orientation to the United Nations' transformation is emerging in Japan as well. While the first and the second generations have been striving to promote UN diplomacy, what may be called the "third generation" has grown up. They are those who participated in election monitoring groups led by Mr. Akashi or in Camp Sadako in Africa when they were young, and have gone on doing research or have acquired experience in international organisations or NGOs afterwards. It is necessary for us to build a social system in which these people can work easily within international organisations, governments, and NGOs.

The third issue that must be tackled is the transformation of our own ways of thinking about the way to support this new generation of leaders. We are mistakenly prone to think of issues such as peace-building and humanitarian aid as non-political issues. There are, however, numerous cases of international organisations, NGOs, and even ordinary people which have to make new kinds of political decisions. When Sadako Ogata was heading the UNHCR, for example, both Serbs and Muslims tried to use humanitarian aid as a political tool in Bosnia. And naturally, Ms. Ogata had to take a political gamble[9].

---

8 Ri Sho Gen (Lee Jon Won), "Chiiki Keisei Purosesu toshiteno Rokusha Kyogi (Six-Party Talks as a Process for Making an Asian Regional Framework)," *Sekai*, October 2005.

9 Sadako Ogata, *The Turbulent Decade: Confronting the Refugee Crises of the 1990s*, New York, W.W. Norton, 2005.

Regionalisation, Regionalism and Institutionalism

The Prospects and Limits of Institutionalisation in East Asia

Richard HIGGOTT

Warwick University & GARNET Network

Introduction

There is a large range of literature on regionalism (the creation of formalised regions with agreed membership) and regionalisation (the process by which regional economies and societies become more integrated)[1]. There is a large body of literature on regionalism and regionalisation in East Asia and the Pacific; notably on ASEAN and APEC, and of late on 'East Asia' as a voice of regional. Indeed, if the volume of literature written on a region was an indicator of the strength of regional institutional development then the Asia Pacific would be a highly institutionalised region. There is also a growing body of literature comparing regionalism and regionalisation in Europe with East Asia in particular[2]. Finally, there are also large bodies of scholarly literature in economic and political science on the theory and practice of institutionalism and international organisation[3]. This last body of literature is evolving and on many issues not settled.

There is as yet, however, little or no substantial analysis of the importance of the theory and practice of institutionalism located in a specifically East Asian context. There is a range of reasons for this.

1 See *inter alia*, Coleman and Underhill, 1998; Fawcett and Hurrell, 1995; Gamble and Payne, 1996; Grugel and Hout, 1998; Mansfield and Milner, 1997; Mattli, 1999.

2 For reviews of this literature see Beeson, 2005; Higgott, 1998a and 2005 and Acharya, 2005.

3 Katzenstein, *et al.*, 1998; Simmons and Martin, 2002; Kratochwil and Mansfield, 2005; Higgott, 2006.

From the perspective of the scholar of institutionalism and international organisation, East Asia was simply not a region where they could ply their craft in a meaningful way. The laboratories were to be found either in the multilateral organisations, or at the regional level specifically in the study of the European project; for many, the one exercise in regionalisation worthy of theoretical study. For the analyst-cum-practitioner involved in the various regional discourses taking place in the Asia Pacific, and East Asia in particular, during the closing decades of the 20th century, the very idea of institutionalising this dialogue in a meaningful way, or certainly on the basis of some European model was largely unthinkable. Indeed, senior members of the Asian regional policy community were often heard to rail against what they saw as the dangerous excesses of European legal formalism and the prospect of a 'Brussels in Asia'.

In more recent times, there seems to be an emerging feeling, implicit and explicit, that a change of mood might be coming about in East Asia. Driven by a number of factors in the wake of the financial crises in the region in the closing stages of the 20th century, observers have focused on the enhanced dialogue on regional monetary cooperation, especially following the Chiang Mai agreement, and the development of the ASEAN+3 (or APT) process as a sign of a new interest in enhanced cooperation in the region. As we move to the first East Asian Summit in December 2005, it is then perhaps appropriate that a conference such as this should take stock of how significant these activities really are. It is the aspiration of this paper to contribute to this stock-taking.

The paper is not, however, meant to be just another review of the state of East Asian regionalism[4]. Rather it will attempt to take the theory and practice of institutions and institutionalisation seriously and ask exactly what the prospects of such institutionalism really are in East Asia in the early 21st century. This, the paper argues is better done in a comparative context. Thus the analysis of the theoretical literature on institutionalism is embedded in the empirical context in which it has found strongest expression to-date – the European project. At this time in the history of the EU, the comparison with East Asia warrants further interrogation especially since the normative advocacy of institutionalism in East Asia would appear to be strengthening at the very time when limits of this process in Europe, in the wake of the defeat of the constitution, are being questioned more strongly than at any time in the last 25 years.

4 The literature on the state of the contemporary regional project in East Asia is large. For a flavour see Beeson, 2004; Higgott, 2005; Pempel, 2005; Ravenhill, 2005; Stubbs, 2002; Knight, 2004.

Does the history of the European project tell us anything about the utility and limits of regional institutionalism to enhance understanding of East Asia? If so, does it do so in a way that takes us beyond the early 1990s dichotomous analytical impasse that gave us the 'No Brussels in Asia' school of thought on the one hand and the 'No serious regional cooperation in Asia until it adopts the European model' on the other (for discussions see Segal, Maull and Wanadi, 1995 and Breslin, 2005). Does a comparative reading of the European and East Asian institutional projects instead now allow us to offer a more dynamic explanation or regionalisation in East Asia that sees a process of adaptation, or what Acharya (2004) call 'norm localisation', rather than one of either mere rejection or mimicry? The answer, in my best judgment is yes. But not in the mechanistic way outlined in some of the literature of the 1990s. Those pessimistic, and at times Eurocentrically smug, contrasts of the 1990s that saw Europe and Asia on different paths with European regionalism overcoming the negative constraints of state sovereignty on the one hand while Asia hovered on the edge of perilous security and regional disorder on the other (Friedberg, 2003-2004; Buzan and Segal, 2004) were far too stylistically overdrawn.

Specifically, the paper is in 4 parts. Firstly it will say something about the theory and practice of regionalism in comparative perspective. Secondly, it will address the issue of the theory and practice of institutionalism in a regional setting. Finally in parts three and four, on the basis of an examination of these two established bodies of literature it will ask how relevant contemporary European institutional cooperation might be for understanding the way forward in East Asia. In so doing, it will suggest that we recognise not only the significance of the European project to-date, but also what appear to be the limits of that project as a vehicle for transcending sovereignty and advancing supranationalism on the one hand and the potential for regional transformation in East Asia on the other. Europe, certainly for the time being, would appear to have gone about as far as it can down the institutional path. East Asia is only at the first step on that path. The interesting policy question is not whether East Asia will become more institutionalised rather than what form that institutionalisation might take. The interesting scholarly question is what are the key drivers that might assist or impede that process of regional institutionalisation? Just as Europe is questioning the status of the institutions and practices that characterised the European project in the closing decades of the 20th century, so too is Asia, especially since the financial crises of 1996-1997. The 'Asia Pacific way' characterised by weak informal norms of consensus based decision making and non-interference are giving way to more serious calls to establish substantive institutional practices of decision-making especially in the domains of trade and monetary relations at both regional and bilateral levels even though the practical direction and application of initiatives such as ASEAN+3 and a putative East Asian Community remain to be determined.

Sections one, two and three rehearse some of the insights gained in to the role of institutions and institutional theory and ask how they are salient in practical terms to an understanding of enhancing cooperation in East Asia. This is no mere scholarly exercise. It will demonstrate that the debate over the role of institutions *qua* institutions – especially in their capacity as transaction cost reducers and vehicles for the enhancement of transparency and as agents to ensure the credibility of commitments and norm compliance – cast increasingly long policy shadows over current regional activities in East Asia.

Section four explores the issue of regional 'leadership' and institution building. In the context of the East Asian regional dialogue, this is identified as the key issue for the early 21st century. At its core, the degree and the nature of regional leadership in the emerging Asian integration process that can be provided by China *and/or* Japan will prove crucial to the success of the current endeavours to secure enhanced regional economic (and political) institutional cooperation in the region. The presence of, or absence of, the emergence of some kind of collective leadership, or at least consensual cooperation, is the major instrument for, or obstacle to, any advancement of regionalism in Asia. Without a 'historic compromise' between China and Japan economic integration will be severely delayed, if not made impossible.

1. Theorising Regionalism: Europe and Asia Compared

Policy-makers (rightly or wrongly) often conceptualise regionalism with reference to the European. But, while we are not dealing with functionally equivalent entities, it is clear that policy learning and the politics of emulation (or in many cases the politics of avoidance) are major features of current deliberations about regionalism in other parts of the world, and especially East Asia. This is especially the case as regionalism is increasingly seen as a response to the growing internationalisation of the division of labour and production, or what we now call globalisation.

The time lag between European developments and the construction of regional orders elsewhere has meant that region-building elites have had the opportunity to learn from the European experience. As often as not this has led to a desire for avoidance of, rather than the emulation of, the 'Brussels model'. The less institutionalised approach that emerged in Asia in the early 1990s represented a deliberate choice to avoid the perceived 'Cartesian' legal formalism of the EU (see Higgott, 1998a).

So, whether viewed negatively or positively, the European experience looms large. It is, ironically, the EU as an exercise in regional integration that is a major obstacle to the development of analytical and theoretical studies of regional integration elsewhere (Breslin, 2005). The oft-repeated characterisation of Asian regionalism as 'loose' or 'informal' reflects a teleological prejudice informed by the assumption that 'progress' in regional organisation is defined in terms of EU-style institutionalisation.

An assumption remains that the EU is *the* paradigmatic case of regionalism against which all other regional projects are judged. For some, the Union's longevity, institutional complexity and policy reach means that it is more than just an international organisation. Indeed, Hix (1994 and 1999) argues that the EU is a political system rather than an integration project. This is an extreme position (see Rosamond, 2000), but it raises the issue of whether the EU is in fact an instance of integration, and thus of regionalism, at all and thus of any comparative use for trying to explain the direction of regionalism in Asia in the 21st century.

This dominance of the EU on our mental maps imposes an understanding of regionalism as bound up with 'formal institutionalisation'. But to equate mature regionalism with the creation of supranational politico-institutional bodies equivalent to the European Commission, the European Parliament and the European Court of Justice prejudices any conclusions we might want to make about the emergence of a world order based on alternative forms of regional organisation and co-operation. This approach also assumes that key political economy questions pertaining to economic cooperation can only be addressed in this context. This emphasis on institutional regionalism proceeding through a mixture of intergovernmental dialogue and treaty revision is at the heart of the now classic model of economic integration developed over forty years ago by Bela Balassa (1962). Balassa used the term 'economic integration' to refer to the creation of formal co-operation between states and the forward movement from a free trade area to a customs union, a common market, a monetary union and finally total economic integration.

Balassa's Four Stages of Regional Economic Integration

- Free trade area (with the removal of trade restrictions).
- Customs Union (with a common external trade policy towards non-members.)
- Common Market (with free movement of factors of production between member states).
- Economic Union (Harmonisation of economic policies under supranational control)

This view of regionalism, with its teleological reasoning, also informed the early neo-functionalist versions of integration theory emanating from American political science (Webb, 1983). In these explanations of regional cooperation neo-functionalists saw 'spillovers' leading to economic and (ultimately) political integration. They theorised the transcendence of the state system rather than its survival and the process of economic and political integration being driven by *rational actors*, be they supranational institutions or self-regarding producer groups. Neo-functionalists used the European experience to generalise about the prospects for regional integration elsewhere (Haas, 1956 and 1964; Lindberg, 1966; Schmitter, 1971; Nye, 1968 and 1971). But this was all short-lived. The publication of Haas's devastating auto-critique, *The Obsolescence of Regional Integration Theory* (1975), suggested the very idea of producing replicable models of *regionalism* was misconceived. Two problems with integration theory had emerged:

- The European experience from the time of the creation of the European Coal and Steel Community through to the achievement of the Common Market was not replicated. Analogous projects such as the Latin American Free Trade Area and the East African Common Market failed.
- Integration theory in Europe had under-estimated the pervasiveness of nationalist sentiment and the inter-governmental direction community policy making had taken (Wallace, 1996 and Moravcsik, 1994 and 1998).

Indeed, explanations of European integration remained complicated by the domestic politics of the member states. But, the dissolution of 'integration theory' was not just a consequence of the discrepancies between theoretical predictions and empirical 'reality'. It was also marginalised by a growing distaste for grand predictive social theory and a growing interest in explanations that privileged international 'interdependence' as the forerunner to globalisation (see Katzenstein, Keohane and Krasner, 1998).

It was only with the emergence of the single market programme in the mid-1980s that we saw a partial revival of neo-functionalist integration theorising. An activist Commission, under Jacques Delors, offered an empirical reinstatement of the neo-functionalist idea of supranationalism. The single market was suggestive of a number of spill-overs into social policy, economic and monetary union and political integration more generally (Tranholm-Mikkelsen, 1991). More traditional state-centric accounts of integration, clinging to outdated realist state theory, failed to capture the 'everyday' regulatory complexity of the European policy process (see Rosamond, 2000.)

Interestingly, this reawakening of European integration occurred more or less simultaneously with the appearance of regional free trade areas elsewhere. The appearance of schemes in North and South America, the Asia Pacific and Southern Africa were suggestive of a new regionalised world order, which would be triadic, with Europe, the US and East Asia as the nodal points. The drivers of this process were twofold:

- The revised geopolitical security structure that followed the end of the Cold War loosened the possibilities of trans-border activity and inter-state exchange.
- The growth of globalisation: especially, but not only, in its key economic forms of the liberalisation of global trade and the deregulation of global financial markets questioned economic relations founded on the premise of national territory (Held *et al.*, 1999; Scholte, 2005).

Both drivers stressed the fuzziness of the distinction between the 'domestic' and the 'international'. Regional cooperation was thought to enhance global competitiveness. This general assumption is crucial to comparative analysis of the European and emerging Asian Experience. Nowhere did regionalism appear to be getting stronger throughout the first half of the 1990s than in East Asia and the Pacific. For many, the growth of ASEAN and the so-called 'Asian way' to regional cooperation was a new form of regionalism explained by the need to respond to globalisation (see Acharya, 1997 and 2001). The development of APEC in the early 1990s strengthened this view (see Higgott, Leaver and Ravenhill, 1993). But the financial crises of the late 1990s challenged this view.

2. Beyond Europe: Regionalism in Asia after the Financial Crises

The financial crises of the late 1990s proved to be watershed for both the analysis and practice of regionalism in East Asia. It provided clarity of observation and represented a political reality check on a number of issues of regional and global economic management that had been obscured, or at least seemed less obvious, during the heady 'emerging market', 'Asian miracle' era of the early 1990s. Most obviously, and despite the now well-known hype that accompanied its development throughout the 1990s, the much-vaunted APEC initiative seemed incapable of even delivering short-term palliative responses to the regional financial crises This posed serious questions about APECs efficacy as an emergent mode of regional organisation in the Asia-Pacific (see Ravenhill, 2001). This reading was further justified by the abortive Japanese initiative to establish an Asian Monetary Fund in the wake of the crises. The collapse of this plan in the face of US opposition highlighted the fragility of a Pacific-wide regional project that seemed dependent on the hegemonic blessing of the US.

It can, of course, be argued that APEC was only ever a trade-led initiative, neither intended nor equipped to deal with financial crises (Harris, 2002). On the other hand, an argument can be made that the crises opened the way for clearer and less idealistic thinking about regionalism in Asia (see Higgott, 1998). In the longer term the crises may have pushed states to think again about how best to build a regional order capable of preventing financial crises (or at least competent to deal effectively with those crises when they arise). The creation of a network of currency swaps and other financial arrangements arising from, and subsequent to, the Asian Development Bank meetings in May 2000 reflect this approach to regional cooperation.

Even if such initiatives amount to nought, at the very least, the discussions that have taken place since that time suggest a growing regional self-definition of 'East Asia' as a valid economic space with a discernible political voice. Analytically, this suggests that such policy initiatives do not simply arise merely as rational spillovers from financial integration. Rather they depend upon an emergent sense of collective identity that frames the way in which policy elites respond to exogenous shocks. This highlights the centrality of two important variables in the study of regionalism often over-looked in the economic literature on regional integration.

- The importance of identities in region building;
- The catalytic impact on regionalisation of exogenous political as well as economic challenges emanating from the rapid growth of globalisation.

Regions, by their very existence, mediate between national and global effects. Recent events in Asia allow us to identify roles that nascent regional organisations play as mediating layers of governance between the nation-state and global institutions. In the Asian case this is as likely to involve the deflection of dominant Western ideologies, preferences and economic models that are bound up with the philosophies and actions of the international financial institutions as it is to accept such preferences. Even in Europe, a purpose of such a mediating layer, certainly in the late 20th century and possibly until the collapse of the Constitutional initiative in 2005, involved the protection of the 'European social model' against the assimilating tendencies of deregulated Anglo-American capitalism (Hay and Rosamond, 2000).

We also need to treat institutions (such as regular forums for regional dialogue) as 'social' venues rather than just capsules in which rational action takes place. Observers of regional cooperation in Asia need to recognise the salience of the relationship between institutionalised interaction on the one hand and the emergence of regional identities and interests on the other. Rationalists need not follow well-worn state-centric paths. Strategic action by state actors may be, indeed certainly is, still important, but such action must continue to be placed within a wider complex of actors (both state and non-state) and institutional venues that conspire to influence the development of regionalism (Hurrell, 1995a). It is in this context that the role of institutions and, indeed the theory that underpins institutional growth and activity is more important than has traditionally been thought to be the case in the dialogue on regionalism that prevailed in Asia prior to the Asian financial crises.

3. Why Institutions Matter and Why Europe is Different

> Institutions are the rules of the game in a society or, more formally, the humanly devised constraints that shape human interaction. (…) Institutions reduce uncertainty by providing structure to everyday life (…) institutions define and limit the set of choices of individuals. (Nobel Laureate in economics, Douglass North, 1990: 3-4)
>
> Institutions are '(…) persistent and connected sets of ruled (formal and informal) that prescribe behavioural roles, constrain activity and shape expectations.' (Princeton political scientist, Robert Keohane, 1989: 3)

As processes of economic globalisation deepen they need to be institutionalised if they are to avoid increased hostile and negative responses. The continued liberalisation of trade, the deregulation of finance and a limited role for the state in the process of market globalisation requires trusted and legitimated structures (institutions) if globalisation is to continue. The level at which these institutions will flourish is yet to be fully determined. What is clear is that this cannot be either/or global or regional. It is a multi-level enterprise in which the failure of institutionalism at the global level is likely to enhance institutional thinking at the regional level. As problem solving at the global level becomes more difficult, attempts to enhance collective action problem solving at the regional level become more attractive.

But much that we have learned about institutions is in danger of being unlearned. We are correct to point to deficiencies in the UN. We are correct to want to reform it and the international economic institutions such as the IMF, World Bank and WTO. What is alarming however is a growing willingness to question the very utility of institutions – as ways or organising international behaviour – that is growing in key quarters of the global policy community. Social science has demonstrated the theoretical and practical importance of institutions as the reducers of uncertainty and transactions costs and the importance of their role in making promises credible. We may be cynical about institutions and distrust them but most of us recognise that if they did not exist we would be re-inventing them in one way or another. Institutions facilitate deal-making between actors that may be in adversarial situations. But, institutionalism as a trust-enhancing commitment to principled behaviour lacks support at the global level. It is difficult for societal actors to give loyalty to transaction cost reducers!

Institutional Principles developed in the 20th century

- Institutions lower transactions costs by the provision and sharing of information
- Institutions reduce uncertainty
- Institutions help make promises and commitments credible
- Institutions facilitate deal-making
- Institutions enhance compliance
- Institutions are vehicles for learning and socialisation
- Institutions help shape collective identities[5].

5 See for discussions of institutions and institutional theory see Keohane, 1984, 1989, 2002; Simmons and Martin, 2002; Higgott, 2006.

These principles do not give us a clear-cut definition of what constitutes an institution. It is not, for example, always easy to distinguish, in practice, between an institution and a norm of behaviour. Moreover, for some analysts the concepts of 'organisation' and 'institution' are interchangeable while for others not all institutions are organisations. For economists for example, 'property rights' are an institution, and an important one in explaining stability and predictability of market behaviour under conditions of globalisation. For political scientists a key institution for global problem solving is multilateralism.

It is, therefore, worth recalling the standard definition of multilateralism as the management of trans-national problems with three or more parties making policy on the basis of a series of acceptable '(...) generalised principles of conduct' (Ruggie, 1993: 11). The key principles identified by Ruggie are indivisibility, non-discrimination and diffuse reciprocity. It was expected that overtime, decision-making underwritten by these principles would lead to collective trust amongst players within an institution. A key element in the development of trust would come from the willingness of the institutional hegemon – that is the strongest member of the institution – to agree to be bound by these principles. That is, to accept the principle of 'self-binding' (Martin, 2003).

But it is not sufficient simply to identify the principles inherent in multilateralism. We must also understand the degree to which these processes deliver outcomes; the prominence of an international organisation (*pace* APEC) does not always correlate with a high rate of success in problem solving in a given area of international relations. Ambitious organisations might try to structure rules and behaviour in some of the key policy areas of contemporary global politics but often to little avail. Thus, the decreasing salience of the principal international institutions in the late 1970s-early 1980s has been a growing factor in the search for regional solutions to collective action problem solving since that time.

Recently, insight has moved beyond the 'institutionalist' literature on institutions to take more account of history, culture and identity. Explanations of the inter-subjective socio-legal context for inter-state behaviour have emerged (see Kratochwil and Ruggie, 1986.) These approaches, finding fullest expression in the constructivist theorising of the late 20th century (see Wendt, 1992 and 2000) which focused less on the role of international institutions as actors and more on their as norm brokers (see Finnemore, 1996.) States not only use international institutions to reduce uncertainty and transaction costs. They also use them '(...) *to create* information, ideas, norms and expectations (...) [and]

(...) to legitimate or delegitimate particular ideas and practices' (my emphasis) (Abbott and Snidal, 2001: 15). Institutions are thus more than arbiters, and trustees, they are also norm brokers and 'enforcers'. This is an important theoretical insight that has only partially found its way into the analysis of East Asian regionalism to-date (see Acharya, 2004). It is an area of policy relevant, but theoretical, scholarship in need of development.

This discussion of institutionalism has clear implications for the prospects of enhanced institutionalisation taking place in East Asia in the contemporary era in other ways too. We need, for example, to ask to what extent we are seeing movement in the direction of a 'Ruggiesque' definition of multilateralism as institutionalisation in East Asia at this point in time. In the language of institutional theory, to what extent are the processes that are in train in East Asia maximising information sharing, generating transparency in decision-making and advancing the institutional ability to generate credible collective action problem solving in a given issue area, eventually (in some if not all instances) leading to the development of enforcement/compliance mechanisms and dispute resolution procedures?

This is not only a question for East Asia. There is a general issue at stake. Are we in danger of unlearning these principles in the early 21st century? Specifically, is the USA unlearning the message about the role of institutions at the very time when other parts of the world (including Europe, and notwithstanding the current problems with the constitutional settlement) are learning of their importance? The need for institutions is particularly important in those regions of the world in which the market economy is less embedded and where these questions will continue to cast massive policy shadows. East Asia needs to learn the principles of institutionalism that flourished in the 20th century. This is not to suggest that their implementation will follow the paths adopted in the 21st century. Indeed, what makes East Asia so interesting is precisely the fact that it is a vehicle for adaptation of some of the key principles of governance behaviour that developed countries have took on board during the 20th century. The approach adopted by the EU to institutionalisation is not going to be adopted in Asia, but the European experience is important.

If we look at the EU, then a major purpose of it as an institution has been to create 'credible commitments' amongst its member states in areas where the need for collective action problem solving has been accepted (see Moravcsik, 1998). It has done so via a pooling and delegation of sovereignty in key areas. This is the main difference between the EU and other regional integration schemes in the modern era. Pooling and delegating sovereign decision-making is what has given the EU institutional capacity. The key elements of the development of the EU that makes it different from other systems to date can be noted in point form:

1. Europe does have an integrated governance system, linking institutional structures, policies, legal instruments that bring together the national and supranational level of decision-making and policy-implementation. Such integration is key to the overall success of *any* governance system.
2. In individual policy areas (for example, trade and competition policy) Europe has a sophisticated regulatory framework that is unequalled at the global level. To-date, only Europe has managed to develop a competition framework based upon the adoption by each state of common standards, procedures and laws. This is a framework that will not pass easily to the global trade community embodied in the WTO.
3. The EU governance model relies heavily on the rule of law (see Stone Sweet, 2004). The role of the European Court of Justice (ECJ) is crucial in ensuring a system that is both effective and fair at the same time. The ECJ has a key role to play in ensuring the legal provisions of the Treaty of Rome (and subsequent amending treaties) are upheld by the member state governments, the supra-national institutions, and by organisations and individuals. In this regard, the ECJ is a political actor, as much as a legal one. It aims not only to produce more efficient governance in Europe. Increasingly, it is also the conduit through which individuals, organisations as well as states seek redress for infringement of their rights.
4. Access to the ECJ for private individuals as well as member states and the supranational institutions makes it distinctive from other international governance models. Contrast it with the WTO, where only states can make a complaint to the Dispute Settlement Body. If these legal principles of direct effect and supremacy were to be fully incorporated into other international agreements, and particularly in systems of global governance, there would be a radical change in the effectiveness, the capacity and the fairness of international and global governance.
5. The EU, for all its shortcomings has managed to instill a spirit of cooperation amongst a diverse group of member states, succeeded in showing the benefits of cooperation for its members and proving that cooperation need not be zero-sum and can be learned. In essence, cooperation within the context of an interna-

tional governance system produces results where the participants can perceive cooperative action as a public good. This is not to suggest, of course, that cooperation among sovereign states or between states and non-state actors in the establishment of a governance system is either automatic or easy. Successful cooperation to-date has depended on a public-sector push and an emerging supranational structure.

6. The EU has evolved towards a model of governance with a degree of democratic legitimacy. Despite real criticisms and a literature on the democratic deficit (for a discussion see Bellamy, 2005 and Moravcsik, 2004) the EU continues to address the imbalance between the supranational and the national democratic structures.
7. Europe exhibits both common and distinctive features in its national social models. Its models of the welfare state face common internal and external challenges arising from globalisation. Within the academic and the policy communities, the debate about European socio-economic convergence versus national diversities, and stimulated by the "Lisbon strategy" (2000-2001), was aimed at building a competitive 'European knowledge-based society' consistent with social cohesion. Such a modernisation process does impact (if only in a limited way) on the coordination of national social, economic, employment, research, technology, public health and enterprise policies.
8. While the European Union has emerged as a major actor in the world economy, with a reasonably developed and coherent set of trade policies, it is not so successful as a global political actor. For the EU to be taken seriously in the international arena, and to exert influence in the international institutions that currently form the global governance system, it needs a regional political identity as an effective and legitimate actor able to represent the interests of all member states. But finding legitimacy among its citizens and in public discourse within the EU on the one hand, and among the actors and institutions of global governance on the other has proved difficult and events can and do derail these processes (see Reuber and Wolkersdorf, 2002).
9. The European Union has built up a dense web of cooperative relations with countries and regions in other parts of the world. These form a set of bilateral and multilateral relations linked to trade, aid, investment and other forms of development cooperation. Determined by historical, political and geographical factors, these links demonstrate distinctive priorities, value systems and

normative considerations in the negotiation processes and decision-making frameworks, all of which shape the European approach to reform of the global governance system. Inter-regional cooperation has increased in both the scope and density of the agreements. Although often misunderstood, the Asia-Europe (ASEM) process, EU-Mexico, EU-Mercosur, and the Cotonou Agreements constitute examples of the increased aspirations of regional group to build a density of relations and foster trust and understanding fundamental to a global governance framework.

These developments, and the networking and bargaining surrounding them, provide many lessons for regional and global governance in general and for the prospects of institutionalisation at the regional level in particular. European experience (and European scholarship, see Higgott, 2005b) can make a serious theoretical and practical contribution to the emerging notion of sovereignty. European approaches to governance have developed flexible and multidimensional concepts of sovereignty in the international system. As suggested earlier, these ideas of sovereignty contrasts with the often bounded, state-based/intergovernmental characterisations of sovereignty and international relations as understood by most US practice and scholarship and reflected in many other parts of the world where state consolidation rather than sovereignty pooling remains a principle pre-occupation of a governing regime. Institutions, especially regional ones, are the essential conduits between the state and the global economic and political orders. Enhanced global economic integration requires innovation in thinking about governance.

It remains important to make an intellectual leap to overcome these more bounded notions of sovereignty that beset decision makers in all East Asian states. The repressive potential of the state remains considerable, especially given the changing dynamics of international security in the post 9/11 era. We need to escape from a bounded notion of sovereignty and narrow definitions of security and state-interest if the global and regional integration process is to deliver better governance at both regional and global levels. Central to overcoming these limitations must be the recognition that sovereignty can be disaggregated and redistributed across institutional levels from the local to the global with the regional level, if the EU experience is anything to go by, capable of playing an important intermediary role. Thus the importance of institutionalism is no mere theoretical indulgence. How seriously we take it, and in what domains, will determine the nature of regional cooperation in the early years of the 21st century. Institutions will be important interlocateurs in the relationship between globalisation and regionalisation, especially as the recourse to regionalism becomes an increasingly common response to globalisation.

Some early depictions of globalisation missed the complex interplay in the relationship between the 'global' and the 'regional' in the foreign economic policies of states. These analyses made judgments on technical and economic change and then extrapolated from them into the socio-political sphere in a manner for which the evidence was, at best, flimsy. Nowhere was this better illustrated than in what is often called the 'hyperglobalist' literature (*pace* Oman 1999) which saw the declining salience of state actors and state borders in the rise of what Kenichi Ohmae (1995), with a breathless McKinseysque cartography, labelled 'region states'. In so doing he prematurely reduced the state to the role of mere passive actor and victim of cross-border processes. The 'hyperglobalisation' thesis misconstrued how economic space is politically and socially (re) constructed over time. At the very least, economic regionalisation requires governments to sanction the relaxation of barriers to trade and investment, or, more proactively, to facilitate the provision of incentives to investment and trade sponsorship.

We did not witness the end of the nation state although we have seen a transition in its role (Weiss, 2001). States are reasserting themselves, but not in the same way in all parts of the world. In some parts of the world regionalisation, as a meso-level process of state-led governance and regulation, has grown in influence, and will continue to grow in influence in the early stages of the 21st century, but that this regionalism will not necessarily follow the European model leading eventually to some form of 'sovereignty pooling'. Europe's regional present is not Asia's regional future. Rather, we are seeing the rise of what some call 'regulatory regionalism' (Jayasuriya, 2004) in East Asia as state actors develop selective, issue-specific, strategies to manage regional stability and enhance regional competitiveness in the face of recognised limitations in the institutional structures of global economic and political management that emerged throughout the second half of the 20th century.

4. The New Regionalism: Some Important Lessons from and for East Asia[6]

What do the preceding discussions offer us in terms of an enhanced understanding of what is happening in East Asia in the current era? How do we draw on a discussion of comparative regionalism and the

[6] There is a plethora of activity in East Asia in the current era. It is difficult to keep up with the panoply of bilateral initiatives to secure FTAs in the region. For reviews see Dent, 2004; Soesastro, 2005 and Defraigne *et al.*, 2005.

importance of the institutionalisation process in Europe? Do we look for parallels? Do we look for models? Do we look for differences? Do we look for processes of adaptation? The not very precise or robust answer is, I am afraid, a bit of all of these. It may help if we embed our discussion in the wider context of what has come to be known as the 'new regionalism' that, as Breslin (2005: 6) rightly notes, is 'a framework, not a theory'[7].

At its core, new regionalism is a response to globalisation and especially a recognition of the inseparability of what Wallace (1990) called 'informal' and 'formal' integration and Higgott (1997) identified as *de facto* and *de jure* integration. The former refers to integration via the emergence of transnational space among private market actors. The latter sees integration led by the formal authority of governmental actors through agreement or treaty. New regionalism also captures the importance of the ideology of regionalism; that is region building as a political project rather than one driven simply by gravity models of increasing economic integration. The new regionalism also has structural consequences beyond the region in which it has taken place. For example, we increasingly see the growth of institutions and organisations, or at least discourses, attempting to mediate between regions (such as the ASEM process). If this occurs in a formalised way we speak of inter-regionalism.

It is increasingly accepted that *regionalisation* refers to those processes of integration that arise from markets, private trade and investment flows, and from the policies and decisions of companies rather the predetermined plans of national or local governments. *Regionalism* refers to those state-led projects of cooperation that emerge as a result of intergovernmental dialogues and treaties. But, as in the relationship between regionalisation and globalisation, these are not mutually exclusive processes. Failure to recognise the dialectic between globalisation and regionalisation can mean that we impose a regional level of analysis on something that is actually global or vice versa. We must also consider the salience of extra-regional relations when considering regionalisation. Failure to do was a principal past deficiency of early theories of integration. It is especially important to avoid this mistake in the Analysis of the East Asian region

7 A term first used, according to Breslin (2005) by Andrew Hurrell (1995). The growing body of literature that we can gather under the rubric of the 'new regionalism cannot be reviewed here. But see *inter alia*, Gamble and Payne, 1996; Hettne *et al.*, 1999, 2000 and 2001; Breslin *et al.*, 2000; Soderbaum and Shaw, 2003 and Breslin, 2005.

For example, the growth in intra-regional trade in East Asia is the consequence of the fragmentation of production across national boundaries. With components produced across a region, the traded component in the production of a commodity increases dramatically. But the final goods produced as a result of intra-regional trade still have to be sold somewhere, be it inside or outside the region. Is this regionalisation or globalisation? The dichotomy does not help. The answer is both: the processes of developing regional production networks are themselves driven by global processes and are contingent on global markets.

How we map economic and political space is also a concern. Strict national or sovereign parameters should be avoided when identifying regionalisation. In addition to looking for a correlation between the national state and regional membership, we should also examine the wider groups and classes of actors that are involved in processes of integration. The growth of trans-national networks and alliances that integrate elites, but not usually the wider populations, of a given country is the key here. Nowhere is this better illustrated than in the context of the development of APEC, where throughout the 1990s and early 21st century there has been a clear disjuncture between the enthusiasm for the process amongst intellectual, corporate and bureaucratic elites (if not all political ones) and the lack of knowledge and disinterest, if not hostility, towards the project in the wider communities of the member states.

New regionalisms are invariably defined in rejection of the old, 'old' in terms of both theory and practice. At the level of practice, the first key feature of the 'new' is the sheer number of formal regional arrangements. There are few countries that are not members of at least one regional organisation and most are members of more than one. This upsurge in regional activity can be explained in several ways:

- The promotion of export growth strategies has advanced the reality of increased economic regionalisation. In this regard, the increased adoption of varieties of domestic neo-liberal policies is an explanatory variable for regional initiatives.
- An understanding that state actors are but one set of agents among many is at the heart of newer approaches. Moving away from this old 'statist' approach is a defining characteristic of 'new regionalisms'. Newer perspectives recognise the complex cocktail of state actors, interstate and global institutions and non-state actors (especially multinational corporations, emerging civil society organisations and NGOs) that all have an effect upon regional outcomes.

- The need to respond to globalisation or *participate* in the global economy is a driving factor for governments, both weak and strong.

Hence it is the meso-level, between globalisation and the nation-state, especially in a European context, that most effort has been applied to the management of trans-territorial, or multi-territorial collective action problem solving. While moves toward regionally integrated problem solving have been more active in Europe than in other parts of the world, this is not only a European phenomenon. Elsewhere, the growing linkages between different regional integration schemes, such as the FTA between the EU and Mercosur, or the development of the ASEAN Free Trade Area, for example, are evident (Sampson and Woolcock, 2003).

There is also a growing tendency to devolve competencies from state-level to local levels in countries participating in integration processes. As a result, political authority becomes increasingly dispersed while economic activities become more globalised. In addition, non-state actors become increasingly involved in governance. This is not simply an academic observation. It is also replete with policy implications. We should stop thinking in terms of hierarchical layers of competence separated by the subsidiarity principle. We cannot ignore the strong tendency towards networking arrangements at all levels of governance shaping, proposing, implementing and monitoring policy together. In this context, can identify at least four different ways of trying to explain contemporary regionalism:

Four Contrasting Approaches to Regionalism
1. **De facto *Regionalism***: Informal, market-led and leading to enhanced economic integration. This is principally *rationalist-economic* in analytical orientation.
2. **De Jure *Regionalism***: Formal, rule governed, state led and leading to enhanced institutionalised cooperation. This, is principally *legal-political* in analytical orientation.
3. ***Instrumental Regionalism***: Initially informal, interest led. Built on the identification of the interest to be gained by the development of a common policy towards third parties in a given issue area. This is principally power politics *realist* in analytical orientation.
4. ***Cognitive Regionalism***: Initially informal. Built on shared cultural, historical and emotional affiliations that distinguish 'insiders' from 'outsiders'. This, is principally *socio-cultural* in analytical orientation.

The salience of these approaches varies. Trying to find a 'one size fits all' explanation is pointless and rather than building (or joining) regional arrangements to enhance independence from the global economy (as they once did), many developing states now see regionalism as a measure to ensure continued participation in the global economy. Thus, and by extension, the distinction between *de facto* and *de jure* regional activity also becomes more problematic. While markets are the key drivers of regionalisation, state-led initiatives to enhance integration into the global economy lead to the pursuit of more strongly politico-strategic regional policies. But, for a range of reasons that we are only just coming to understand, East Asia, notwithstanding a growing keenness for enhanced regional cooperation, is unlikely to repeat the four-stage sequential process of integration as described by Balassa in a European context and outlined earlier in this paper. Globalisation has had the effect of enhancing trans-border activities and inter-state exchange. Moreover, the security driven disciplines of the Cold War era that ensured tight bi-polarity have disappeared and the growth of a neo-liberal ideology (and practice) of freer trade and financial deregulation amongst global economic actors have combined to challenge traditional economic relations once founded on the premises of 'national economies'. In their place we had a growing recognition in the last quarter of the 20th century of regional projects as a response (both defensive and offensive) to the power of global markets and the need to ensure the flow of FDI in the search for competitiveness.

The difference of the Asian regional experiment in the 21st century is that it is less trade-led than the European project of the 20th century. Of course, *de facto* market led integration is strong. Intra regional trade at 26.5% of regional GDP in 2002 is larger than that for any developing region (Evian, 2005: 5). But such has been the success in liberalising trade in goods under the GATT that the need to free up trade on a regional basis has become less pressing. This is not to suggest that trade is not the motor of growth in East Asia. It remains so. Rather, it is to suggest that it is not the only motor of the regional economic discourse.

Much of the hyperbole surrounding the evolution of APEC in the first half of the 1990s saw only the benefits of free trade. But the export-oriented countries of East Asia have needed very little convincing of the virtues of trade. But discussions in APEC missed the major changes taking place in the global economy and the potentially adverse effects they could have. What was not understood until the financial crises of 1997-1998 was the manner in which dramatic increases in deregulated, unrestricted capital mobility could lead to the kind of catastrophic volatility seen in these crises. Since that time we have seen two seemingly opposing, but nevertheless compatible, trends. These trends are the gradual, movement towards enhanced monetary cooperation in East Asia on the one hand, and the growing interest in bilateral trading arrangements on the other. What makes them compatible is that both are wrapped up in the wider recognition of the importance of 'East Asia', as opposed to the 'Asia Pacific', as the 'voice' of region.

Of course, the US remains the dominant presence in the region, defined as the Asia Pacific (in both economic and military terms), but it is also an unwitting exogenous catalyst in the 'East Asianisation' of the Western Pacific seaboard. APEC, rather than being a potential instrument for trade liberalisation at the Asia Pacific level, has come to be seen in large sectors of the policy communities of East Asia as but an additional site at which the US might advance its own agendas, such as for further capital market liberalisation and, since 9/11 as a vehicle for advancing the US security agenda (see Higgott, 2004).

As is well known, since the late 1990s, regular ASEAN summits have been expanded by the participation of Japan, China and South Korea in ASEAN+3 meetings. The first East Asian summit is scheduled for Kuala Lumpur in December 2005. Asian policy elites appear no longer to want their policies controlled from Washington when economic crises occur; hence the search for 'purpose-designed', East Asian responses to economic policy uncertainty. In this regards, 'instrumentalism regionalism' is driving the growing regional interest in monetary cooperation. There is recognition of the need to cooperate in the face of the shared common problem of financial volatility. This is a stronger urge than a desire to liberalise trade on a regional level. Recent initiatives emanating from this mode of thinking, especially those in the monetary domain discussed in include not only the 2001 Chiang Mai Initiative to create a regional liquidity (swap) fund but also the Asian Bond Fund Initiative (ABF), proposed in June 2003, and the suggestion of a regional stock exchange, both of which have the aim of reducing the distances between the individual national markets and exchanges. One clear benefit of this process is the raising of standards and regulatory norms and practices in the region. The CMI and the ABF collectively enhance, although they do not guarantee, the regional capability of resisting financial volatility.

In terms of 'cognitive' influences in East Asia, the changing leadership role of the United States is important. It represents a growing 'other' in the Asian regional foreign policy context as regional players move to secure greater autonomy *vis-à-vis* the erstwhile regional hegemon. The nascent nature of regional cooperation, when accompanied by the fear of being on the receiving end of asymmetrical agreements in times of low trust in the multilateral trading system, has also seen governments in Asia developing bilateral strategies. This can be seen in the proliferation of preferential trading agreements in the region.

What the Asian crisis told us was that there was no consensus on how to manage the international economic order in the closing stages the 20th and the early stages of the 21st centuries. The major financial institutions were caught between competing nationalist and liberal views of how the world should work. The international financial institutions (IFIs) were found wanting in both theory and practice by the events in East Asia and the crisis provided a learning experience at the multilateral level – globalisation requires institutional capability for prudential regulation and it does so at a range of different levels. While most regional analysts recognise that regulation is best pursued at the global level, regional level initiatives of the type outlined in the Manila framework and discussion of an Asian Monetary Fund will continue to evolve.

Where early regionalism might have been identified as a defensive mechanism to reduce dependence on the international economy, the 'new regionalism' sees it as more pro-active. It is a means of greater access to global markets, not securing regional autarchy. Regionalism is also now more multifaceted and multidimensional than in the past. States engage in any number of overlapping endeavours without sensing contradictions in such a process. Where the defensive legacies of the earlier phase remain – among political elites sceptical of the unregulated nature of contemporary global capitalism – this does not imply a growing regional resistance to all elements of the globalisation process. Indeed, the extent to which regional organisations act as a spur to global economic liberalisation is an important question. APEC was designed to facilitate wider global processes and could be read as a (failed) attempt on the part of its Caucasian members to prevent the emergence of a specific 'East Asian' regionalism.

We should also consider the changing rationale for joining (or forming) regional organisations for many developing states. On one level, the formal criteria established for membership by organisations – *pace* EU requirements in 2004 – force policy change on aspirant members. In the process of liberalising to meet EU standards, these economies have become more open to the global economy. Thus regionalism can be seen as a pathway to globalisation. This is a key distinction between current and old explanations for regional projects. Rather than building (or joining) regional arrangements to enhance independence from the global economy, many developing states now see regionalism as a measure to ensure continued participation in it but with emerging regionalism as a meso-level comfort zone.

Thus regionalism can be simultaneously a response to, and a dynamic behind, globalisation. We are dealing, in short with mutually reinforcing and co-constitutive rather than contending processes. Regional regimes are not barriers to globalisation, but rather 'in-betweens'. The regional project is both part of and a facilitator of globalisation and a regional counter-governance layer in the world political economy. This relationship between regions and neo-liberal paradigms and economic policies stands at the heart of the new assessments of regionalism and regionalisation at the beginning of the 21st century.

Trends in East Asian Regionalism

Since the turn of the century several broad trends have emerged:

- The growing malaise of APEC as the foremost regional construct has continued.
- The growth of bilateral Free Trade or Preferential Trade Areas (PTA or FTA) in the region continues to strengthen.
- The development of an East Asian understanding of regionalism (embodied in the development of the ASEAN+3) and subsequent moves along a path towards the first East Asian Summit
- Closely linked to the above point, the development of an East Asian interest in mitigating the prospects of further financial volatility at a regional level via the gradual development of policies promoting monetary regionalism.

The defining issue in the development of these regional trends is not 9/11. Rather, it is the Asian financial crises of 1997/8. For most Asian states these crises, their aftermath, and Asian responses to US policy in the period since then provide the most salient component of an explanation of current trends and policies.

Bilateral Trade Policy and Regional Theory

While the rhetorical support for markets remains strong, the impact of politics on markets is never far away. And the growing interest in bilateral trade arrangements is determined by a number of factors. In the economic domain, the WTO had not fared well since its inception and the unbalanced diet that is the Doha MTN Round has proved particularly indigestible in many parts of the world giving rise to the growth of interest in bilateral preferential trading relationships (PTAs). This interest was (is) not simply a US phenomenon. But, if the Europeans started it, and other, smaller and weaker states also began to explore it, it has been the role of the US, as the strongest partner in any bilateral relationship, which has been disproportionately influential. In the politico-security domain, the offer of preferential bilateral trading relationships in return for support in Iraq in particular and the war on terror in general has been a major instrument of US foreign policy.

The Asian interest in bilateral agreements reflects a general appreciation of the success of GATT in reducing tariffs and, albeit to a lesser extent, non-tariff barriers in the second half of the 20th century on the one hand, but a concern about the direction of the WTO in the 21st century on the other. But the benefits of regional-multilateral free trade agreements are much less significant in economic terms than they were thought to be. Industry leaders in the region (*de facto* agents of market-led economic integration) are acutely aware of the degree to which manufacturing is now more global than regional. Building large, multi-member, regional trade blocs in an era of globalisation is deemed less relevant. Rather bilateral trade arrangement – in many ways a defining feature of the regional political economy in the early 21st century – are felt to give regional policy elites greater control over national trade policies. This reflects Asian fears that their influence over deliberations at the WTO is not always as great as they would wish. As such, bilateral free trade agreements are statements of sovereignty. East Asian leaders also see them as a useful policy tool with both extra-regional and inter-regional payoffs for the states concerned. The effects of this trend can be, at one and the same time, to enhance regional convergence in one area of activity yet exacerbate regional divergence in another area of economic activity

If bilateral economic cooperation in the trade domain is a fact of life in East Asia in the early years of the 21st century, the key issue for this paper is the degree to which it might enhance the regional project overall or detract from greater regional economic policy coordination and integration. This is clearly not an either/or situation. Elements of both enhanced cooperation and increased competition are present in the contemporary regional policy process. In a 'structural argument', bilateralism can bolster the economic foundations of the region with the prospect of enhanced cooperation at the regional level. It can provide a regional 'lattice' of technical and institutional arrangements to reinforce the regional project (Dent, 2004).

By contrast, a 'process-led argument' in favour of bilateralism suggests that it has the effect of enhancing the broader discourse on regional economic cooperation and integration. No state it is argued, pursues just a bilateral or multilateral trade policy. The two arms can surely be reinforcing. Bilateral activity should be seen as a compliment to other initiatives such as the development of an ASEAN Economic Community and the APT, both of which have different, but complementary agendas and functions. This is a position advanced, for example, by Singapore and Thailand as part of their trade strategies (see Desker, 2004).

In sum, support for enhanced economic cooperation and integration at the regional level is a possible outcome of the trend towards bilateralism in East Asia, but it is not inevitable and strong counter-veiling tendencies and outcomes are equally possible. We have little or nothing in the historical or scholarly armoury to make a strong prediction one way or the other at this stage. The risks may outweigh the opportunities. The degree to which the positive outcome might prevail will in part be determined by the success or failure of activities in other areas of the policy domain and with other putative economic initiatives, such as monetary cooperation, where the collective regional urge in East Asia is currently stronger. But the jury will remain out on the strength of these arguments for the foreseeable future.

Opponents argue that the increasing recourse to bilateral initiatives has the effect of undermining the wider regional project in East Asia. Intellectual and technical capability and political will (key components of institution building) are finite resources that cannot be indefinitely sub-divided without diminishing their utility and effectiveness. At the ASEAN level, bilateral activities must inevitably be in competition for attention with attempts to upgrade the ASEAN (AFTA) to the ASEAN Economic Community (AEC) by 2020 (Hew and Soesastro, 2003). A longer-term outcome of this competition in the trade domain could be the consolidation of existing asymmetries, enhanced inter-state rivalry amongst regional neighbours and a diminution of the region's ability to present a united front to other global actors in other policy domains.

Monetary Regionalism and Cooperation

Narratives of the development of cooperation in this area abound (Deiter and Higgott, 2003; Hamilton-Hart, 2005; Pempel, 2005a) but several points about regional monetary policy as an example of cooperation can be drawn out. Nascent regional cooperation, when accompanied by the fear of asymmetrical agreements in times of low trust in the multilateral trading system, has seen governments developing bilateral strategies. The search for a new voice of Asian regionalism, remains problematic. Dialogue at the Asia Pacific level has faltered. APEC's identity crisis persists. However, the regional dialogue has moved on dramatically since the time of the financial crises of 1997/8. It is the crises of late 1990s that have contributed to the evolution of a new type of regionalism in Asia. Before the crises trade-led regionalism in the Asia-Pacific had been driven by the Caucasian members of APEC. But even prior to 9/11, Asian observers had increasingly evaluated APEC as a tool of American foreign policy. The resistance of Asian policy makers to a strengthened APEC was caused by their fear of American dominance (Kahler, 2000: 568). They became increasingly critical of the lack of tangible benefits that APEC provided (Ravenhill, 2001). The manner in which the US has treated APEC in the wake of 9/11 has confirmed these initial Asian perceptions.

The debate about cooperation at the level of East Asia, writ small to mean ASEAN, continues with discussions about the creation of an AEC to integrate the activities of AFTA, the ASEAN Framework Agreement on Services, and the ASEAN Investment Agreement. But it is at the level of East Asia – writ large to include ASEAN, China, Japan and South Korea – that a dialogue on how best to mitigate the kind of volatility experienced during the financial crises of 1997/8 has developed most rapidly. Notwithstanding the failed attempt to establish an AMF in 1998, the principle behind the proposal did not die. By the end of 1999, the worst of the Asian crisis was over and East Asian policy circles once again addressed the topic of regional co-operation. The regular ASEAN summits were expanded by the participation of Japan, China and South Korea, the new body being called ASEAN+3 (or APT) with the first East Asian Summit taking place in Kuala Lumpur in December 2005. Since then, steps in the search for a new monetary regionalism have been have been frequent and numerous. They represent a contribution to a regional institutional economic architecture that departs from previous cooperation models in Asia.

Efforts to secure monetary cooperation are very much part of the wider exercise of soul searching that has been taking place both within ASEAN, and between ASEAN and its other East Asian partners, since the turn of the century. The crucial point of these exploratory exercises is not their immediate significance. Nor is the point to under-estimate the difficulties of such policy coordination in the region. Rather I suggest we would be naive to think that Asians will not continue to develop greater regional institutional mechanisms for the common management of financial questions. To see ASEAN+3 as but an exercise in extended conference diplomacy, reflecting weakness rather than strength, would be misleading. True, in the opening years of the 21st century, it is too early to see what kinds of institutional structures will eventually be embedded in the region, but the range of interactions developing is unprecedented. ASEAN+3 have moved on from initial leadership meetings. Considerable deepening has taken place with regular ministerial meetings across most policy domains (economics and finance, agriculture, forestry, tourism etc.) (see Stubbs, 2002; Suzuki, 2004 and Thomas, 2004). In T.J. Pempel's perceptive view,

> ... a strikingly contradictory view of the East Asian region emerges. ... [D]espite the overwhelming structural impediments to integration, East Asia has in recent years become considerably more interdependent, connected and cohesive. [It is] ... a region that has developed an increasingly dense network of cross border cooperation, collaboration, interdependence and even formalised institutional integration (Pempel, 2005: 2).

In keeping with earlier analysis of the importance of a concept of 'East Asia' (Higgott and Stubbs, 1995) what we are seeing is a trend picked up by others (Bergsten, 2000; Webber, 2001; Rapkin, 2001); namely, the emergence of a voice of region beyond that of the sub-regions – Southeast and Northeast Asia – but more restricted than that of the Pacific as a mega region. The Asian voice of region that is emerging in the global political economy is an "East Asian" one. When looked at collectively the processes in train actually represent a more systematic package of activities than would at first sight appear to be the case. The whole will be greater than the mere sum of its parts provided the momentum can be maintained. The degree to which this is likely to be the case will be conditioned by the structures of regional leadership that emerge over the coming years.

5. Institutionalising East Asia: The Leadership Issue

Leadership is one of the most difficult analytical concepts in the lexicon of the modern day policy sciences. It is one of those popular and populist concepts that everyone thinks they understand. Few do. The key distinction drawn in this section is between what we might call structural/institutional leadership and agency oriented/political leadership. The two are of course not distinct but the do provide a useful way of identifying the problems and prospects for leadership in the enhancement of Asian regional cooperation over the short to medium term. Specifically, a twofold classification allows us to distinguish between leadership and hegemony.

Leadership is not the same as hegemony (that is economic and military preponderance). Leadership can be intellectual and inspirational. If we look at the development of the EU, for example then we can see both kinds of leadership over the life of the organisation, *pace* the intellectual leadership of figures such as Schuman and Monnet in the crucial agenda setting period of the 1950s and a quasi co-operative hegemony of France and Germany, as the economic core of Europe in the following era. From such a judgment it is easy to suggest that part of the problem that Europe face at the moment is the absence of either kind of leadership. From this position we can also ask a series of similar questions about leadership in Asia in the early 21st century. Several specific questions come to the fore in this context:

- From where will the leadership come to take the cooperative dialogue in East Asia forward at this time? Where are the necessary actors to be found? Where are the Schumans and Monnets?
- What are the structural constraints on actor based leadership emerging and can they be overcome? To-date, the leadership and political resolve required to advance regional institutional cooperation, of the kind seen in Europe in the second half of the 20th century has yet to emerge in East Asia.
- What roles for the principal actors in the region over the short (5 years) to medium (20 years) period. Will the USA play a supportive role in building East Asian cooperation in the 21st century as in the building of the European Union in the second half of the 20th century? Can China and/or Japan play the kind of role that Germany and France played in the evolution of the EU?

The USA and the Question of Hegemony

To talk of regionalism in East Asia without addressing the specific question of the role of the USA is rather like a performance of Hamlet without the Prince. To do so is to miss the context of the US in East Asia since World War II, especially when compared with its role in the reconstruction of Western Europe. This is especially, but not solely, the case since the advent of the Bush administration and the policy changes emanating from the events 9/11/2001. Quite clearly US policy towards the regional agenda is more significantly shaped by its own agenda which since 9/11 has become increasingly a security driven agenda at the expense of what we might call the neo-liberal economic agenda that underwrote its bilateral and multilateral policies towards the region prior to then.

In historical terms the US role, as an exogenous actor, in the development of a European community was pivotal (see Latham, 1997). Within a Cold War context US foreign policy pro-actively supported the European project. True, enhanced regional cooperation in Europe may have taken place without US support in any circumstances, but we will never know one way or the other. But we do know that the US, via a range of initiatives, gave considerable impetus and assistance to the early collaborative efforts of the European project. This is not the contemporary case in East Asia. Indeed, Mark Beeson (2005: 978-81) would argue that one of the key reasons for the slowness of enhanced economic cooperation in East Asia has been precisely because of the constraining role played by the USA in the Cold War context. Moreover, American hegemony and the geo-political setting in the contemporary era remain, as Beeson notes:

> … still crucial influences on regional processes, they are having an inadvertent rather than intentional impact. Whereas the EU sprang from a highly successful attempt to reconstruct Western Europe on a new integrated basis, in East Asia American foreign policy is having a more ambivalent impact on the region that is gradually moving to assume greater autonomy despite, rather than because of, American policy (see Beeson, 2005: 970. But see also Beeson and Higgott, 2005).

If the Cold War in Europe was centripetal, in East Asia it was centrifugal. For fifty years, US policy split the region along ideological grounds and built a structure of bilateral hub and spoke relationships between it and its major East Asian partners on the one hand and propagated Cold War divisions on the other that rendered impossible any leadership pretensions of the regions two major powers. Japan for the second half of the 20th century subordinated any leadership ambitions to its asymmetrical bilateral relationship with the USA. Japan's rise to become the world's second largest economic power in the 1980s and 1990s was achieved at the expense of its own regional leadership ambitions. Similarly, the absence of China (for Cold War reasons) was not in a position to contribute to East Asian wide regional cooperation. For most of the second half of the 20th century, both states, China for ideological reasons, Japan for its own particular debilitating historical reasons, were effectively denied regional leadership ambitions. But in the 21st century the bilateral strategic architecture of the region is undergoing a process of gradual dismantlement that requires that they think positively about leadership issues.

The historical balance sheet on US economic leadership in the post World War II era is mixed, or perhaps more precisely divided into two eras. In the first era it provided massive reconstruction funding, especially for Korea and Taiwan (see Stubbs, 2005). It also provided relatively open market access for the rapidly growing Japanese economy and other NICS in the first tree decades after World War II without receiving a reciprocal openness from these trading partners. This is traditionally explained as part of a wider grand strategy in the Cold War context. From the early 1970s, however, this benign (Kindleberger-esque) reading of US hegemony needs to be revised. Straightened economic circumstances in the US from that time have seen a well documented recourse to aggressive economic policy to restrict access to the US economy for East Asian exports and open East Asian markets to US exporters. This has taken place through a range of strategies variously described as 'aggressive unilateralism' (Bhagwati and Patrick, 1990), strategic trade policy (Krugman, 1986) and the recourse to sectoral protectionist activities with euphemistic names such as Voluntary Export Restraints, Orderly Marketing Arrangements, Structural Impediments Initiatives and the like and, since the 1980s a more or less permanent pressure on the major countries of the region to progressively de-regulate their financial markets.

In contemporary terms, it is perhaps inevitable in the wake of 9/11 that we should see the robust reassertion by the US of the geo-security agenda over the geo-economic agenda that prevailed in the 1990s. US attitudes towards regional projects are now, ambiguous, to say the least. This is not only the case with regards to Europe in the wake of the war in Iraq but also in its attitudes towards enhanced regional cooperation in an East Asian context. While keeping a sense of perspective, we should note that the principal contemporary trends are not substantially different to those that were developing prior to 9/11. The US, since the time of the Asian financial crises and the attempts to establish an AMF, opposes (or at best feigns indifference to) regional initiatives that run counter to its perceived interests in the region.

But there is evidence that suggests that changes in the relationship between the USA and East Asia are becoming less economically asymmetrical and, as a consequence, the ability of the US to set the regional agenda is becoming less convincing than at anytime in the last two decades. As such, the likelihood that it will actively support greater institutional cooperation in the region should not be taken for granted. Indeed, as Marcus Noland, East Asia specialist at the International Institute of International Economics in Washington notes, there are obvious signs of concern in the US foreign economic policy community that events in East Asia, especially closer regional economic cooperation, have the capacity to '… develop in a way that excludes the US' (*The Financial Times*, 14 September 2005: 6; but see also Munakata, 2003: 10).

Resulting from a secular trend over the last 30 years, US GDP is now only 80% of that of East Asia. East Asia's share of total world trade is, at approximately 25% almost double that of the US at 13%. As of 2003, East Asian exports are double those of the US; inter-regional trade in East Asia is strengthening rapidly and the US share of East Asian export trade has declined to 25%. Holdings of foreign currency reserves in East Asia are now more than 20 times those of the United States. It would also seem obvious, US technological superiority notwithstanding and judged by the increase in its share of patent registrations, that East Asia is making some inroads into US preponderance (see Ravenhill, 2005: 12-13).

Of course, quantitative indicators alone are not definitive, especially when dealing with a concept as illusive as hegemony. East Asian aggregate performance does not axiomatically find its way into enhanced political leverage over the US given that the region does not formulate policy towards the US on the basis of an 'East Asian' interest or via a regional institutional policy-making machinery capable of reflecting any such aggregate interest. Decision-making resides firmly at the level of the constituent states not at the level of the wider regional collective. In this context the agenda setting abilities of the US far outweigh those of any single East Asian state individually or, even given the probability of some enhanced cooperative decision-making emerging in the region from a successful EAS, collectively for a few years to come. For East Asia to bring about a closure of the asymmetry in decision-making process with the USA to accompany the declining gap in material capability, it needs to enhance its collective decision making capabilities. For this to occur, leadership endogenous to the region needs to strengthen. How this might be achieved is, of course, the single most important regional policy issue for the future.

Geo-Politics, Leadership and East Asian Cooperation

East Asian responses to US economic policy are not insignificant. Major strides have been made by East Asian states in using existing institutional opportunities to defend sectoral interests, for example, via the WTO Dispute Settlement Mechanism (see Pekkanen, 2004) although the region remains basically under-represented in the Bretton Woods institutions that still reflect the configuration of global power at the end of World War II. However, Japanese and Chinese leadership aspirations continue to grow and the discursive practices of regionalisation continue to evolve in a non-trivial manner. Whether the Asians will be successful or not in their endeavours, there can be little doubt that the continued exploration of cooperation as a way to combat vulnerability is an established item on the regional policy agenda in the early 21st century and it demonstrates a marked contrast with the late 20th century. Take three examples.

Firstly, if we consider APEC as the dominant regional initiative of the closing decade of the last century, then during this period we saw the US strongly pro-active; Japan as a passive/reactive actor in the organisation; and China giving its support to the EAEC initiative of the Malaysians rather than APEC. But the Asian financial crises exposed the limitations of the progressively excessive expectations that were heaped on APEC from the time of the first summit in 1993 until the crises of 1996-1997. Secondly, the AMF initiative of the late 1990s, initiated by the Japanese met with resistance (albeit low key) from the Chinese and outright hostility from the USA.

From that time on rose tinted lenses and soft rhetoric were replaced by harder realist lenses as APEC lost is appeal for Asian policy makers in particular. No significant economic initiatives have emerged from APEC since that time. Other factors diminished its attraction as an 'institution' for Asian leaders; especially the 'securitisation' of APEC following 9/11 (Higgott, 2004). APEC's potential to be anything more than a vehicle for general dialogue, notwithstanding detailed technical work in its sub-groups and committees and by some of its members (especially Australia), has always been over-hyped. Without accepting Mahathir-style rhetoric, East Asian regional support for APEC has always been constrained by national interest concerns that eschew any serious commitment to its core analytical and policy concepts of 'open regionalism' and 'concerted unilateral liberalisation'.

Thirdly, and most significantly, in the early 21st century the major regional agenda item to-date has been the attempt to develop enhanced monetary cooperation, especially since the Chiang Mai initiative, as the major exercise in regional cooperation in the 21st century. In this initiative we see, for the first time, a position where both the Japanese and the Chinese are strongly supportive of this regional project. While the USA is opposed, it is not minded to develop strong countermeasures. China and Japan are not it should be stressed, engaged in a concerted coordination of their foreign policies. Rather, we see a coincidence where both powers recognise that the regional agenda for enhanced monetary policy coordination can be supported and advanced comfortable in the knowledge that it is a positive sum, not a zero sum, game. It is the primacy of instrumental regionalism. At the risk of labouring the point, in contexts where Japanese and Chinese instrumental interests cohere, this will be a massively powerful force for regional cooperation in East Asia. As we understand, in contexts where they are at odds, it will be very counter-productive.

China and Regional Cooperation

How this will relationship between China and the rest of the region plays out in the long run is the key to security, cooperation and institution building in East Asia. This issue is best approach by posing a question rather than offering unsustainable propositions regarding future behaviour. 'Does increased wealth and power lead to greater cooperation or greater competition?' This is a perennial question of international relations. It is central to the relationship between China and Japan. The evolution of their respective economies, over the last two decades at least, has been complementary, rather than competitive in terms of what they produce for the global market and what they take bilaterally from each other. China is Japan's second largest trade partner after the USA and Japan the largest partner for China and in Japan the largest source of ODA to China and, since 2001, Japanese FDI third only to that of Hong Kong and the USA (Taniguchi, 2003).

Longer-term, however, it is likely that the relationship will become increasingly competitive as they compete (both bilaterally and with the USA) in their search for inputs into their respective economies – especially in their search for sources of energy and other resources. 2004 saw China overtake Japan as the world's second largest oil importer. It is also now, depending on statistical interpretation, the world's second largest economic power in PPP terms and the world's third largest trading power. It can also be argued that US policy fuels rather than cools the competition between the two Asian superpowers as it grapples to adjust to changes in the global power structure brought about by China's rising role). To-date all the signs are that it is not doing this well, or even responsibly (see Johnson, 2005).

And of course there are also still strong, residual nationalistic antagonisms between the two countries that cannot be assigned to the historical past. Aaron Friedberg's (1993/4) suggestion that the region is 'ripe for rivalry' could be countered by T. J. Pempel's (2005) recent assertion that the region could just as easily be 'ripe for cooperation'. How it turns out will depend on how the regional conversation is managed in the coming decades. To say that the discussion could and should be rationalist and instrumental is not to say that the regional dialogue cannot be derailed. In essence there are thus two scenarios for consideration.

In the worst-case scenario, contemporary strains in the relationships between the regional great powers are seen as fundamentally irresolvable. There are several factors that we might anticipate in this scenario:

1. The unwillingness of Japanese policy makers to distance themselves and their country sufficiently from the atrocities of World War II continues, and remains unacceptable to the rest of the region. The historical roots are deep and continue to cast ominous policy shadows over its relationships with the key players in East Asia in a way that has long ceased to be the case in Germany's relationships with the rest of Europe for example.
2. Japan sides with US in attempting to block China's greater participation in the regional economic order and political orders and this is seen as a fundamental act of hostility by the Chinese government. Note here certain signaling activities by Japan such as

its support for the US approach towards Taiwan and other factors such as Japan blocking Chinese participation in the Inter-American Development Bank.

3. A conflictual rather than peaceful outcome to the increasing contest for energy supplies amongst the US, China (and Japan) must remain a possibility if not necessarily a probability. Demand in both countries and the region in general (not to mention India) will grow rapidly. Provided the increased pressure is 'lateral', that is pressure that brings on gradual structural reform of the system rather than provokes direct confrontation between the hegemon and the rising great powers, then there is hope for a non-conflictual outcome.

The worse case scenario also assumes certain, resistant, courses of action by the USA towards greater regional economic cooperation in East Asia. In grand strategic terms, Asian economic co-operation is not nearly as useful to the USA in the 21st century as European integration was in the second half of the 20th century. There is no longer any need to demonstrate the superiority of the market economy. The alternative has vanished. But successful economic integration in Asia today from China (more so than Japan notwithstanding parallels with the 1980s) is a challenge to US competitiveness (and for some analysts its security). Indeed, Asian regionalism is seen by much of the current US policy community as but a vehicle for China's ambitions. If Asia were to emancipate itself from American 'guidance', Washington's hold on the region would deteriorate sharply. Most importantly, US-China competition for scarce energy supplies could impact adversely on the US's wider geo-political objectives in say the Middle East or Latin America (Venezuela). As Shambaugh persuasively argues (2005: 90-91), the Sino-US relationship, notwithstanding China's strengthening position in the region, does not have to be zero-sum. But how the US takes it forward is yet to be determined, although the omens are not promising.

Thinking more positively, there is an alternative, more favourable scenario that can be developed around the rise of regulatory regionalism. The key elements of which are enhanced regional economic dialogue and interaction both *amongst* the states of Northeast Asia (China, Japan and South Korea) and *between* these states and the states of Southeast Asia through the development of the ASEAN+3 process leading to an East Asian Community.

Regulatory Regionalism

This is not the kind of regional cooperation that has its antecedents in a European intellectual context. Rather it links national and global understandings of regulation via the region as a 'meso'-level. Effectively, regionalism is a transmission belt for global disciplines to the national level via the de-politicising and softening process of the region in which regional policy coordination – evolving regional governance – becomes a link between the national and the global. It is emerging as a genuinely multi-level exercise. It reflects several trends where:

1. Regional policy coordination to mitigate risk is delegated to the state. It is sovereignty enhancing. Indeed, there is a strong relationship between state form, the global economic and political orders and the nature of regional governance emerging. This compromise is inevitable if the continuing tension between nationalism and regionalism in East Asia is not to jeopardise the cooperative endeavour. Again, it is instrumental regionalism.
2. The meshing of multilevel process of regulation reinforce the connections between the international institutions (especially the IMF and World Bank) and regional institutions such as the ADB and the emerging instruments of regulation developing in the context of monetary regionalism at the level of ASEAN+3, such as the ASEAN regional surveillance process (ASP) and the regularised (dare one say institutionalised) meetings of regional central bankers.
3. The transmission of internationally agreed codes, emanating from the perceived best practice of international institutions such as the IMF, help enforce market standards, and do so much more than sceptics concede (see Manupipatpong, 2002).

It is in the area of monetary regionalism, not regional trade liberalisation, where cooperation is advancing most rapidly. It is not *de facto* trade led regionalism driving the agenda – this is taken care of now much more at the global multilateral and bilateral levels. The key to monetary regionalism is closer integration through the development of *common* national 'regulation' rather than regional institution building. Nor is it *de jure* state-led cooperation driving the agenda. The discourse of regulatory regionalism carries fewer negative connotations for sovereignty and regime autonomy than 'regional institution building'. Institution building throughout the pre-crisis days in East Asia carried with it the implications of sovereignty pooling of the European Cartesian legal formalist variety that alarmed Asian regional elites. Regulatory regionalism does not have the same echoes. It is instrumental regionalism.

While it reflects a different understanding of regionalism to that which prevails in Europe, it nevertheless demonstrates perhaps a greater interest in the development regional institutions and inter-regional relationships to enhance collective action problem solving under conditions of globalisation than is to be found in contemporary US foreign economic policy as the brief comparison set out below suggests.

Americans and Europeans project sharp differences in their approaches towards world politics in general and global and regional institutional cooperation in particular. The US and the EU, for example, differ on questions of 'partnership', 'burden sharing', and 'exceptionalism' as approaches to global management. For the Bush Administration, what drives contemporary world order is 'primacy', '*real-politik*' and freedom to manoeuvre. For Europeans it is 'globalisation' and 'interdependence'. The EU disposition for multi-level-governance and 'sovereignty pooling' is incomprehensible to US policy makers. The '*acquis communautaire*' (the body of common standards and regulations that have developed over the life of the European project) notwithstanding perpetual complaints about excessive bureaucracy and the rejection of the constitution, are generally accepted in Europe. Europe, in theory if not always in practice, exhibits a stronger normative attitude towards multilateral governance structures and constitutional and regulatory frameworks that transcend the nation state.

Those states of greater Europe that are not members of the EU, for all its shortcomings, are still keen to join it. With the benefit of the longer term historical perspective, what looks like weakness through traditional state-centric, realist, power politics lenses actually looks like strength through the newer lenses of the increasingly diffused and networked nature of power in the contemporary global era (see Hall and Biersteker, 2002 and Slaughter, 2004).

Without over-stating this case either, differences with the US towards, regionalism and multilateralism may also be found in East Asia in the early 21st century. East Asia too places a greater stress on multilateral and regional cooperation than the US although, as in Europe, there may be a marked disconnect between theory and rhetoric on the one hand and application and practice on the other. But we live in an era of the 'new regionalism' in East Asia that has progressed apace since the financial crises of the latter part of the 1990s. The key elements of this new regionalism are enhanced regional economic dialogue and interaction both *amongst* the states of Northeast Asia (China, Japan and South Korea) and *between* these states and the states of Southeast Asia. This tendency is not, of course unproblematic and the behaviour of

China in East Asia over the medium to longer term is crucial. The continual war of words between China and Japan over the past has not stopped China replacing the USA as Japan's major trading partner. It is possible to identify potential pitfalls standing in the way of the longer term consolidation of the relationship. If we privilege the security relationship at the expense of the economic one, then neighbours attracted by China's market potential and willingness to enter into regional partnerships in the economic domain are much more sanguine about China's growing regional military might.

In this positive scenario, while the USA remains the dominant presence in the region, defined as the Asia Pacific (in both economic and military terms), it does so as a more passive actor, but also, ironically, as an exogenous catalyst in the 'East Asianisation' of the Western Pacific. At the risk of a post-modern turn, the USA becomes the 'other' enhancing the growth of a cognitive understanding of East Asian regionalism! Similarly, while the growth of bilateral initiatives may be sub-optimal in terms of pure economic theory, they should not cause alarm if they lead to competitive liberalisation, domestic reform and enhanced regional knowledge and transparency. This is the positive gloss that might be put on what one scholar calls the 'Sino-Japanese FTA Race' (Munakata, 2003: 6).

When looked at collectively the processes in train East Asia may actually represent a more systematic package of regional governance activities than would at first sight appear to be the case. The APT process is being institutionalised through the evolution of an over lapping multi-dimensional process of regional conference diplomacy strengthening, and indeed creating, links between the states of Northeast Asia and Southeast Asia (Suzuki, 2004). Whether Asians will be successful or not in their endeavours, there can be little doubt that the continued exploration of cooperation as a way to combat vulnerability is an established item on the regional policy agenda in the early 21st century, as even the normally sceptical *Economist* in a recent editorial was prepared to acknowledge (26-27 March 2005).

Of course, the future of successful regional discourse seems dependent not only on Japanese economic reform, but also on a willingness of the PRC to continue its new found regional cooperative economic role that has developed since 1997 (see Shambaugh, 2005). If this continues in a positive way and trust can be built in the region between the major actors, then regionalism will grow as an important activity as a meso-level instrumental expression of the desire to optimise sovereign decision-making by states confronting the rigors of global competition. If Japanese and Chinese *instrumental interests* can be privileged over *cognitive differences* this could be a massively powerful force for regional cooperation in East Asia. Without their input and indeed eventual leadership, ASEAN-driven attempts to secure East Asian regionalism will amount to little. The extent to which either player is committed remains problematic and for both, but especially Japan, it is in many ways a function of their relationship with the United States. Japan remains a reluctant regional institutionalist and the US does nothing to dissuade it from that position

These alternative scenarios are not merely determined regionally. They need to be located in the overall discussion about globalisation and regionalisation in the early 21st century. There is a general principle that we can draw about power and regionalism from a comparative discussion of Europe and Asia. It is better put as a question than offered as an assertion. 'Is it likely that we are entering an era where large sections of the global community look less to the major multilateral institutions – so much the playthings of the major powers – as vehicles for collective action problem solving and more towards the development of regional activities and communities?' If so, then the growing salience of the regional dialogue is a positive trend in international relations in general and in East Asia in particular.

Regionalism is an effort to transcend a uni-polar world in which the hegemonic power shows an increasing reluctance, in contrast to times past, to engage as an 'altruistic', as opposed to what Jagdish Bhagwati (2003) calls a 'selfish' hegemon. To this extent, although this is not the intended outcome, contemporary US foreign policy can act as a catalyst to regional consolidation in Asia. Growing discontent with US policy in, and towards, the East Asian region (especially since the Asian financial crises) has been a significant factor in the enhanced regional dialogue of the 21st century. Taken to extremes, it is not impossible to envisage a situation in which the world does become more multi-polar. Not necessarily multi-polar in the traditional realist sense of other regions combining to 'balance' against the US, but multi-polar in the sense that the US becomes less salient as an actor in the development and activities of other regions. That we even raise these questions is testament to the magnitude of change that has taken place in thinking about the strength of the glue holding contemporary global order together in the early 21st century.

The US having won the Cold War through a combination of hard power and soft power now seems to hope that raw material power will be sufficient to intimidate other great powers. This assumes that China, Japan (and East Asia) as well as Europe, Russia, India, Brazil and Latin America are not capable of developing policies and strategies to mitigate the influence of US economic and military power. US hegemony, or primacy in the military sphere, is not preventing the development of multi-polar initiatives in geo-political and economic domains, as the nature of regional institution building without US participation attests.

None of this should allow us to under-estimate the continuing power and influence of the USA in the East Asia. A growing Asian rhetorical resistance to US policy in the region (agency driven sources of power and leadership) should not cause us to neglect the residual and continuingly strong structural influences from the US, what Nye (2002) would call 'soft power', especially strong support for the broad neo-liberal economic agenda. Moreover, for most states of the region, notwithstanding the increasingly role of China, the US remains the major bilateral relationship. It is not an easy one. The Bush administration is the most self-regarding US administration any Asian post-colonial leaders have known.

Conclusion: Towards Regulatory Regionalism in East Asia in the 21st Century

Both the practice and theory of regionalism are undergoing a period of significant change. The key element is a shift from a Cold War to post Cold War/globalisation era. During the Cold War, regional theory was statist, European-influenced and stressed inter-governmental bargains. In the era of globalisation it is more complex, multidimensional and, notwithstanding the increased salience of security issues post 9/11, still primarily economic focused. In the first era, the 'economic' and the 'political' were largely treated as separate issue areas for investigation and action. In the second era, politics and the economics are more clearly linked and the state is joined by a series of other significant, non-state actors in the practice of regionalism as the relationship between state authority and market power becomes fuzzier.

In addition, the early Balassian model, based on a reading of the evolution of the EU, no longer stands scrutiny in the context of globalisation, where guarding against the volatility and erratic mobility of capital is in many ways now a factor of as great, if not greater, regional concern than guaranteeing the openness of the trade regime. Balassian style theory pays insufficient attention to the possibility of different routes to, or different agendas for, regional cooperation. It is also silent on the significance of socio-cultural factors – especially the role of identity in region building – to be relevant in an era of globalisation. In this sense, the contemporary discussion in East Asia illustrates the differences between the two eras and two approaches to theorising and offers us an alternative reading of regionalism in a wider global context.

East Asia is a region of economic experimentation. The glue of regionalism at the level of the Asia Pacific – embodied in APEC – has come unstuck since the time of the Asian financial crisis. Events post-9/11 have exacerbated this trend. Moreover, Asian policy communities have learned that globalisation and regionalisation are not mutually exclusive activities but rather exist in a dialectical relationship. Regionalism is not an alternative to globalisation. Following this logic allows us to explain the emergence of a multiplicity of policy responses to recent economic issues in the Asia-Pacific. These responses reflect, in part at least, Asian resistance to western driven models. Specifically, the financial crises of the late 1990s forced regional scholars and policy makers alike to examine not only their national economic policies, but also their very understanding of regionalism.

The regionalism we see emerging in East Asia in the 21st century is not the kind of regional cooperation with a European intellectual pedigree. It is clearly unrealistic to imagine the development of institutions involving the transfer of elements of state sovereignty to regional institutions. Rather it is a 'regulatory regionalism' that links national and global understandings of regulation via the intermediary regional level. This regulatory urge is not simply restricted to trade. Indeed, it is in the area of monetary regionalism that it is advancing most rapidly. The key to monetary regionalism is closer integration through common national 'regulation' rather than regional institution building. In discursive terms, 'regional regulation' carries fewer negative connotations for sovereignty and regime autonomy than 'regional institution building'. Institution building throughout the pre-crisis days in East Asia carried with it the unwanted implication of European style 'sovereignty-pooling'.

In the absence of global structures of economic governance (not a real prospect) we must expect policy makers to explore more manageable alternatives. Traditional state-centric, power politics approaches to the management of the world order under conditions of globalisation are becoming less salient. More diffuse networked understandings of power, with loosely institutionalised regulatory actions providing a *modus operandi* for cooperation are becoming increasingly attractive. In this context, the role of institutional capacity – especially institutions as transaction cost reducers and vehicles for the enhancement of transparency and norm compliance – cast increasingly long policy shadows over current regional activities in East Asia. It is here that the current discourse on regionalism (and multi-level governance for all its faults and all its detractors) offers the bones of an alternative model. The European experience, or that of the multilateral international organisations, is not simply an 'off the shelf' export model. Some key elements, especially those of a sovereignty pooling nature will be resisted. But other elements will be adjusted and/or localised in a specifically East Asian fashion. The degree to which East Asia can develop institutional capacity in the absence of some sovereignty pooling is the key research and policy question for the future. "Meso"-level, regulatory regionalism can enhance cooperation only so far. East Asia will not mirror what we understand by the term institutionalism in Europe in the second half of the 20th century, but neither will it be trivial. For both the scholar and the practitioner of regionalism and institutionalism, these are indeed interesting times in East Asia.

References

Acharya, A. (1997), "Ideas, Identity and Institution Building: From ASEAN Way to the Asia Pacific Way", *The Pacific Review*, 10(2).

—— (2001), *Constructing a Security Community in Southeast Asia: ASEAN and the Problem of Regional Order*, London, Routledge.

—— (2004), "How Ideas Spread: Whose Norms Matter? Norm Localization and Institutional Change in Asian Regionalism", *International Organisation*, 58 (2), p. 239-75.

—— (2005), "Europe and Asia: Reflections on a Tale of Two Regions", in Webber, D. and Fort, B. (eds.), *Regional Integration in Europe and East Asia: Convergence or Divergence*, London, Routledge.

Balassa, B. (1962), *The Theory of Economic Integration*, Homewood (Illinois), Richard Irwin.

Beeson, M. (2005), "Rethinking Regionalism: Europe and East Asia in Comparative historical Perspective", *European Journal of Public Policy*, 12 (6), p. 969-85.

—— and Higgott, R. (2005), "Hegemony, Institutionalism and US Foreign Policy: Theory and Practice in Comparative Historical Perspective" (with Mark Beeson), *Third World Quarterly*, 26(7), 2005, p. 1173-88.

Bellamy, R. (2005), "Still in Deficit: Rights, Regulation and Democracy in the EU", for the Democracy Task Force of the EU 6th Framework Integrated Project on New Modes of Governance, p. 1-31.

Bergsten, C. F. (2000), "East Asian Regionalism: Towards a Tripartite World", The Economist, 15 July.

Bhagwati, J. (2002), *Free Trade Today*, Princeton, Princeton University Press.

—— and Patrick, H. (1990) (eds.), *Aggressive Unilateralism: America's 301 Trade Policy and the World Trading System*, Ann Arbor, University of Michigan Press.

Breslin, S. (2005), "Studying Regions: Comparativism and Eurocentrism", Conference on China and Asian Regionalism, Shanghai, Fudan University, January, p. 1-39.

—— Higgott, R. (2000), "Studying Regions: Learning from the Old, Constructing the New", *New Political Economy*, 5 (3), p. 333-352.

—— Hughes, C., Phillips, N. and Rosamond, B., (2002) (eds.), *New Regionalism in the Global Political Economy: Theories and Cases*, London, Routledge.

Buzan, B. and Segal, G. (1994), "Rethinking East Asian Security", *Survival*, 36 (2), p. 3-21.

Coleman, W. and Underhill G. (1998) (eds.), *Regionalism and Global Economic Integration: Asia, Europe and the Americas*, London, Routledge.

Defraigne, J.-C., Dieter, H., Higgott, R. and Lamy, P. (2005), *East Asian Integration: Opportunities and Obstacles for Enhanced Economic Cooperation*, Report for JETRO, Paris, Notre Europe.

Dent, C. (2004), *The New Economic Bilateralism and Southeast Asia: Region Convergent or Region Divergent*, British International Studies Association, IPEG Papers in Global Political Economy, No.7, April, 2004.

Desker, B. (2004), "In Defence of FTAs: From Purity to Pragmatism in East Asia", *The Pacific Review*, 17 (1), 2004, p. 3-26.

Deiter, H. and R. Higgott (2003), "Exploring Alternative Theories of Economic Regionalism: From Trade to Finance in Asian Co-operation", *Review of International Political Economy*, 10 (3), 2003, p. 430-54.

Evian Group (2005), "East Asian Regionalism: Integrative versus Disintegrative Forces", 2005 Evian Hong Kong Initiative, Hong Kong, 17-18 May, p. 1-12.

Fawcett, L. and Hurrell, A. (1995 (eds.), *Regionalism in World Politics: Regional Organisation and International Order*, Oxford, Oxford University Press.

Finnemore, M. (1996), "Norms, Culture and World Politics: Insights from Sociology's Institutionalism", *International Organisation*, 50(2), p. 887-918.

Friedberg, A. (1993/4), "Ripe for Rivalry: Prospects for Peace in Multi-Polar Asia", *International Security*, 18(3), p. 5-33.

Gamble, A. and Payne, A. J. (1996) (eds.), *Regionalism and World Order*, Basingstoke, Macmillan.

Gavin, B. (2001), *The European Union and Globalisation: Towards Global Democratic Governance*, Aldershot, Edward Elgar.

Grugel J., and Hoult, W. (1999) (eds.), *Regionalism across the North-South Divide: State Strategies and Globalisation*, London, Routledge.

Haas, Ernst (1958), *The Uniting of Europe: Political Social and Economic Forces, 1950-57*, Stanford CA, Stanford University Press.

—— (1964), *Beyond the Nation-State: Functionalism and International Oganisation*, Stanford CA, Stanford University Press.

—— (1975), *The Obsolescence of Regional Integration Theory*, Berkeley CA, Institute for International Studies.

Hall, R. B. and Biersteker, T. J. (2002) (eds.), *The Emergence of Private Authority in Global Governance*, Cambridge, Cambridge University Press.

Hamilton-Hart, N. (2005), "The Chiang Mai Initiative and the Prospects for Closer Monetary Cooperation in East Asia", in Webber, D. and Fort, B. (eds.), *Regional Integration in Europe and East Asia: Convergence or Divergence*, London, Routledge.

Harris, S. (2002), "Asian multilateral institutions and their response to the Asian economic crisis: regional and global implications", in Breslin S. *et al.*, *New Regionalisms in the Global Political Economy*, London, Routledge.

Hay, C. and Rosamond, B. (2002), "Globalisation, European Integration and the discursive construction of economic imperatives", *European Journal of Public Policy*, 9, 2.

Held, D. and A. McGrew, (2000) (eds.), *The Global Transformations Reader: An Introduction to the Globalization Debate*, London, Polity.

Hew, D. and Soesastro, H., "Realising the ASEAN Economic Community by 2020: ISEAS and ASEAN ISIS Approaches", *ASEAN Economic Bulletin*, 20 (3), 2003.

Hettne, B., Inotai, A. and Sunkel, O., (1999) (eds.), *National Perspectives on the New Regionalism in the Third World,* London, Palgrave.

—— (2000) (eds.), *National Perspectives on the New Regionalism in the North,* London, Palgrave.

—— (2001) (eds.), *Comparing Regionalisms: Implications for Global Development*, London, Palgrave.

Higgott, R. (1997), "*De facto* or *De Jure* Regionalism: The Double Discourse of Regionalisation in the Asia Pacific", *Global Society: Journal of Interdisciplinary International Relations*, 11(2), 1997, p. 165-83.

—— (1998), "The Asian Financial Crisis: A Study in the Politics of Resentment", *New Political Economy*, 3(3), p. 33-56.

—— (1998a), "The International Political Economy of Regionalism: Europe and Asia Compared", in Coleman, W. and Underhill, G. (eds.), *Regionalism and Global Economic Integration: Asia, Europe and the Americas*, London, Routledge.

—— (2004), "The 'Securitisation' of U.S. Foreign Economic Policy in East Asia", *Critical Asian Studies*, 36 (3), 2004, p. 425-44.

—— (2005), "Economic Regionalism in East Asia: Consolidation with Centrifugal Tendencies", in Stubbs, R. and Underhill, G. (eds.), *Political Economy and the Changing Global Order*, Oxford, Oxford University Press.

—— (2005a), "The Theory and Practice of Regionalism in a Changing Global Context", in Webber, D. and Fort, B. (eds.), *Regional Integration in Europe and East Asia: Convergence or Divergence*, London, Routledge, p. 17-38.

—— (2005b), "The Theory and Practice of Global Governance: Accommodating American Exceptionalism and European Pluralism", *European Foreign Affairs Record*, October 2005.

—— (2006), "International (Political) Organiszation(s)", in Rhodes, R. and Rockman, B. (eds.), *The Oxford Handbook of Political Institutions*, Oxford, Oxford University Press, 2006.

—— Leaver, R. and Ravenhill, J. (1993) (eds.), *Pacific Economic Relation in the 1990s: Cooperation and Conflict,* Boulder, CO, Lynne Reinner.

—— and Stubbs, R. (1995), "Competing Conceptions of Economic Regionalism: APEC versus EAEC", *Review of International Political Economy*, 2(3).

Hix, S., (1994), "The Study of the European Community: The Challenge for Comparative Politics", *West European Politics*, 17(1).

—— (1999), *The Political System of the European Union*, Basingstoke, Macmillan.

Hurrell, A. (1995), "Explaining the Resurgence of Regionalism in World Politics", *Review of International Studies*, 21 (4).

—— (1995a), "Regionalism in Theoretical Perspective", in Fawcett, L. and Hurrell, A. (eds.), *Regionalism in World Politics: Regional Organisation and International Order,* Oxford, Oxford University Press.

Hurst, P. and Thompson, G. (2001), *Globalisation in Question*, Cambridge, Polity, 2nd edition.

Jayasuriya, K., (2004) (ed.), *Asian Regional Governance: Crisis and Change*, London, Routledge.

Johnson, C. (2005), "No Longer the 'Lone' Supoerpower: Coming to Terms with China", *Japan Policy Research Institute, Working Paper 105*, San Francisco, March, 1-12. www.jpri.org/publications/wp105.html.

Katzenstein, P., Keohane, R. O. and Krasner, S. (1998), "International Organisation and the Study of World Politics", *International Organisation*, 52 (4).

Kahler, M. (2000), "Legalization as a Strategy: The Asia Pacific Case", *International Organization*, 54 (3), 2000, p. 549-71.

Keohane, R. (1984), *After Hegemony: Cooperation and Discord in the World Political Economy*, Princeton, Princeton University Press.

—— (1989), *International Institutions and State Power: Essay in International Relations Theory*, Boulder Co, Westview Press.

—— (2001), "Governance in a Partially Globalised World", *American Political Science Review*, 95 (1), p. 1-13.

—— (2002), *Power and Governance in a Partially Globalized World*, Routledge.

—— (2004), "Global Governance and Democratic Accountability", in Held, D. and Archibugi, M. K., *Taming Globalization: Frontiers of Governance*, Cambridge, Polity Press.

Kooiman, J. (2003), *Governing as Governance*, London, Sage.

Kratochwil, F. and Ruggie, J., (1986), "The State of the Art on an Art of the State", *International Organisation*, 40 (4), p. 753-75.

—— and Mansfield, E. (2005) (eds.), *International Organisation: A Reader*, New York, Longman Publishers, 2005.

Krugman, P. (1986) (ed.), *Strategic Trade Policy and the 'New' International Economics*, Cambridge, MA, MIT Press.

Latham, A. (1997), *The Liberal Moment: Modernity, Security, and the Making of Postwar International Order*, New York, Columbia University Press.

Leonard, M. (2005), *Why Europe Will Run the 21st Century*, London, Fourth Estate Books.

Lindberg, L. (1966), *The Political Dynamics of European Economic Integration*, Stanford CA, Stanford University Press.

Manupipatpong, W. (2002), "The ASEAN Surveillance Process and the East Asian Monetary Fund", *ASEAN Economic Bulletin*, 19 (1), p. 114-15.

Mansfield, E. D. and Milner, H. (1977) (eds.), *The Political Economy of Regionalism*, New York, Columbia University Press.

Martin, L. (2003), *Multilateral Organisations after the US-Iraq War of 2003*, Harvard University, Weatherhead Centre for International Affairs, August, p. 1-17.

Mattli, W. (1999), *The Logic of Regional Integration*, Cambridge, Cambridge University Press.

Moravcsik, A. (1994), "Preferences and Power in the European Community: A Liberal Intergovernmental Approach", in Bulmer, S. and Scott, A. (eds.), *Economic and Political Integration in Europe,* Oxford, Blackwells.

—— (1998), *The Choice for Europe: Social Purpose and State Power: From Messina to Maastricht*, Ithaca, Cornell University Press.

—— (2004), "Is there a 'Democratic Deficit' in World Politics? A Framework for Analysis", *Government and Opposition*, 39 (3), p. 344-46.

Munakata, N. (2003), "The Impact of the Rise of China and Regional Economic Integration in Asia: A Japanese Perspective", *Statement to US-China Economic and Security Review Commission Hearings on China's Growth as a Regional Economic Power*, Washington DC December, p. 1-13.

Nesadurai, H. (2003), *Globalisation, Domestic Politics and Regionalism: The ASEAN Free Trade Area,* London Routledge, 2003.

North, Douglass (1990), *Institutions, Institutional Change and Economic Performance*, Cambridge, Cambridge University Press.

Nye, J. (1968), "Comparative Regional Integration: Concepts and Measurement", *International Organisation*, 22(4).

—— (1971), *Peace in Parts: Integration and Conflict in International Organisations*, Boston MA, Little Brown.

—— (2002), *The Paradox of American Power: Why the World's Only Superpower Cannot Go it Alone,* New York, Oxford University Press.

Ohmae, K. (1995), *The End of the Nation State: The Rise of Regional Economies*, New York, Harper Collins.

Oman, C. (1999), "Globalisation, Regionalisation and Inequality", in Fawcett, L. and Hurrell, A. (eds.), *Regionalism in World Politics: Regional Organisation and International Order,* Oxford, Oxford University Press.

Pekkanen, S. (2004), "At Play in the Legal Realm: The WTO and the Changing Nature of US-Japan Anti-Dumping Disputes", in Krauss, E. and Pempel, T. J., *Beyond Bilateralism: US-Japan Relations in the New Asia Pacific*, Stanford C, Stanford University Press.

Pempel, T. J. (ed.) (2004), "Emerging Webs of Regional Connectedness", *Remapping East Asia: The Construction of a Region*, Ithaca, Cornell University Press.

—— (2005), "Firebreak: East Asia Institutionalizes its Finances", *Institutionalizing North East Asia: Making the Impossible Possible?* Tokyo, UNU and Aoyama-Gakuin University, Sept. 20-22, 2005.

Rapkin, D. P. (2001), "The United States, Japan, and the Power to Block. The APEC and AMF cases", *The Pacific Review*, 14 (3), p. 373-410.

Ravenhill, J. (2001), *APEC and the Construction of Pacific Rim Regionalism.* Cambridge, Cambridge University Press, 2001.

—— (2005), "US Economic Relations with East Asia: From Hegemony to Complex Interdependence", in Beeson, M. (ed.), *Bush and Asia: America's Evolving Relations with East Asia*, London, Routledge.

Soderbaum F. and Shaw, T. J, (2003) (eds.), *Theories of New Regionalism: A Palgrave Reader,* Basingstoke, Palgrave.

Reuber, P. and G. Wolkersdorf (2002), "The Transformation of Europe and the German Contribution: Critical Geopolitics and Geopolitical Representations", *Geopolitics*, 7 (3), p. 39-60.

Rosamond, B. J. (2000), *Theories of European Integration*, Basingstoke, Palgrave.

Ruggie, J. G. (1993), "Multilateralism: The Anatomy of an Institution", in Ruggie, J. G. (ed.), *Multilateralism Matters: The Theory and Praxis of an Institutional Form*, New York, Columbia University Press.

Sampson, G. and Woolcock, S. (2003) (eds.), *Regionalism, Multilateralism and Economic Integration: The Recent Experience*, Tokyo, UNU Press.

Sandholtz, W. and Stone Sweet, A. (1998) (eds.), *European Integration and Supranational Governance*, Oxford, Oxford University Press.

Scholte, J. A. (2005), *Globalisation: A Critical Introduction*, London, Palgrave, 2nd edition.

Schmitter, P. (1971), "A Revised `Theory of European Integration", in Lindberg, L. and Scheingold, S. (eds.), *Regional Integration: Theory and Research*, Cambridge MA, Harvard University Press.

Segal, G., Maull, H. and Wanandi, J. (1998) (eds.), *Europe and the Asia Pacific,* London, Routledge.

Shambaugh, D. (2005), "China Engages Asia", *International Security*, 29 (3), p. 64-99.

Simmons, B. and Martin, L. (2002), "International Organisations and Institutions", in Carlsnaes, W., Risse, T. and Simmons, B. (eds.), *Handbook of International Relations*, London, Sage, p. 192-211.

Slaughter, A. M. (2004), *A New World Order*, Princeton, Princeton University Press.

Soesastro, H. (2005), "Realizing the East Asian Vision", *CSIS Economics Working Paper Series*, Jakarta, www.csis.or.id/papers/wpe090.

Stiglitz, J. (2002), *Globalisation and its Discontents*, London, Penguin.

Stone Sweet, A. (2004), *The Judicial Construction of Europe*, Oxford, OUP.

Stubbs, R. (2002), "ASEAN Plus Three: Emerging East Asian Regionalism", *Asian Survey*, 42 (3), 2002, p. 440-55.

—— (2005), *Rethinking Asia's Economic Miracle: War, Prosperity and Crisis*. Basingstoke, Palgrave.

Suzuki, S. (2004), *East Asian Cooperation through Conference Diplomacy: Institutional Aspects of the ASEAN Plus Three (APT) Framework*, Tokyo, Institute for Developing Economies, APEC Study Center, JETRO, *Working Paper* 03-04, No. 7.

Taniguchi, M. (2003), "Towards the Establishment of an East Asian Economic Zone: How can Japan, China and Korea Cooperate to Attain This Aim?", *Working Paper* 171, Tokyo, Research Institute of Economy, Trade and Industry, June, p. 1-11.

Thomas, N. (2004), *An East Asian Economic Community: Multilateralism Beyond APEC*, Conference on Asia Pacific Economies: Multilateral versus Bilateral Relationships, Hong Kong, City University, 19-21 May.

Tranholm-Mikkelsen, J. (1991), "Neo-functionalism: Obstinate or Obsolete?", *Millennium: A Journal of International Studies*, 20 (1).

Verdun, A. (2000), *European Responses to Globalisation and Financial Market Liberalisation: Perceptions of Economic and Monetary Union in Britain, France and Germany*, Basingstoke, Macmillan.

Wallace, H. (1996), "The Institutions of the EU: Experience and Experiments", in Wallace, H. and Wallace, W. (eds.), *Policy-Making in the European Union*, Oxford, Oxford University Press, 3rd edition.

Wallace, W. (1990), "Introduction: The Dynamics of European Integration", in Wallace, W. (ed.), *The Dynamics of European Integration*, London Pinter/ Chatham House.

Webb, C. (1983), "Theoretical Approaches and Problems", in Wallace, H. and Wallace, W. (eds.), *Policy-Making in the European Union*, Chichester, John Wiley, 2nd edition.

Webber, D. (2001), "Two Funerals and a Wedding? The Ups and Downs of Regionalism in East Asia and the Asia pacific after the Asian Financial Crisis", *The Pacific Review*, 14 (3), p. 339-72.

Weiss, L. (2002) (ed.), *States in the Global Economy: Bringing Domestic Institutions Back In*, Cambridge University Press, New York and Cambridge

Wendt, A. (1992), "Anarchy is What States Make of it: The Social Construction of Power Politics", *International Organisation*, 46 (3), p. 391-425

—— (2000), *Social Theory of International Politics,* Cambridge, Cambridge University Press.

Institutionalisation in East Asia after the 1997 Crisis

Frederik PONJAERT

As Higgott rightly points out in the previous chapter, regional studies have emerged as a particularly dynamic and fruitful field, fuelled by a contemporary flux of mutually reinforcing conceptual innovations and empirically observed evolutions. The very "hot" nature of regional studies seems particularly true in the East Asian case, where both innovative theoretical frameworks as well as decisive political developments have briskly emerged over the past decade. The speed at which this rapidly changing region of the world has grown into one of the hubs of the global economy has fundamentally altered its internal dynamics as well as the ways in which we have come to think of it. This transformation is an on-going and volatile process, allowing one to constantly shed new light on the regional cooperation structures emerging in East Asia. The budding and increasing nature of regional institutionalisation in East Asia brings with it a need for continual reappraisal of past observations and conclusions. Thus, at the hand of the most recent evolutions and building on the insightful and illuminating points and questions raised by Higgott in this paper, which was presented in October 2005, one can already tentatively test a number of conclusions and formulate some new perspectives.

As argued above, the 1997 Asian financial crisis "opened the way for clearer and less idealistic thinking about regionalism in Asia" as it clearly emerged as the defining issue in the development of contemporary regional trends in Asia. As time has passed and other major crises, such as the 9/11 attacks, have affected the region, the Asian financial crisis has emerged as a "critical juncture" (Mahoney, 2000) marking a new historical sequence in the history of East Asian regional cooperation. The continued and even increasing importance of regional practices introduced following the 1997 crisis has strengthened Higgott's suggestion that novel and structural institutional practices are emerging and consolidating in East Asia. The continued feverish trade talks within the region, once again illustrated by Tokyo's recent uncommonly frank appeal to its ASEAN partners to intensify efforts in creating an

East Asian Free Trade Area, as well as the sustained regional dialogue on monetary affairs have confirmed the *path dependent* nature of regional initiatives since 1997.

The original and structural nature of the new forms of cooperation that have emerged in East Asia since 1997 seem to be confirmed by empirical observation; the constant accretion of new regional initiatives therefore allows one to gradually draw a better picture of the "practical direction and application of such [emblematic regional] initiatives such as ASEAN+3 and […] the East Asian Community." As suggested in Higgott's contribution, beyond the economic nature of regionalism there are two important variables which have emerged as key factors in determining a regional institution's practical implementation: *identities* and *exogenous challenges*. Both these factors have recently undergone important evolutions supporting and clarifying the paths along which East Asian regionalism will most likely progress.

The cognitive dimension of regionalism in East Asia, as stated by Higgott, has always been intimately linked to the changing role of the only remaining major external actor in East Asia: the United States. The fundamentally reactive nature of the "[East]Asian identity" has been one of its constituent features since its materialisation in the late 19th century as a reaction to the eruption of the Western imperial powers onto the Asian scene (Cameroux, 2006). Consequently, in line with its origins, "East Asian identity-building" continues to express a will to circumscribe external influences within the region. Recent evolutions have only confirmed and even strengthened the conviction among Asian leaders that their region requires a stronger independent voice in world affairs. Both Washington's continued focus on geo-security matters and its willingness to utilise every venue, such as APEC or trade talks, to further its security agenda as well as the recent collapse of the Doha which marked another step in the gradual marginalisation of global multilateral institutions have highlighted the need for new regional forums focusing on East Asia's specific needs thus allowing a partial emancipated from the leading role the United States has played since World War II. This continued process of cognitive region-building has resulted in the creation of a new, loosely united regional grouping, including India and Australia, aimed at working together to combat Asia's economic, security and political problems. The formation of the new group, decided in December 2005 at the first East Asian Summit (EAS), which will hold annual summit conferences, significantly widens the circle of cooperation among countries represented by the 10-member Association of Southeast Asian Nations and its sister group, ASEAN+3. The defensive nature of the EAS *vis-à-vis* Washington was obvious, as illustrated by Richard Armitage's wry comment:

> My view is this is a thinly veiled way to make the point the United States is not totally welcomed in Asia (Richard Armitage in Asahi Shinbun, 1 May 2005).

But by accepting Australia, New Zealand and India into the new group, East Asian leaders left unanswered questions about what goals they would pursue. If the function and usefulness of the East Asian regional cognitive process as a shield guaranteeing a greater margin of maneuverability for East Asian elites in the face of external pressures has been recognised by most actors, the exact contours of the East Asian region and the resulting internal power balance remain unclear. If the need for an East Asian dimension appears to be largely accepted the evolving power relationships continue to drive the debate on the future composition of such a community as China becomes stronger and increasingly willing even eager to exercise regional leadership and Japan moves strategically closer to the United States.

Beyond the cognitive dimension, several new or strengthening external factors have also continued to shape the emerging regional institutions in East Asia. Crucially, the recent collapse of the Doha Round talks within the WTO have reinforced existing regional strategies in East Asia. The apparent failure of the Doha Round has further undermined global multilateral institutions as viable and effective policy tools, and this in turn has led to an increase in alternative initiatives, most notably within East Asia. The recent flurry of FTAs in East Asia (about 20 have already been signed, and over 60 are still being negotiated) is a corollary both of the 1997 crisis and of the protracted breakdown of the Doha Round[1]. The consolidation and multiplication of discriminatory FTAs, at the cost of the unilateral indiscriminate liberalisation previously espoused within the APEC context, has led to the emergence of a region characterised by a "hub-and-spoke" configuration (Scollay, 2005). The resulting system of interwoven arrangements lacking any overarching coherence has been characterised as the East Asian "Noodle Bowl" (Baldwin, 2006). Although these arrangements, limited both in scope and membership, are relatively less beneficial then broader options – such as global multilateral deals, or even the creation of a regional common market – East Asian elites have increasingly come to favour discriminatory FTAs since they insure that the control of the evolutions in trade flows remain influenced by the national elites. This has allowed the various East Asian actors to increasingly tailor their trade policies in function of various specific national strategic

---

1 *The Economist*, "In the Twilight of Doha," The Economist Group-Time Warner, 29 July-4 August 2006, London, p. 65-66.

concerns (Sally, 2006). Thus, this incoherent yet increasingly sweeping collection of East-Asian FTAs has clearly been fuelled by national political and strategic considerations which are not ultimately aimed at creating a regional East Asian market but are the result of the novel approach in East Asia towards trade liberalisation. Such a politically motivated "hub-and-spoke" approach is ill-equipped to favour a coherent regional integration. It could only possibly lead to further trade regionalisation if one of two scenarios is played out (Scollay, 2006):

- the continued spread of East Asian FTAs finally encompasses all trade areas and their regulatory stipulations converge significantly
- the various FTAs are amalgamated within a new overarching agreement aimed at reinforcing region-wide coherence.

Contrary to the mounting pressures on trade-related regionalisation, monetary regional cooperation has been consolidating since its emergence in 1998. Relative international financial stability, a sustained recovery in most countries in East Asia, an exponential growth of national reserves held by East Asian countries and a growing uneasiness with the structural imbalances of the US economy have all conspired to strengthen East Asian regional cooperation in monetary and financial affairs. The foray into a new field of regional cooperation born from the 1997 crisis has clearly reached a level of noteworthy institutionalisation which is starting to show some specific characteristics. The institutionalisation of a regional monetary dialogue can be observed at four levels (Dieter, 2006): the institutionalisation of tentative currency swaps through the Chiang Mai initiative; increased regional overview of short-term capital flows; other forms of regulatory cooperation such as Best Practice learning; and several measures aimed at strengthening the regional bond market. Policy options selected in the aftermath of the Asian financial crisis have become entrenched and have institutionalised new forms of regional cooperation. The two main region-wide monetary policies are the continued accumulation of massive currency reserves to act as a buffer for any future shock, and the establishment of a structural and continued dialogue amongst the East Asian central banks. The consolidation of these forms of cooperation have on the one hand led to new challenges (e.g. how should East Asian countries maximise the use of their vast reserves without causing any major imbalances?). On the other, they have helped to better define the practical implementation of regional cooperation in East Asia as informal yet regular, technical but conditioned by perceived "strategic national interests" and interest-driven while still remaining fragmented and isolated from other policy areas which might remain controversial. Therefore, Higgott's concept of

Regulatory Regionalism, understood as "selective, issue bound [regional cooperation] [...] aimed at enhancing regional stability and competitiveness," still appears as relevant as ever.

The broad trends underlying Regulatory Regionalism in East Asia have largely continued and even strengthened over the last year and a half, thereby clarifying East Asia's emerging institutional arrangements. Growing malaise with external influences and an increasing distrust of global multilateral institutional arrangements have further coaxed the East Asian down the road of regionalism, but have left them with the need to define the exact nature of such an entity. This increased interest in regional approaches, combined with varying definitions of the final goal, has led to an increasing number of loose regional consultation and cooperation forums. The forms of regional cooperation have been broadened to include new fields, such as monetary and financial matters, leading to an increased institutionalisation of certain cooperative practices associated with Regulatory Regionalism. Furthermore, the increased reliance on East Asian policy options has incited the East Asian actors to reevaluate their trade policy in function of national strategic interests. These evolutions, considerably strengthened over the last few years, have led to the emergence of a specifically East Asian form of regional institution formation.

Comparison of the main drivers of regionalism in Europe and East-Asia[2]

Contemporary drivers of Regionalism	Europe	East-Asia
***De Facto* Regionalism** Market-driven informal regionalism based on a rational utilitarian logic	first	second
***De Jure* Regionalism** Formal regionalism led by regional institutional arrangements pulled ahead by functionalist logics	second	third
Instrumental Regionalism Elite-driven regionalism dictated by perceived national interests, resulting from an instrumentalisation of regional cooperation	fourth	first
Cognitive Regionalism Reaction towards external actors' influence aimed at promoting alternative regional solutions through the logics of cultural legitimisation	third	fourth

2 Higgott Richard, "Leadership and Institutions," in Report on East Asian Integration. Opportunities and Obstacles for Enhanced Economic Cooperation," *Notre Europe Research Paper*, No.47, Paris, p. 27.

The question becomes whether this novel East Asian approach can produce lasting, stable and efficient regional arrangements. Confronting the institutionalised practices within East Asia to the "Ruggiesque" definition of an institution Higgott alludes to in his analysis, one can venture to offer an initial evaluation. In terms of *information sharing*, East Asian regional institutions have become increasingly effective as they have broadened their scope and continued to rely on technocratic forms of collaboration. Nevertheless, the continued efficiency of these communication channels depends on the actors' ability to isolate spheres of cooperation from other areas of disagreement. On the issue of *transparency in decision-making*, East Asian institutional arrangements have increased predictability within the various separate fields of regional cooperation by isolating "region-wide preferred practices," but the overall transparency of regional governance mechanisms has probably decreased over the last few years in light of a multiplication of diverging politically-motivated national strategies towards the Region. Finally, concerning the Region's ability to generate *credible collective action problem solving* has been consolidated and even increased as specifically East Asian forms of cooperation have emerged and become generally accepted which China's integration and increased involvement in the various Regional institutions has come to illustrate. Although the various options might not lead to the optimal solution concerning certain problems (e.g. questions related to efficient trade liberalisation), Regulatory Regionalism has become an efficient meso-level tool allowing regional elites to address the various challenges born from opposing national and global imperatives. However, Regulatory Regionalism has consistently been incapable of producing enforcement/compliance mechanisms and dispute resolution procedures other than co-opting those existing within the global multilateral institutions. This lack of coordination is the main drag on regionalism in East Asia and is the result of weak intra-regional leadership.

As stated above, the current uncertainty surrounding leadership in East Asia boils down to the question of whether intra-regional leadership will be strong enough to offer/impose regional arrangements as a credible alternative to faltering multilateral institutions and the weakening legitimacy of American actions within the region. Although the answer to this crucial question remains uncertain, one can isolate certain key variables and evaluate the impact of the latest empirical observations. Historical experiences as well as more recent developments have illustrated that endogenous leadership in East Asia can only emerge if the United States remains a good-faith and objective external arbiter whose main contribution to East Asian stability is a strengthening of the strategic status quo, and also only if China does not emerge as a dominant power within East Asia but is persuaded through rational and self-serving arguments to engage Japan in a form of combined regional leadership (Buzan, 2003) – of course Tokyo, in turn, must be willing to collaborate. Most recent evolutions within East Asia therefore do not bode well for the emergence of a form of shared regional leadership between Tokyo and Beijing. In spite of the consolidation and the further institutionalisation of Regulatory Regionalism, far-reaching evolutions in regional cooperation seem unlikely for the nearby future, barring some unforeseen major contingent event such as the 1997 crisis. Previous increases in regional cooperation have been the result of fortuitous convergence of interests between Tokyo and Beijing that were successfully isolated from other areas of conflict. Yet currently, one clearly sees both an increase in the level of disagreement between Tokyo and Beijing (e.g. in strategic and historic matters) as well as a blurring of certain separations between various foreign policy fields as several East Asian countries favour a more holistic approach (e.g. integrating strategic concerns within trade talks). This has led to a formal breakdown in cooperation between Beijing and Tokyo as various grievances have stalled – but not wrecked, as informal contacts continue – the dialogue between the two regional powers. Beyond a change of leadership, particularly in Tokyo where Koizumi's Yaskuni shrine visits have made him *persona non grata* in Beijing, a renewed cooperation will rest upon a convergence of fundamental commonalities born from the increased interdependence between both countries and changing national political cultures.

Since the questions surrounding Regional Leadership have continued to disrupt the emergence of regional institutions in East Asia even as a commonly accepted form of regional cooperation was increasingly being institutionalised, Regulatory Regionalism marks the institutionalisation of a certain regional *praxis*, though regionalism has not emerged as a political goal in itself. Therefore the evolution within the Japanese and Chinese polities will be a determining factor in the future direction of regional integration in East Asia, as these two powers will largely decide the objectives that will be pursued through these regional practices. Hitherto, recent evolutions have highlighted diverging strategic considerations in Tokyo and Beijing. On the one hand, Tokyo increasingly leans towards Washington's policy of "*constrainment*" *vis-à-vis* China (Segal, 1999), as was dramatically illustrated by the intended creation of an integrated military command for the East Pacific between Japan and the United States. On the other, in spite of China's increased willingness to operate within multilateral institutions, its aims remain geared toward the strengthening of its ascending global status and not towards regional or even global governance (as Beijing's timid stance on both the Iranian and North Korean nuclear questions have continuously illustrated). The doubts surrounding China's future regional impact spring from two uncertainties: how China's increased power will influence its policies and those of its neighbours, and how a potential democratisation of China's political system would influence regional power balances. Regulatory Regionalism, as an instrumental *praxis* which is at the disposal of national elites, remains bound by the East Asian actors' drive to safeguard the effectiveness of their national sovereignty. Therefore, the relative importance of various sources of legitimacy and perceived sovereignty with the various East Asian polities will be a determining factor in their willingness to provide the necessary regional leadership.

However one can state that several path dependant reactive sequences that have been elaborated in East Asia make the emergence of any regional leadership, be it collaborative or unipolar, particularly difficult and exceptionally contingent to exogenous factors. On the one hand, the historical processes that have lead, since the end of World War II, to the constitution of collective memories in East Asian countries have produced a particularly fragmented memory which has become an increasing source of conflict. On the other hand, in spite of their rather young age and the continued importance given to the notion of "strong national sovereignty," most East Asian regimes have seen the sources of legitimisation on which they rest change dramatically.

Notwithstanding the regions contentious memories and its fluctuating legitimacy mechanisms, the various East Asian States have elaborated similar process through which to legitimise and strengthen their political regimes and preserve their national sovereignty.

One can identify the following elements as commonalities amongst most East Asian political cultures: a tendency towards centralisation, conservative and technocratic since a given elite often nearly unremittingly holds the reins of power. A political regime offering such a constellation of characteristics must rely upon two main sources of legitimacy: out put legitimacy and nationalism (identity based legitimacy) because the various mechanisms guaranteeing in put legitimacy remain quite weak (e.g. political alternation, transparency, clear political competition decided through contentious elections, etc.).

Path dependent reactive sequence illustrating the elaboration of a collective memory within most East Asian political cultures

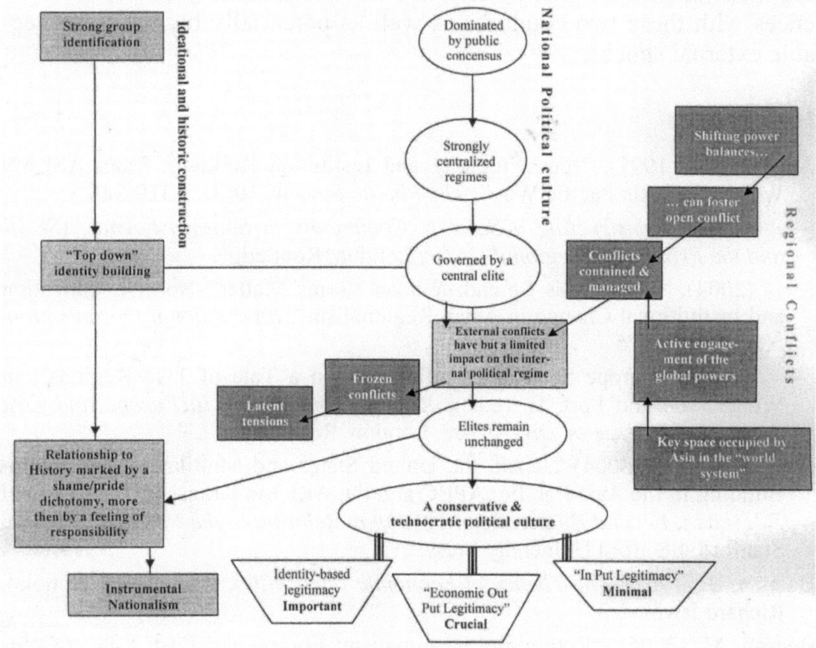

Typology of the main sources of legitimacy in East Asian political regimes

Nationalism / **Socio-Economic**	**Strong** Ideational Legitimacy	**Weak** Ideational Legitimacy
Strong Output Legitimacy	**1.** Strong and confident regional profile ➢ Potential **STRONG** & **Pro-active** contribution to regional leadership	**2.** Discreet yet efficiently self-serving regional profile ➢ Potentially **STRONG** support but **Passive** regional leadership
Weak Output Legitimacy	**3.** Unilateralist and provocative regional profile ➢ **STRONG** opposition to any form of regional leadership	**4.** Weak and ineffectual Regional ➢ **No significant** impact on regional leadership ("bandwagoning" tendencies)

Currently, with both China and Japan in a state of flux, hovering between various categories, the future evolution and development of regional institutions will most likely be determined by domestic influences with these two countries as well as potentially by but unforeseeable external shocks.

References

Acharya, A. (1997), "Ideas, Identity and Institution Building: From ASEAN Way to the Asia Pacific Way", *The Pacific Review*, 10(3), p.319-346.

—— (2001), *Constructing a Security Community in Southeast Asia: ASEAN and the Problem of Regional Order*, London, Routledge.

—— (2004), "How Ideas Spread: Whose Norms Matter? Norm Localization and Institutional Change in Asian Regionalism", *International Organisation*, 58 (2), p. 239-75.

—— (2005), "Europe and Asia: Reflections on a Tale of Two Regions", in Webber, D. and Fort, B. (eds.), *Regional Integration in Europe and East Asia: Convergence or Divergence*, London, Routledge.

Ashizawa K. P. (2004) "Japan, the United States and Multilateral Institution-Building in the Asia-Pacific. APEC and the ARF" in Krauss E. S. & Pempel T.J. (eds.), *Beyond Bilateralism. US-Japan Relation in the New Asia-Pacific*, Stanford, Stanford University Press.

Balassa, B. (1962), *The Theory of Economic Integration*, Homewood (Illinois), Richard Irwin.

Beeson, M. (2005), "Rethinking Regionalism: Europe and East Asia in Comparative historical Perspective", *European Journal of Public Policy*, 12 (6), p. 969-85.

—— and Higgott, R. (2005), "Hegemony, Institutionalism and US Foreign Policy: Theory and Practice in Comparative Historical Perspective" (with Mark Beeson), *Third World Quarterly*, 26(7), 2005, p. 1173-88.

Bellamy, R. (2005), "Still in Deficit: Rights, Regulation and Democracy in the EU", for the Democracy Task Force of the EU 6th Framework Integrated Project on New Modes of Governance, p. 1-31.

Bergsten, C. F. (2000), "East Asian Regionalism: Towards a Tripartite World", *The Economist*, 15 July.

Bhagwati, J. (2002), *Free Trade Today*, Princeton, Princeton University Press.

—— and Patrick, H. (1990) (eds.), *Aggressive Unilateralism: America's 301 Trade Policy and the World Trading System*, Ann Arbor, University of Michigan Press.

Breslin, S. (2005), "Studying Regions: Comparativism and Eurocentrism", Conference on China and Asian Regionalism, Shanghai, Fudan University, January, p. 1-39.

—— Higgott, R. (2000), "Studying Regions: Learning from the Old, Constructing the New", *New Political Economy*, 5 (3), p. 333-352.

—— Hughes, C., Phillips, N. and Rosamond, B. (2002) (eds.), *New Regionalism in the Global Political Economy: Theories and Cases*, London, Routledge.

Buzan, B. and Segal, G. (1994), "Rethinking East Asian Security", *Survival*, 36 (2), p. 3-21.

Coleman, W. and Underhill, G. (1998) (eds.), *Regionalism and Global Economic Integration: Asia, Europe and the Americas*, London, Routledge.

Defraigne, J.-C., Dieter, H., Higgott, R. and Lamy, P. (2005), *East Asian Integration: Opportunities and Obstacles for Enhanced Economic Cooperation*, Report for JETRO, Paris, Notre Europe.

Dent, C. (2004), *The New Economic Bilateralism and Southeast Asia: Region Convergent or Region Divergent*, British International Studies Association, IPEG Papers in Global Political Economy, No.7, April, 2004.

Desker, B. (2004), "In Defence of FTAs: From Purity to Pragmatism in East Asia", *The Pacific Review*, 17 (1), 2004, p. 3-26.

Deiter, H. and Higgott, R. (2003), "Exploring Alternative Theories of Economic Regionalism: From Trade to Finance in Asian Co-operation", *Review of International Political Economy*, 10 (3), 2003, p. 430-454.

Evian Group (2005), "East Asian Regionalism: Integrative versus Disintegrative Forces", 2005 Evian Hong Kong Initiative, Hong Kong, 17-18 May, p. 1-12.

Fawcett, L. and Hurrell, A. (1995) (eds.), *Regionalism in World Politics: Regional Organisation and International Order*, Oxford, Oxford University Press.

Finnemore, M. (1996), "Norms, Culture and World Politics: Insights from Sociology's Institutionalism", *International Organisation*, 50(2), p. 887-918.

Friedberg, A. (1993/4), "Ripe for Rivalry: Prospects for Peace in Multi-Polar Asia", *International Security*, 18(3), p. 5-33.

Gamble, A. and Payne, A. J. (1996) (eds.), *Regionalism and World Order*, Basingstoke, Macmillan.

Gavin, B. (2001), *The European Union and Globalisation: Towards Global Democratic Governance*, Aldershot, Edward Elgar.

Grugel J., and Hoult, W. (1999) (eds.), *Regionalism across the North-South Divide: State Strategies and Globalisation*, London, Routledge.

Haas, Ernst (1958), *The Uniting of Europe: Political Social and Economic Forces, 1950-57*, Stanford CA, Stanford University Press.

—— (1964), *Beyond the Nation-State: Functionalism and International Oganisation*, Stanford CA, Stanford University Press.

—— (1975), *The Obsolescence of Regional Integration Theory*, Berkeley CA, Institute for International Studies.

Hall, R. B. and Biersteker, T. J. (2002) (eds.), *The Emergence of Private Authority in Global Governance*, Cambridge, Cambridge University Press.

Hamilton-Hart, N. (2005), "The Chiang Mai Initiative and the Prospects for Closer Monetary Cooperation in East Asia", in Webber, D. and Fort, B.

(eds.), *Regional Integration in Europe and East Asia: Convergence or Divergence*, London, Routledge.

Hänggi, Heiner *et al.* (eds.) (2006), *Interregionalism and International Relations*, London, Routledge.

Harris, S. (2002), "Asian multilateral institutions and their response to the Asian economic crisis: regional and global implications", in Breslin S. *et al.*, *New Regionalisms in the Global Political Economy*, London, Routledge.

Hay, C. and Rosamond, B. (2002), "Globalisation, European Integration and the discursive construction of economic imperatives", *European Journal of Public Policy*, 9, 2.

Held, D. and McGrew, A. (2000) (eds.), *The Global Transformations Reader: An Introduction to the Globalization Debate*, London, Polity.

Hew, D. and Soesastro, H., "Realising the ASEAN Economic Community by 2020: ISEAS and ASEAN ISIS Approaches", *ASEAN Economic Bulletin*, 20 (3), 2003.

Hettne, B., Inotai, A. and Sunkel, O., (1999) (eds.), *National Perspectives on the New Regionalism in the Third World*, London, Palgrave.

Hettne, B. and Söderbaum, F. (2005), 'Civilian Power or Soft Imperialism? The EU as a Global Actor and the Role of Interregionalism', *European Foreign Affairs Review*, 10 (4), pp.535 – 552.

—— (2000) (eds.), *National Perspectives on the New Regionalism in the North*, London, Palgrave.

—— (2001) (eds.), *Comparing Regionalisms: Implications for Global Development*, London, Palgrave.

Higgott, R. (1997), "*De facto* or *De Jure* Regionalism: The Double Discourse of Regionalisation in the Asia Pacific", *Global Society: Journal of Interdisciplinary International Relations*, 11(2), 1997, p. 165-83.

—— (1998), "The Asian Financial Crisis: A Study in the Politics of Resentment", *New Political Economy*, 3(3), p. 33-56.

—— (1998a), "The International Political Economy of Regionalism: Europe and Asia Compared", in Coleman, W. and Underhill, G. (eds.), *Regionalism and Global Economic Integration: Asia, Europe and the Americas*, London, Routledge.

—— (2004), "The 'Securitisation' of U.S. Foreign Economic Policy in East Asia", *Critical Asian Studies*, 36 (3), 2004, p. 425-44.

—— (2005), "Economic Regionalism in East Asia: Consolidation with Centrifugal Tendencies", in Stubbs, R. and Underhill, G. (eds.), *Political Economy and the Changing Global Order*, Oxford, Oxford University Press.

—— (2005a), "The Theory and Practice of Regionalism in a Changing Global Context", in Webber, D. and Fort, B. (eds.), *Regional Integration in Europe and East Asia: Convergence or Divergence*, London, Routledge, p. 17-38.

—— (2005b), "The Theory and Practice of Global Governance: Accommodating American Exceptionalism and European Pluralism", *European Foreign Affairs Record*, October 2005.

—— (2006), "International (Political) Organiszation(s)", in Rhodes, R. and Rockman, B. (eds.), *The Oxford Handbook of Political Institutions*, Oxford, Oxford University Press, 2006.

—— Leaver, R. and Ravenhill, J. (1993) (eds.), *Pacific Economic Relation in the 1990s: Cooperation and Conflict*, Boulder, CO, Lynne Reinner.

—— and Stubbs, R. (1995), "Competing Conceptions of Economic Regionalism: APEC versus EAEC", *Review of International Political Economy*, 2(3), p.516-535.

Hix, S. (1994), "The Study of the European Community: The Challenge for Comparative Politics", *West European Politics*, 17(1), p.1-30.

—— (1999), *The Political System of the European Union*, Basingstoke, Macmillan.

Hughes, W. Christopher (2008), "Europe and Japan Facing the Challenges of Peace and War: Declining Prospects for Cooperation in the Management of US Hegemony?" in Ueta, T., Remacle, E. and Ponjaert, F. (eds.), "*Japan-European Union: A Partnership in the Making*", *Studia Diplomatica*, LXI(4), pp.55-73.

Hurrell, A. (1995), "Explaining the Resurgence of Regionalism in World Politics", *Review of International Studies*, 21 (4), p.331-358.

—— (1995a), "Regionalism in Theoretical Perspective", in Fawcett, L. and Hurrell, A. (eds.), *Regionalism in World Politics: Regional Organisation and International Order*, Oxford, Oxford University Press.

Hurst, P. and Thompson, G. (2001), *Globalisation in Question*, Cambridge, Polity, 2nd edition.

Jayasuriya, K. (2004) (ed.), *Asian Regional Governance: Crisis and Change*, London, Routledge.

Johnson, C. (2005), "No Longer the 'Lone' Superpower: Coming to Terms with China", *Japan Policy Research Institute, Working Paper 105*, San Francisco, March, 1-12. www.jpri.org/publications/wp105.html.

Katzenstein, P., Keohane, R. O. and Krasner, S. (1998), "International Organisation and the Study of World Politics", *International Organisation*, 52 (4), p.646-686.

Katzenstein Peter J. (2005), *A World of Regions*, Ithaca, Cornell University Press.

Kahler, M. (2000), "Legalization as a Strategy: The Asia Pacific Case", *International Organization*, 54 (3), 2000, p. 549-71.

Keohane, R. (1984), *After Hegemony: Cooperation and Discord in the World Political Economy*, Princeton, Princeton University Press.

—— (1989), *International Institutions and State Power: Essay in International Relations Theory*, Boulder Co, Westview Press.

—— (2001), "Governance in a Partially Globalised World", *American Political Science Review*, 95 (1), p. 1-13.

—— (2002), *Power and Governance in a Partially Globalized World*, London, Routledge.

—— (2004), "Global Governance and Democratic Accountability", in Held, D. and Archibugi, M. K., *Taming Globalization: Frontiers of Governance*, Cambridge, Polity Press.

Kooiman, J. (2003), *Governing as Governance*, London, Sage.

Kratochwil, F. and Ruggie, J. (1986), "The State of the Art on an Art of the State", *International Organisation*, 40 (4), p. 753-75.

—— and Mansfield, E. (2005) (eds.), *International Organisation: A Reader*, New York, Longman Publishers, 2005.

Krugman, P. (1986) (ed.), *Strategic Trade Policy and the 'New' International Economics*, Cambridge, MA, MIT Press.

Kupchan, Charles, A. (2000), "After Pax Americana: benign power, regional integration and the sources of stable multipolarity", in Hansen, Birthe & Heurlin, Bertel (eds.), *The New World Order: Contrasting Theories*, Basingstoke, Palgrave, pp. 134-66.

Latham, A. (1997), *The Liberal Moment: Modernity, Security, and the Making of Postwar International Order*, New York, Columbia University Press.

Leonard, M. (2005), *Why Europe Will Run the 21st Century*, London, Fourth Estate Books.

Lindberg, L. (1966), *The Political Dynamics of European Economic Integration*, Stanford CA, Stanford University Press.

Manupipatpong, W. (2002), "The ASEAN Surveillance Process and the East Asian Monetary Fund", *ASEAN Economic Bulletin*, 19 (1), p. 114-15.

Mansfield, E. D. and Milner, H. (1977) (eds.), *The Political Economy of Regionalism*, New York, Columbia University Press.

Martin, L. (2003), *Multilateral Organisations after the US-Iraq War of 2003*, Harvard University, Weatherhead Centre for International Affairs, August, p. 1-17.

Mattli, W. (1999), *The Logic of Regional Integration*, Cambridge, Cambridge University Press.

Moravcsik, A. (1994), "Preferences and Power in the European Community: A Liberal Intergovernmental Approach", in Bulmer, S. and Scott, A. (eds.), *Economic and Political Integration in Europe*, Oxford, Blackwells.

—— (1998), *The Choice for Europe: Social Purpose and State Power: From Messina to Maastricht*, Ithaca, Cornell University Press.

—— (2004), "Is there a 'Democratic Deficit' in World Politics? A Framework for Analysis", *Government and Opposition*, 39 (3), p. 344-46.

Munakata, N. (2003), "The Impact of the Rise of China and Regional Economic Integration in Asia: A Japanese Perspective", *Statement to US-China Economic and Security Review Commission Hearings on China's Growth as a Regional Economic Power*, Washington DC, December, p. 1-13.

Nesadurai, H. (2003), *Globalisation, Domestic Politics and Regionalism: The ASEAN Free Trade Area*, London, Routledge, 2003.

North, Douglass (1990), *Institutions, Institutional Change and Economic Performance*, Cambridge, Cambridge University Press.

Nye, J. (1968), "Comparative Regional Integration: Concepts and Measurement", *International Organisation*, 22(4).

—— (1971), *Peace in Parts: Integration and Conflict in International Organisations*, Boston MA, Little Brown.

—— (2002), *The Paradox of American Power: Why the World's Only Superpower Cannot Go it Alone*, New York, Oxford University Press.

Ohmae, K. (1995), *The End of the Nation State: The Rise of Regional Economies*, New York, Harper Collins.

Oman, C. (1999), "Globalisation, Regionalisation and Inequality", in Fawcett, L. and Hurrell, A. (eds.), *Regionalism in World Politics: Regional Organisation and International Order*, Oxford, Oxford University Press.

Pekkanen, S. (2004), "At Play in the Legal Realm: The WTO and the Changing Nature of US-Japan Anti-Dumping Disputes", in Krauss, E. and Pempel, T. J., *Beyond Bilateralism: US-Japan Relations in the New Asia Pacific*, Stanford C, Stanford University Press.

Pempel, T. J. (ed.) (2004), "Emerging Webs of Regional Connectedness", *Remapping East Asia: The Construction of a Region*, Ithaca, Cornell University Press.

—— (2005), "Firebreak: East Asia Institutionalizes its Finances", *Institutionalizing North East Asia: Making the Impossible Possible?*, Tokyo, UNU and Aoyama-Gakuin University, Sept. 20-22, 2005.

Ponjaert, F. (2008), "Cross-Regional Dynamics: Their Specific Role and Contribution to Global Governance Efforts within the International System", in Seidelmann, R. and Vasilache, A. (eds.), *European Union and Asia. A Dialogue on Regionalism and Interregional Cooperation*, Baden-Baden, Nomos, p. 177-196.

—— Rapkin, D. P. (2001), "The United States, Japan, and the Power to Block. The APEC and AMF cases", *The Pacific Review*, 14 (3), p. 373-410.

Ravenhill, J. (2001), *APEC and the Construction of Pacific Rim Regionalism*. Cambridge, Cambridge University Press, 2001.

—— (2005), "US Economic Relations with East Asia: From Hegemony to Complex Interdependence", in Beeson, M. (ed.), *Bush and Asia: America's Evolving Relations with East Asia*, London, Routledge.

Reuber, P. and Wolkersdorf, G. (2002), "The Transformation of Europe and the German Contribution: Critical Geopolitics and Geopolitical Representations", *Geopolitics*, 7 (3), p. 39-60.

Rosamond, B. J. (2000), *Theories of European Integration*, Basingstoke, Palgrave.

Ruggie, J. G. (1993), "Multilateralism: The Anatomy of an Institution", in Ruggie, J. G. (ed.), *Multilateralism Matters: The Theory and Praxis of an Institutional Form*, New York, Columbia University Press.

Sampson, G. and Woolcock, S. (2003) (eds.), *Regionalism, Multilateralism and Economic Integration: The Recent Experience*, Tokyo, UNU Press.

Sandholtz, W. and Stone Sweet, A. (1998) (eds.), *European Integration and Supranational Governance*, Oxford, Oxford University Press.

Scholte, J. A. (2005), *Globalisation: A Critical Introduction*, London, Palgrave, 2nd edition.

Schmitter, P. (1971), "A Revised Theory of European Integration", in Lindberg, L. and Scheingold, S. (eds.), *Regional Integration: Theory and Research*, Cambridge MA, Harvard University Press.

Segal, G., Maull, H. and Wanandi, J. (1998) (eds.), *Europe and the Asia Pacific*, London, Routledge.

Shambaugh, D. (2005), "China Engages Asia", *International Security*, 29 (3), p. 64-99.

Simmons, B. and Martin, L. (2002), "International Organisations and Institutions", in Carlsnaes, W., Risse, T. and Simmons, B. (eds.), *Handbook of International Relations*, London, Sage, p. 192-211.

Slaughter, A. M. (2004), A New World Order, Princeton, Princeton University Press.

Soderbaum, F. and Shaw, T. J, (2003) (eds.), *Theories of New Regionalism: A Palgrave Reader*, Basingstoke, Palgrave.

Söderbaum, Fredrik & van Langenhove, Luk (2006) (eds.), *The EU as a Global Player. The Politics of Interregionalism*, London, Routledge.

Soesastro, H. (2005), "Realizing the East Asian Vision", CSIS Economics Working Paper Series, Jakarta, www.csis.or.id/papers/wpe090.

Solingen, Etel (2005), "East Asian Regional Institutions: Characteristics, Sources, Distictiveness", in Pemple T.J. (ed.), *Remapping East Asia. The Construction of a Region*, Ithaca, Cornell University Press.

Stiglitz, J. (2002), Globalisation and its Discontents, London, Penguin.

Stone Sweet, A. (2004), *The Judicial Construction of Europe*, Oxford, OUP.

Stubbs, R. (2002), "ASEAN Plus Three: Emerging East Asian Regionalism", *Asian Survey*, 42 (3), 2002, p. 440-55.

—— (2005), *Rethinking Asia's Economic Miracle: War, Prosperity and Crisis*. Basingstoke, Palgrave.

Suzuki, S. (2004), *East Asian Cooperation through Conference Diplomacy: Institutional Aspects of the ASEAN Plus Three (APT) Framework*, Tokyo, Institute for Developing Economies, APEC Study Center, JETRO, *Working Paper* 03-04, No. 7.

Taniguchi, M. (2003), "Towards the Establishment of an East Asian Economic Zone: How can Japan, China and Korea Cooperate to Attain This Aim?", *Working Paper* 171, Tokyo, Research Institute of Economy, Trade and Industry, June, p. 1-11.

Terada, Takeshi (2003), "Constructing an 'East Asian' concept and growing regional identity: from EAEC to ASEAN+3", *The Pacific Review*, 16 (2).

Telò, Mario (ed.) (2001), *European Union and New Regionalism*, Aldershot, Ashgate.

Telò, Mario (2005), *Europe: A Civilian Power?*, Basingstoke, Palgrave.

Thomas, N. (2004), *An East Asian Economic Community: Multilateralism Beyond APEC*, Conference on Asia Pacific Economies: Multilateral versus Bilateral Relationships, Hong Kong, City University, 19-21 May.

Tranholm-Mikkelsen, J. (1991), "Neo-functionalism: Obstinate or Obsolete?", *Millennium: A Journal of International Studies*, 20 (1).

Vanoverbeke, D. and Ponjaert, F. (2008), "Japan in East Asia: the Dynamics of Regional Cooperation from a European Perspective", in Ueta, T., Remacle, E. & Ponjaert, F. (eds.), *"Japan-European Union: A Partnership in the Making"*, *Studia Diplomatica*, LXI(4), pp.97-117.

Verdun, A. (2000), *European Responses to Globalisation and Financial Market Liberalisation: Perceptions of Economic and Monetary Union in Britain, France and Germany*, Basingstoke, Macmillan.

Wallace, H. (1996), "The Institutions of the EU: Experience and Experiments", in Wallace, H. and Wallace, W. (eds.), *Policy-Making in the European Union*, Oxford, Oxford University Press, 3rd edition.

Wallace, W. (1990), "Introduction: The Dynamics of European Integration", in Wallace, W. (ed.), *The Dynamics of European Integration*, London, Pinter/ Chatham House.

Webb, C. (1983), "Theoretical Approaches and Problems", in Wallace, H. and Wallace, W. (eds.), *Policy-Making in the European Union*, Chichester, John Wiley, 2nd edition.

Webber, D. (2001), "Two Funerals and a Wedding? The Ups and Downs of Regionalism in East Asia and the Asia pacific after the Asian Financial Crisis", *The Pacific Review*, 14 (3), p. 339-372.

Weiss, L. (2002) (ed.), *States in the Global Economy: Bringing Domestic Institutions Back In*, New York and Cambridge, Cambridge University Press.

Wendt, A. (1992), "Anarchy is What States Make of it: The Social Construction of Power Politics", *International Organisation*, 46 (3), p; 391-425.

—— (2000), *Social Theory of International Politics*, Cambridge, Cambridge University Press.

Japan's Nuclear Disarmament and Non-Proliferation Policy

Multilateral Approaches, Regional Efforts and Region-to-Region Cooperation

Sukeyuki ICHIMASA*

Research Fellow, Centre for the Promotion of Disarmament and Non-Proliferation (CPDNP), Japan Institute of International Affairs (JIIA)

Introduction

For the past many years, Japan has most ardently supported the disarmament and non-proliferation activity of the international community. Indeed, nuclear disarmament and non-proliferation are among the priorities for Japan within its foreign policy even up to today. Actually, there are approaches at various levels in the pursuit of nuclear disarmament and non-proliferation as well as other diplomatic issues.

In the current environment, nuclear disarmament and non-proliferation business are in a political and technical turmoil. The achievements of these goals depend upon an efficient verification system, the universal application of nuclear non-proliferation regime; it is also necessary to maintain the momentum for promoting nuclear disarmament and non-proliferation among the international community by all the possible means.

On the basis of such ideas, this article describes features of the current nuclear disarmament and non-proliferation policy of Japan and covers recent events concerning such issues as the UN General Assembly, Nuclear Non-Proliferation Treaty (NPT), the International Atomic Energy Agency (IAEA), Comprehensive Nuclear Test-Ban Treaty

* The view and analysis expressed on this article is that of the author's personal remark and do not necessarily represent those of CPDNP.

(CTBT), Fissile Material Cut-off Treaty, cooperation for the elimination of nuclear weapons and Japan's commitment in the international framework of nuclear export control, in the case of the Nuclear Suppliers Group (NSG) especially. Then this article evaluates Japan's regional efforts to the nuclear issues of the DPRK (Democratic People's Republic of Korea) and Iran in particular. Then finally, it touches upon the recent case of Japan-EU cooperation in the area of nuclear disarmament and non-proliferation as a matter of example.

I. Japan's Nuclear Disarmament Policy in Recent Years

A. General Policy

1. Renewed Determination towards the Total Elimination of Nuclear Weapons (60th session of the UN General Assembly (2005))

On 8 December 2005 Japan has proposed a 'Renewed determination towards the total elimination of nuclear weapons'[1] to the 60th session of the UN General Assembly. This proposal was adopted by the large majority of the 168 states, 2 opposite (the US and India) and 7 abstentions (Bhutan, China, Cuba, the DPRK, Israel, Myanmar, Pakistan). This acknowledges that the approach of Japan has never changed since 1994 (Japan's first proposition), that it has proved to be effective and has been widely supported among the international community.

In the light of nuclear disarmament and non-proliferation, 2005 was a year when substantial mutual agreement were neither obtained in NPT review conference nor at the Summit meeting in the UN headquarters. However, 2005 also illustrates a turning point for Japan which celebrates its 60th anniversary of the atomic bombing of Hiroshima and Nagasaki. Japan hence prepared a concise, powerful resolution and emphasised the importance of compliance with NPT, the early entry into force of CTBT and the continuity of nuclear test moratorium, by starting the negotiation of FMCT and reaching an agreement at the early stage[2].

As the only nation that was the victim of atomic bomb, it is very important to take an initiative related to the total elimination of nuclear

---

1 60th UN General Assembly in 2005, renewed determination towards the total elimination of nuclear weapons. http://www.mofa.go.jp/policy/un/disarmament/arms/un0510.html.

2 Statement by Ambassador Yoshiki Mine, Representative of Japan to the 2005 NPT Review Conference at the Plenary Meeting. http://www.mofa.go.jp/policy/un/disarmament/npt/conf0505-4.html.

weapons in such a tangible manner. This evidences that a long-time contribution of Japan within the United Nations General Assembly bring results. It seems that the longstanding diplomatic effort of Japan to the Article VI of NPT[3] should be highly evaluated.

2. NPT

2005 NPT review conference was a major turning point for most of the Weapons of Mass Destruction (WMD), disarmament and non-proliferation work. On the nuclear issue especially, the rights and obligations of the P5 states have been broadly acknowledged again. It is also important to remember that the intrinsic right to exercise the peaceful use of atomic energy has been claimed for by the developing countries.

Needless to say, for many years NPT was one of the major diplomatic agenda for Japan. This conference has offered the Japanese government prime opportunities to give its strong view on the importance of accelerating the nuclear weapons control and disarmament. In this way, failure of the 2005 NPT review conference was a kind of test-stone for Japan on whether to carry on its efforts towards nuclear weapons control and disarmament.

In March 2006, the US-India Civil Nuclear Agreement was concluded. The agreement of cooperation about nuclear power between US and India means that India's virtual possession of the nuclear weapons is approved of and that India is excluded from the countries list of export restriction stipulated by the NSG. It means that the result of the US-India Nuclear agreement may be directly linked to the permission of sharing the sensitive technologies which relates to the development of nuclear power that has been prohibited up to now. The US-India nuclear cooperation agreement does not only matter between these two countries. This kind of arrangement might consequently lead to the collapse of the NPT regime. As a member of NPT and a major promoter of the nuclear weapons abolition and the reinforcement of the NPT regime, Japan should not adopt a detached attitude to this case.

However, in April 2006, the Iranian President Mahmoud Ahmadinjad stated that the uranium enrichment for peaceful purposes should continue in the face of international pressure. After all, the role that Japan should play at the next NPT Review Conference does not get

[3] Article VI: Each of the Parties to the Treaty undertakes to pursue negotiations in good faith on effective measures relating to cessation of the nuclear arms race at an early date and to nuclear disarmament, and on a Treaty on general and complete disarmament under strict and effective international control.

clear, but Japan's willingness to contribute to the nuclear disarmament and non-proliferation is all the more expressed in its actions within the IAEA, CTBT and others.

3. *IAEA*

In the light of the implementation of peaceful use of atomic energy, Nuclear Safeguards operated under the IAEA are also an important matter, for Japan's nuclear disarmament and non-proliferation policy. Japan has signed the IAEA Nuclear Safeguards Additional Protocol (AP, INFCIRC/540[4]) on 4 December 1998, and the AP has come into effect on 16 December 1999. The number of countries that ratified the AP on 28 February 2006 reaches 74. Japan was among those latter and was the 8th country with nuclear power generation to ratify the AP the first. Outreach activity to promote the universalisation of the AP has positively worked on Japan's nuclear disarmament and non-proliferation policy through the various opportunities, for instance the consultation between Japan-Iran is typical bilateral approach, AP working-level conference, improving the opportunity of multilateral meeting such as G-8, Association of Southeast Asian Nations (ASEAN), Asia Pacific Economic Cooperation (APEC), Asian Senior-level Talks on Non-Proliferation (ASTOP)[5] and of course in the occasion of 2005 NPT review conference are the cases in point of improving the opportunity of multilateral meetings. In short, Japan called for the importance of the Safeguards AP, because it will contribute to the reinforcement of the verification regime. On the other hand, it is necessary to understand that the various obligations are newly required along with a ratification of the AP.

In fact, the countries which have concluded the Safeguards AP, owes an obligation to declare the nuclear power as a relevant activity that is not declared in the present Safeguards agreement[6]. Moreover, sometimes the country will be required to admit the 'complementary access' by the IAEA inspectors to the site, where access is not permitted in the present Safeguards agreement.

---

4 INFCIRC/540 (Corrected) Model Protocol Additional to the agreement(s) Between State(s) and the International Atomic Energy Agency for the application of safeguards. http://www.iaea.org/Publications/Documents/Infcircs/1998/infcirc540 corrected. pdf.

5 Japan is positively appealing to the country of an Asian region aiming at the universalisation of an AP on 3 February 2006. The Third Asian Senior-level Talks on Non-Proliferation (ASTOP). http://www.mofa.go.jp/announce/event/2006/2/ 0203-3.html.

6 The safeguards system of the international atomic energy agency. http://www.iaea.org/OurWork/SV/Safeguards/safeg_system.pdf.

On 3 October 2005, Ambassador Yukiya Amano of Permanent Mission of Japan in Vienna was elected to the Chairman of the IAEA General Conference[7]. This nomination is far from being the result of the international community's appreciation of the Japanese contribution to the IAEA for years.

For the purpose of promoting a peaceful use of nuclear power and strengthening the international system of a nuclear non-proliferation, the championship of the NPT regime is still one of the most important goals of Japan. In the light of the importance of verification effectiveness, the universalisation of the IAEA Nuclear Safeguards AP will remain the most important part of Japanese policy related to the IAEA. It seems therefore that Japan will make further efforts to improve its influence and its *raison-d'être* in the IAEA.

4. CTBT

Japan extremely values CTBT of its early entry into force as a part of the NPT regime along with the IAEA Nuclear Safeguards. Japan sends delegates on the order of foreign ministers to the 'Conference Facilitating the entry into force of CTBT' which is held every two years; it is also carrying out diplomatic efforts to the outreach activity of CTBT through a multiple approach. For instance, Japan has granted major instruments for constructing the International Monitoring System (IMS) of CTBT to 17 countries. Every year since 1995, ten participants from various countries have been accepted to the global earthquake observation training (in total, 107 people have been accepted by the fiscal year 2005). In addition, since 2003 'CTBT Friends Foreign Minister Meeting[8]' which has proposed, has started to maintain and to keep the momentum of CTBT entry into force by Japan. Many countries joined the 'CTBT Friends Foreign Minister Meeting', including the states endowed with nuclear weapon namely the UK, France and Russia. As a political opportunity to promote CTBT entry into force at such a chance, the meeting is expected to promote deterrence to the nuclear test execution.

In CTBT, the IMS monitoring facilities will be set up in 337 places around the world[9]. Countries which accept the IMS monitoring facilities

[7] On 3 October 2005, Japan Governor Elected as Chair of IAEA Board for 2005-2006. http://www.iaea.org/NewsCenter/News/2004/bogchair_2005.html.

[8] CTBT: Launch of Joint Ministerial Statement (Overview and Evaluation). http://www.mofa.go.jp/region/n-america/us/pfmv0209/ctbt-2.html.

[9] CTBTO preparatory commission, An Overview of the Verification Regime, The International Monitoring System. http://www.ctbto.org/verification/overview.html.

have to be in charge of these operations. Actually, ten of those facilities are built up within the territory of Japan. While being prepared to the election of Japan as a member of the Executive Council (EC) of CTBT from Asia, it is necessary to provide a Japanese unique analysis (analysis and evaluation of a radionuclide and a continuous seismic wave form, etc.) that relates to the detection and verification of the nuclear explosion experiment. One of the most critical functions of the EC is the On-Site Inspection (OSI)[10]. As for OSI, that is the 'challenge inspection' in substance, the responsibility of member states of the EC gets extremely important, especially when they are judging the inspection result. Therefore, the Ministry of Foreign Affairs, as the national authority, made the Centre for Promotion of Disarmament and Non-Proliferation (CPDNP[11]) a secretariat of 'CTBT National Operation System of Japan, consisting of National Data Centres (NDCs) under the cooperation of the Ministry of Education, Culture, Sports, Science and Technology and the Japan Meteorological Agency.

Through the arguments, Japan takes particular note of promoting the early entry into force of the CTBT as a subsidiarily important part of the NPT regime. On this behalf, Japan also considers that building the effective method of verification is especially vital to the future CTBT. Regarding the CTBT verification system, whose effective OSI mechanism as the last resort to the nuclear-test-ban, will consequently be the key establishment to pursue.

5. *Cooperation for the Elimination of Nuclear Weapons*

Following the fall of the Soviet Union in December 1991, it was decided that a tremendous number of nuclear weapons devoted to the former Soviet Union will be reduced. In the meantime, with the purpose of maintaining the international nuclear non-proliferation order, it was decided to bring to Russia strategic nuclear weapons assigned to Ukraine, Kazakhstan and Belarus. However, the possibility of delaying the process of abandonment and processing of the reduced nuclear weapons – due to the political disorder resulting from the collapse of the Soviet Union – had become a serious concern for the international

---

[10] CTBTO preparatory commission, An Overview of the Verification Regime, On-Site Inspection. http://www.ctbto.org/verification/onsiteinspection.html.

[11] CPDNP makes efforts to enhance the NDCs' capabilities and monitors their performance by conducting simulation tests on their infrastructure. Furthermore, CPDNP supports human resource development for NDCs and addresses the other activities such as those related to on-site inspection, a component of the CTBT verification regime, that shall be required in the future CTBT National Operation System. http://www.iijnet.or.jp/JIIA-CPDNP/English/e_disarm.htm.

community. Concerning the dismantlement of nuclear weapons, plutonium disposal was also an urgent problem for the maintenance of the nuclear non-proliferation regime.

Therefore, Japan agrees on promoting cooperation with nations such as the USA, the UK, Germany, France and Italy as to find a solution to the nuclear weapons abandonment and processing of the former Soviet Union, as well as relevant environmental problems based on the agreement of the Munich Summit in 1992[12]. In the meantime, those non-nuclear weapon states (Ukraine, Kazakhstan and Belarus) were urged to join NPT and cooperate with the international action for safeguarding the nuclear materials to detect and prevent an illicit transfer or clandestine production of nuclear weapons. Thus international community has given the highest importance to the establishment of such effective safeguards of nuclear related sensitive materials, goods and technologies owned by the former Soviet Union; Japan has shown strong initiatives to this case and was committed to substantially cooperate described as follows.

In April 1993, Japan announced that about 100 million dollars in total would be offered to support the abandonment of nuclear weapons of the former Soviet Union (Russia, Ukraine, Kazakhstan, and Belarus). Moreover, at the Köln Summit (1999), Japan announced granting additional capital of about 115 million dollars in the cooperation for wiping out nuclear weapons. Under the framework of the Committee on Cooperation for the Elimination of Nuclear Weapons[13], Japan provides the facilities of Liquid Radioactive Waste Treatment Plant – "SUZURAN" – in the territory of the Russian Federation. Japan also provides substantial assistance for the establishment of State Systems of Accounting for and Control of nuclear materials (SSACs)[14] to Ukraine, Kazakhstan and Belarus. In addition, for the sake of preventing the brain drain of sensitive knowledge especially related to the production of nuclear weapons from the former Soviet Union, Japan joined the

12 G-7 Summit: Munich, 6-8 July 1992: "New Independent States of the Former Soviet Union". http://www.g7.utoronto.ca/summit/1992munich/communique/russia.html. "Safety of Nuclear Power Plants in the New Independent States of the Former Soviet Union and in Central and Eastern Europe." http://www.g7.utoronto.ca/summit/1992munich/communique/nuclear.html.

13 16th Meeting of the Committee on Cooperation for the Elimination of Nuclear Weapons in February 2003. http://www.mofa.go.jp/region/europe/russia/meet0302.html.

14 IAEA Further Steps in the Development of the Safeguards System. http://www.iaea.org/Publications/Booklets/Safeguards/pia3812.html.

international effort to establish the International Science and Technology Centre (ISTC)[15].

Today, this process has been consolidated with 'G-8 Global Partnership against the Spread of Weapons and Materials of Mass Destrution'[16]. In this regard, Japan has now contributed with 200 million dollars to this framework. Among these contributions, nearly 100 million dollars is used to dismantle the decommissioned nuclear submarines. Moreover, it is assumed that the remaining 100 million dollars will be dedicated to the plutonium disposal plan of weapons surplus: this well illustrates the Japanese effort to contribute to the nuclear disarmament, which will positively produce substantive results.

6. Fissile Material Cut-off Treaty (FMCT)

Japan has made continuous efforts to facilitate a substantial discussion on Fissile Material Cut-Off Treaty (FMCT) in Geneva. Especial contribution that stands out is the working document that has been submitted in Geneva Conference of Disarmament (CD) in 2003[17]. Following the end of the negotiation for CTBT, Japanese government was worried that the current state of the CD was not committed to the disarmament negotiation in shape. Since Japan evaluates FMCT as one of the top priority matters of nuclear disarmament and non-proliferation, the government expects the negotiation on FMCT to be promoted by submitting the working document to the CD. The working document aims at: (i) identifying the range of object of FMCT, (ii) examining the technical feasibility including the verification technique and (iii) identifying the legal/political issue and technological problem. Verification mechanism of FMCT is also a matter to be discussed on the CD. This working document mentions the importance of the IAEA Nuclear Safeguards including the AP as a basis of the future FMCT verification mechanism. It also emphasises that the additional obligations will not be applied to countries which ratified the IAEA Safeguards AP. It has also pointed out the idea of introducing the verification related expert working group of CTBT and protracted experience, infrastructure and appro-

---

15 ISTC. http://www.istc.ru/ISTC/sc.nsf/html/index.htm?OpenDocument& lang=en.

16 Global Partnership Against the Spread of Weapons and Materials of Mass Destruction – A G8 Action Plan http://www.g8.fr/evian/english/navigation/2003_g8_summit/summit_documents/global_partnership_against_the_spread_of_weapons_and_materials_of_mass_destruction_-_a_g8_action_plan.html.

17 Working paper on a Treaty to Ban the production of Fissile Material for Nuclear Weapons and other Nuclear Explosive Devices submitted by Japan on 14 August 2003. http://www.reachingcriticalwill.org/political/cd/speeches03/ FMCTwp.pdf.

priate expertise of the IAEA Nuclear Safeguards to FMCT. It aims then at the conclusion of FMCT negotiation within five years.

The case of FMCT negotiation significantly shows that the nuclear weapon countries unilaterally declare the prohibition of the production of the fissile material for nuclear weapons at an early stage. In the mean-time, Japan held a bilateral consultation with the USA, the UK, Canada and Australia that has facilitated FMCT negotiation and also organised twice FMCT workshops (2001 and 2003) for maintaining the momentum and out reach purposes.

7. *Nuclear Suppliers Group (NSG)*

Japan was an original member when the NSG conference started in 1975 and has positively participated in the conference in charge of laying down the Guidelines[18] for Transfers of Nuclear-Related Dual-Use Equipment, Material and Technology that could become an important contribution to the nuclear fuel cycle or nuclear explosive activity, which has not been covered yet.

After Part 2 of INFCIRC/254 is agreed on, Japan keep on being pro-actively committed to the NSG meetings and Permanent Mission of Japan to the International Organisation in Vienna while playing the role of Point of Contact (POC). Moreover, since 1995, Japan has also taking on the secretariat of the Guidelines for Nuclear Transfers (INFCIRC/254, Part 1).

For further enhancement of the NSG activity, Japan strongly advocates the addition of a condition on the export of the nuclear related materials, machine parts and technology: it should be possible to create a diversion to nuclear weapon development, contingent upon the ratification of the IAEA safeguards AP. Up to now, strengthening the NSG as the comprehensive export control of the nuclear material and nuclear related technologies were a point in dispute. However the current situation in which the NSG is affected by the US-India nuclear agreement warrants no optimism for Japanese government.

---

18 These dual-use guidelines were published as Part 2 of INFCIRC/254, and the original Guidelines published in 1978 became Part 1 of INFCIRC/254. http://www. nuclear-suppliersgroup.org/PDF/infcirc254r6p1-030516.pdf.

B. Japan's Efforts towards the Regional Nuclear Disarmament and Non-Proliferation – Nuclear Issues of the DPRK and Iran

1. DPRK (Democratic People's Republic of Korea)

Since October 2002, the DPRK's uranium enrichment program has not only put the regional security and stability of Far East Asia at risk, but also represented a considerable challenge to the international regime of nuclear non-proliferation. Thereafter, the DPRK began to behave outrageously with the concerned states and resorted to brinkmanship in the following years. After the announcement of its withdrawal from NPT, the DPRK reactivated its frozen nuclear reactor and started re-processing plant for spending nuclear fuel rods by facing up to the international community.

In November 2002, Resolution of the IAEA Board of Governors[19] stated that the DPRK uranium enrichment plan and secret nuclear activity would violate the international agreements and breach the implementation of NPT. Moreover, this resolution requests the DPRK to disclose all of the information related to the secret nuclear activity and ask the DPRK for wiping out the whole nuclear weapons development programme under the control of the IAEA in a prompt and verifiable manner.

As a matter of fact, Japan and the DPRK have not any diplomatic relationship and there was little chance of establishing a dialogue over security including a nuclear issue between Japan and the DPRK. In the past several years, Japan-DPRK inter-governmental conference has been interrupted several times. At the first round of the Six-Party Talks in 2003 (Beijing), Japan stressed on the necessity to wipe out completely and under scrutiny the DPRK's nuclear program. Meanwhile, Japan keeps on arguing that a 'dialogue and pressure' approach should be adopted to cope with the DPRK nuclear issue; comprehensive solution of nuclear, missile to the abduction of Japanese citizen by the DPRK in compliance with the "Pyongyang Declaration"[20]. Japan is deeply involved into the six-party talks as a key member, and has made all the diplomatic efforts with other states in a cooperative way. However, Japan's comprehensive approach to the DPRK, which deals with

---

19 IAEA Board of Governors Adopts Resolution on Safeguards in the DPRK (IAEA Media Advisory 2002/33). http://www.iaea.org/NewsCenter/MediaAdvisory/2002/med-advise_033.shtml.

20 Japan-DPRK Pyongyang Declaration (17 September 2002 Pyongyang). http://www.mofa.go.jp/region/asia-paci/n_korea/pmv0209/pyongyang.html.

the abduction cases of Japanese citizens along with nuclear issues is hardly supported by other states except for the USA. Actually, the DPRK does not only raises a serious concern for the regional security, a nuclear issue related to the nuclear black market – which does exist – and the DPRK's missiles that puts Japan at true risk; the likelihood of refugee's problem and the normalisation of diplomatic relationship also jeopardise the security of Japanese people as the national media often covered it. Besides the nuclear problem, the opinion of the international community is still severe with the DPRK due to the human rights' violations including the abduction issue[21]. In fact, EU and Japan-USA submitted to the United Nations General Assembly 3rd committee the resolution that criticised the abduction of foreigners – including some Japanese people – by the DPRK while calling it a state-sponsored human-right violation. Following this statement, the DPRK's environment has apparently turned into a new phase.

In that respect, Japan needs to seek further enlightenment in a broader perspective in order to pursue a comprehensive resolution, while following a 'dialogue and pressure' approach to bring the DPRK back to the negotiation table concerning this agenda.

2. *Iran*

The nuclear problem of Iran came to be held to account by the IAEA in the wake of construction of a large-scale secret nuclear power facilities in Natanz and Arak, as revealed in August 2002. After the report of the IAEA Director General Mohamed ElBaradei in November 2003[22], Iran's violation of the nuclear safeguards has arose serious concerns to the international community. Given the situation, Japan also joined the other European countries and made some efforts on a couple of diplomatic dialogues with the Iranian government in order to find a solution. In that respect, in January 2004, Japan-Iran consultation on disarmament and non-proliferation issues[23] took place in Tokyo. During this consultation, Japan encouraged Iran to ratify the IAEA Safeguards AP and also

---

21 EU Presidency Statement – Human Rights in the DPRK http://europa-eu-un.org/articles/en/article_5351_en.htm. US Department of State, DPRK Country Reports on Human Rights Practices – 2004 Released by the Bureau of Democracy, Human Rights, and Labor (28 February 2005). http://www.state.gov/g/drl/rls/hrrpt/2004/41646.htm.

22 Implementation of the NPT Safeguards Agreement in the Islamic Republic of Iran (GOV/2003/75). http://www.iaea.org/Publications/Documents/Board/ 2003/gov2003-75.pdf.

23 Summary of Japan-Iran Consultation on Disarmament and Non-proliferation Issues (27 January 2004). http://www.mofa.go.jp/region/middle_e/iran/consult 0401.html.

emphasised the merit of complying with the resolution of IAEA Board of Governors.

After the strenuous consultation, European countries[24] – EU-3 (the UK, France, and Germany) – and Iran agreed on 'Paris accord'[25] in November 2004: Iran pledged a temporal suspension of its uranium enrichment and reprocessing activities. Within the framework of the 'Paris accord', Iran also accepted the IAEA verification over the temporal suspension of its uranium enrichment. Following the 'Paris accord', in August 2005 EU-3 submitted a new proposal of 'long-term agreement'[26]. However, Iran rejected this proposal and hereupon reactivated a part of its uranium-conversion programme which was suspended under the 'Paris accord'. Under such circumstances, the Japanese approach towards Iran's suspected nuclear weapons development is on an equal footing with the IAEA resolutions[27] in theory and makes Iran ready to accept every item on the resolution, *inter alias*:

(a) Cooperation with the IAEA including complete information disclosure concerning the past 18 years of nuclear activity,

(b) Conclusion, complete implementation, and prompt execution of the IAEA Safeguards AP,

(c) Suspension of all the activities related to uranium enrichment and reprocessing,

(d) Return to negotiation process (board of governor's resolution in September 2005).

For the sake of retrieving the situation, it might be necessary for Iran to regain trust of the international society affected by the past violation of the IAEA Safeguards agreement; Japan has consequently to pursue a negotiated political settlement with Iran. On 22 April 2006, right after

---

24 The EU's relations with Iran (General Affairs and External Relations Council). http://ec.europa.eu/comm/external_relations/iran/intro/gac.htm.

25 Communication dated 26 November 2004 received from the Permanent Representatives of France, Germany, the Islamic Republic of Iran and the United Kingdom concerning the agreement signed in Paris on 15 November 2004 (INFCIRC/637). http://www.iaea.org/Publications/Documents/Infcircs/2004/infcirc637.pdf.

26 European Parliament resolution on Iran (B6-0539/2005). http://www.europarl.eu.int/omk/sipade3?PUBREF=-//EP//NONSGML+MOTION+B6-2005-0539+0+DOC+WORD+V0//EN&L=EN&LEVEL=0&NAV=S&LSTDOC=Y.

27 Implementation of the NPT Safeguards agreement in the Islamic Republic of Iran and related Board resolutions Resolution adopted on 11 August 2005 (GOV/2005/59) http://www.iaea.org/Publications/Documents/Board/2005/gov2005-64.pdf. Implementation of the NPT Safeguards agreement in the Islamic Republic of Iran. Resolution adopted on 24 September 2005 ((IAEA Board of Governors, GOV/ 2005/77). http://www.iaea.org/Publications/Documents/Board/2005/gov2005-77.pdf.

the official statement of the Iranian government to achieve a low uranium enrichment[28], Motohide Yoshikawa – Director of Middle Eastern and African Affairs Bureau of Japan Ministry of Foreign Affairs – visited Iran to carry on a conversation with the Vice Foreign Minister Mehdi Safari to convey Japan's regrets and request compliance with the UN Security Council presidential statement while pointing out the importance of Iran's re-establishment of full, sustained suspension of uranium enrichment activities[29]. However, the Iranian government replied that the country has already cooperated at best with the IAEA, and the sole purpose of its uranium enrichment activity is the development of a peaceful use of atomic energy.

Obviously, there is not any doubt that Iran is entitled to achieve a peaceful use of nuclear power; however, Japan monitors the situation while being deeply concerned that 27 countries – including China and Russia – have reached the agreement with the resolution of the IAEA Special Board of Governors in February 2006[30]. The situation does not allow me to reach a definite conclusion as just described and it is still necessary to hold to account Iran's nuclear problem, which is a key case over the principle of peaceful use of the nuclear power approved by NPT.

C. Japan-EU Cooperation

Japan has recently made a series of diplomatic efforts for the disarmament and non-proliferation issues as mentioned below: Japan-China (2003, 2004), Japan-Australia (2004), Japan-South Korea (2003, 2004), Japan-Libya (2004), Japan-Russia (2003), Japan-Israel (2004), Japan-EU (2004), Japan-USA (2002, 2003, 2004) and Japan-Iran (2003, 2004). In some cases, these joint efforts are made towards specific concerns beyond the unilateral regional approach. Regarding the foregoing, this paper particularly focuses on the Japan-EU consultation through examples.

As a matter of fact, Japan and EU are sharing many common features. It is especially the case on nuclear disarmament and non-

28 Presidency of the Islamic Republic of Iran, Ahmadinejad: Gov't firm to restore nation's full nuclear rights (Mashhad, 11 April, IRNA). http://www.president.ir/eng/ahmadinejad/cronicnews/1385/01/22/index-e.htm#b1.

29 UN Security Council (SC/8679). http://www.un.org/News/Press/docs/2006/sc8679.doc.htm.

30 Implementation of the NPT Safeguards agreement in the Islamic Republic of Iran (GOV/2006/13). http://www.iaea.org/Publications/Documents/Board/ 2006/gov2006-14.pdf.

proliferation, not only in terms of political will but also concerning some aspects in the policies' implementation.

In 2001 'an action plan for Japan-EU Cooperation' has been released at the Japan-EU Summit in Brussels. Among the fields of arms control, disarmament and non-proliferation[31], both parties have confirmed the need for launching an immediate initiative in the field of international disarmament and non-proliferation bodies. This action plan makes the extension of nuclear test moratorium and the early entry into force of CTBT key priorities. The importance of enhancing the implementation of Chemical Weapon Convention (CWC) and its universalisation were mentioned. Concerning the negotiation of Biological Weapon Convention (BWC) verification related protocol, the importance of the joint effort has been acknowledged. At several occasions on the CD, diplomatic efforts were made to establish the *ad hoc* Committee to negotiate FMCT. Through the efforts, the need for enhancement of the IAEA safeguard and also for universalisation of the safeguard AP has reached a mutual agreement. Therefore, it is generally understood that Japan and the EU policy of disarmament and non-proliferation are more or less pursuing the same target.

On 22 June 2004 Japan-EU Joint Declaration on Disarmament and Non-Proliferation was released[32]. Historically[33] speaking, such a declaration was a landmark outcome as Japan-EU were actually committed to the 2001 action plan and also to the joint press statement in 2002 of disarmament and non-proliferation. Indeed, both parties have reaffirmed the importance of carry on their strong commitment to the multilateral efforts for NPT, BTWC (Biological and Toxic Weapons Convention), CWC, CTBT, CCW (Convention on Certain Conventional Weapons), MBT (Mine Ban Treaty), HCOC (Hague Code of Conduct against Ballistic Missile Proliferation) and IAEA. In this joint declaration, the most significant aspect that has been recognised by both parties was that Japan and EU have stressed on the assistance they will provide to those international bodies charged with the verification and upholding of

---

31 An action plan for EU-Japan Cooperation, Arms Control and Disarmament initiatives to be launched immediately. http://www.mofa.go.jp/mofaj/area/eu/kodo_k_e.html#1-2.

32 Japan-EU Joint Declaration on Disarmament and Non-proliferation. http://www.mofa.go.jp/region/europe/eu/Summit/joint0406-2.pdf.

33 In advance of this declaration on 17 May 2004, Ambassador Yukiya Amano, director of the science division of the ministry of foreign affairs of Japan and Ms. Annalisa Giannella, the personal representative on weapons of mass destruction to EU high representative Javier Solana has hold a council and promised to continue their close partnership in the area of disarmament and non-proliferation.

compliance with the treaties, protocols and any kind of agreements. In this respect, the joint declaration also inserts the 'priority areas for a specific cooperation'. The main areas of mutual cooperation include nuclear disarmament and non-proliferation, biological and chemical weapons, missiles, export control, conventional weapons, assistance to the needy countries and problems of non-compliance with the obligations under the disarmament and non-proliferation treaties.

On 24 April 2006, the 15th Japan-EU summit meeting took place in Tokyo[34]. At this summit, the heads of Japan and EU reconfirmed the importance of carrying on the execution of the 2004 Japan-EU Joint Declaration on Disarmament and Non-Proliferation. They also reaffirmed the need for maintaining the integrity of NPT and CTBT. Moreover, by making a specific mention of the BWC review conference in 2006, Japan and EU confirmed the importance of mutual cooperation.

Concerning the DPRK situation, Japan and EU requested an emphasis on the importance of the resumption of the six-party talks; they also want the DPRK to cooperate in a prompt implementation of the joint statement of the 4th six-party talks which includes the abandonment of all the nuclear weapons and the existing nuclear development plans. In the light of humanitarian aspect of the DPRK issue, EU confirmed to make all the efforts in order to solve the abduction case.

In the meantime, one of the biggest issues of the summit was a joint statement against the Iranian nuclear problem. In that respect, Japan basically endorses the approach of EU-3, which is already supposed to represent the EU stance; furthermore, it seems that the joint statement has successfully shown to the international community the Japan-EU close partnership.

Finally, it is worth mentioning the possibility of a 'region-to-region' cooperation in a context of disarmament and non-proliferation. In fact, Japan attaches importance to the framework of the Asia-Europe Meeting (ASEM), and more specifically to the 7th foreign ministers' meeting in Kyoto[35] as the first ministerial conference after the enlargement of the ASEM. Then, on 24 July 2005, the "Political Declaration on Prevention of Proliferation of Weapons of Mass Destruction and their Means of Delivery"[36] was released as the result of the 5th ASEM foreign minis-

34 15th Japan-EU summit in Tokyo (24 April, 2006) joint press statement. http://www.mofa.go.jp/region/europe/eu/summit/joint0604.html.

35 The Seventh ASEM Foreign Ministers' Meeting in Kyoto, Japan (May 2005). http://www.mofa.go.jp/policy/economy/asem/asem7/fm.html.

36 The ASIA-EUROPE meeting, Political Declaration on Prevention of Proliferation of Weapons of Mass Destruction and Their Means of Delivery. http://www.mofa.go.jp/policy/economy/asem/asem5/dec.html.

ters' meeting in Bali. Within this meaningful framework, foreign ministers exchanged views on the 'region-to-region' cooperation and discussed on the way to further substantiate the partnership between Asian and European countries in the context of disarmament and non-proliferation.

Conclusion

A general view of the diplomatic effort to the UN General Assembly, NPT review conference, the IAEA, CTBT, the cooperation for the elimination of nuclear weapons, FMCT, the NSG and nuclear issues of the DPRK and Iran, Japan-EU cooperation, Japan's policy for the nuclear disarmament and non-proliferation seem to be quite consistent within the meaning of positive commitment. Although the view of Japan on disarmament and non-proliferation policy still remains implicit for the future to come, Japan can be said to have substantially contributed to the international community in so many cases.

As mentioned in the introductory paragraph, an efficient verification mechanism and the universalisation of a non-proliferation regime will get more important in the future. As a result, it is likely that Japan's ongoing approach to the nuclear disarmament and non-proliferation will remain the same in pursuit of international peace and security. As a victim of atomic bomb, Japan consistently resorted to policies of nuclear disarmament and non-proliferation while getting a strong support from the international community. In all fairness, Japan is expected to endeavour to enhance the verification mechanism in order to make sure that nuclear disarmament and non-proliferation regimes are properly complied with.

The European Union's Policy on Non-Proliferation of Weapons of Mass Destruction[1]

Oliver MEIER

The EU's current approach to weapons of mass destruction non-proliferation was born out of a disaster. In the run-up to the war against Iraq, Europe was deeply divided on the use of force against a suspected proliferator. As a result, transatlantic relations were severely damaged.

In order to avoid a repetition of this debacle, the EU began to develop a coherent security strategy and a joint approach to Weapons of Mass Destruction (WMD) non-proliferation. In December 2003, less than nine months after the invasion of Iraq, the European Council adopted two key documents, the European Security Strategy (ESS)[2] and the associated EU Strategy Against Proliferation of Weapons of Mass Destruction (WMD Strategy)[3]. Both documents for the first time provide a unified European framework on non-proliferation.

The WMD Strategy made non-proliferation of biological, chemical and nuclear weapons a priority goal of the EU's Common Foreign and Security Policy (CFSP), stating that "our objective is to prevent, deter, halt and, where possible, eliminate proliferation programs of concern worldwide."[4]

---

1 This paper is based on a presentation given at the conference "Europe, a quiet power? Looking for a European Identity," Brussels, 4-5 May 2006. It draws heavily on Oliver Meier & Gerrard Quille: "Testing Time for Europe's Non-proliferation Strategy," in *Arms Control Today*, Vol.35, No.4, May 2005, p. 4-12. The author thanks Gerrard Quille for his help with much of the original research and analysis.

2 "A Secure Europe in a Better World: European Security Strategy," Brussels, 12 December 2003, available at http://ue.eu.int/uedocs/cmsUpload/78367.pdf.

3 "EU Strategy Against Proliferation of Weapons of Mass Destruction," Brussels, 12 December 2003, available at http://ue.eu.int/uedocs/cmsUpload/st15708.en03.pdf (hereinafter EU WMD strategy).

4 WMD Strategy, chap. 2, para. 14.

Politically, the ESS and the WMD Strategy together serve three goals:

1. A joint approach on security issues in general and non-proliferation in particular was seen by European leaders as necessary to rebuild intra-European relations after the Iraqi crisis. It was hoped that such unity would enable Europeans to play a larger and more effective role on non-proliferation issues.
2. At the same time, Europeans wanted to reestablish transatlantic unity on non-proliferation issues. It was expected that by identifying areas of common interest, European and US non-proliferation policies would become better coordinated and a repetition of the Iraq experience could be avoided.
3. A unified and coherent strategy was seen as necessary by many Europeans to counter the new, largely unilateralist US security approach, which emphasised counter-proliferation. In particular, Europeans felt uncomfortable with the US inclusion of pre-emptive military action as a non-proliferation tool but had a few new approaches to offer as alternatives.

While the EU has been largely successful in increasing policy cohesion on non-proliferation issues, contradictions between the second and third goal – rebuilding transatlantic bridges and creating a unique European non-proliferation approach – have damaged the effectiveness of European non-proliferation efforts.

The decisive test for Europe's non-proliferation policies, however, will continue to lie in the EU's position on coercive measures to enforce non-proliferation norms. So far, Europe has championed engagement and dialogue as means to fight against the proliferation of weapons of mass destruction. But it is coming under increasing pressure to support sanctions and possibly also military strikes against Iran even without a UN mandate for such actions. This brings back all the painful memories from the war against Iraq and could result in another non-proliferation fiasco if Europeans were again unable to pursue a unified policy that is consistent with international law.

Internal Cohesion of the EU's Non-Proliferation Policy

Policy coordination on WMD matters has greatly improved since the adoption of the ESS and the WMD Strategy. The appointment of Annalisa Giannella as Javier Solana's Personal Representative on non-proliferation of weapons of mass destruction in October 2003 has established a focal point for Council activities on non-proliferation issues. Giannella's six-month progress reports on the implementation of the WMD Strategy and her list of priorities provide an important yardstick against which to measure EU non-proliferation efforts.

Nevertheless, challenges still remain to be faced. In particular the uncertain future of the European draft treaty calls into question the feasibility of much needed institutional reforms. Such a reorganisation of the EU's foreign policy decision-making is badly needed, not least to reduce overlaps and tensions between the Council of the European Union and the European Commission.

The EU was able to find common language on most of the nuclear arms control topics in a Common Position that was agreed shortly before the NPT Review Conference in May 2005[5]. But the wording of the document on some issues simply papered over the differences that exist between Europeans on such an issue: the role of nuclear weapons, the linkage between nuclear deterrence and proliferation and the best way to make progress towards the goal of a world free of nuclear weapons.

The obstacles to a more coherent and effective EU non-proliferation policy remain political. The fact that France and the United Kingdom are continuing to rely on nuclear deterrence weakens European credibility in the fight against proliferation of weapons of mass destruction. The majority of EU non-nuclear weapon states is pushing for progress on nuclear disarmament but the two nuclear weapon states continue to block stronger European positions on issues such as a Fissile Material Cut Off Treaty (FMCT) and tactical nuclear weapons.

France in particular is increasingly turning into a nuclear hawk, overtaking the United Kingdom in that position. In the run-up to the Review Conference of the Nuclear Non-proliferation Treaty (NPT) in May 2005, Paris helped Washington out by openly calling into doubt the value of existing nuclear weapon states' commitments on nuclear disarmament. Jacques Chirac's speech on nuclear deterrence on 19 January 2006 was further proof that Paris is progressively more mirroring US thinking on nuclear matters[6].

The United Kingdom's future nuclear weapons policy is currently on the table because Tony Blair has initiated a debate about a possible follow-on to Britain's Trident system. It will be interesting to see

5 Council of the European Union: Council Common Position 2005/329/PESC of 25 April 2005 relating to the 2005 Review Conference of the Parties to the Treaty on the Non-Proliferation of Nuclear Weapons, Brussels, 25 April 2005.

6 See Oliver Meier: "Chirac Outlines Expanded Nuclear Doctrine," in *Arms Control Today*, Vol.36, No.2, March 2006, p. 43-44.

whether the Anglo-American alliance – which generally agrees on security issues – will continue to extend to nuclear matters[7].

At the same time, a debate seems to be emerging in some non-nuclear EU member states about the continued deployment on their territory of US tactical nuclear weapons under NATO nuclear sharing arrangements. The German Parliament has on its table three resolutions, all calling for the withdrawal of US nuclear weapons from German territory. It remains a possibility that similar debates will take place in Belgium, Italy, The Netherlands and Turkey which also have US nuclear weapons deployed on their territory[8].

Transatlantic Differences and Commonalities on Non-Proliferation

As the only remaining superpower, the US is dominating international security discussions. The EU's WMD Strategy recognises this fact and calls for close cooperation with the US and other key partners on non-proliferation issues. Generally speaking, the EU and the US are closer on non-proliferation than on disarmament, in particular nuclear disarmament[9].

The transatlantic gap on arms control appears to be widening despite attempts to use identical language to describe a common transatlantic approach to non-proliferation. Both, the EU and US favour an "effective multilateralism" but understand and use this term differently. The Bush administration highlights the perceived lack of compliance with treaty-based non-proliferation regimes and argues that effective responses to proliferation are best found outside such regimes, including through sanctions and the use of force. The EU, on the other hand, still wants to improve non-proliferation treaties by strengthening multilateral institutions and fixing loopholes within these regimes. According to the WMD Strategy, the EU wants to focus its efforts on measures to improve compliance and more effective verification and monitoring systems. The

---

7 See Rebecca Johnson: "End of a Nuclear Weapons Era: Can Britain Make History?," in *Arms Control Today*, Vol.36, No.3, April 2006, p. 6-12.

8 See Oliver Meier, "Tied in nuclear knots," in *The Bulletin of the Atomic Scientists*, Vol.62, No.1, January/February 2006, p. 14-16.

9 Annalisa Giannella herself pointed out that communiqués of EU-US summits discuss weapons of mass destruction almost exclusively from a proliferation perspective and contain almost no commitments on disarmament. See Arms Control Association: "The European Union's Non-proliferation Strategy: An Interview with Annalisa Giannella, the Personal Representative on Non-proliferation of Weapons of Mass Destruction to EU High Representative Javier Solana," 26 July 2005, http://www.armscontrol.org/interviews/20050726_Giannella.asp.

EU also insists that the UN Security Council has a central role in treaty enforcement.

The transatlantic track record on strengthening multilateral arms control and non-proliferation regimes is bad. European and US goals on multilateral arms control differ substantially. European attempts to achieve agreement on an agenda for a renewed NPT, efforts to bring the Comprehensive Nuclear Test Ban Treaty (CTBT) into force and attempts to restart discussions on a possible verification mechanism to the Biological Weapons Convention have all been blocked by the Bush administration. By rejecting a verifiable FMCT, Washington has destroyed the transatlantic consensus on another important arms control issue.

Is There a "European" Approach to Non-Proliferation?

Given the transatlantic deadlock on an agenda for strengthening multilateral arms control regimes and given internal European tensions on nuclear disarmament, the EU has begun to shift the focus of its non-proliferation policy. Europe is increasingly silent on disarmament issues and appears to spend less time, less money and fewer efforts on universal, legally binding, multilateral, treaty-based instruments.

Instead, *ad hoc* coalitions and supply-side mechanisms to tackle WMD proliferation are moving towards the centre of the EU's non-proliferation policy. Such approaches are backed by Washington and therefore promise the achievement of tangible results.

Examples of such pragmatic efforts include

- export controls on "dual use"-technology and goods that could be misused to develop or produce weapons of mass destruction.
- cooperative threat reduction efforts to secure and dismantle the nuclear, chemical and biological weapons legacy on the territory of the former Soviet Union[10].
- new mechanisms to better control trade in technology that could be used to develop weapons of mass destruction[11].

---

[10] The EU's financial framework for 2007-13 makes clear that such efforts will continue to consume by far the biggest share of EU financial resources for non-proliferation. See Oliver Meier: "EU Approves Budget Framework," in *Arms Control Today*, Vol.36, No.5, June 2006, p. 37.

[11] The prime example is the *Proliferation Security Initiative*, which was created by the Bush administration in May 2003. Several EU member states are participating in PSI, which aims to interdict illegal shipments and transports of weapons of mass destruction and related technology.

Although technology controls and cooperative threat reduction programmes are worthwhile in themselves and serve to bridge transatlantic differences, they do not live up to the EU's goal of pursuing a non-proliferation strategy that promotes multilateral solutions to arms control problems. In these and other areas, the EU has yet to prove in the words of its WMD strategy that "a multilateralist approach to security, including disarmament and non-proliferation, provides the best way to maintain international order."[12] There is a real danger that the EU's non-proliferation policies are becoming increasingly lopsided by neglecting the demand-side of the proliferation problem. The fact that the EU denies any connection between its own military capabilities – in particular the continued reliance of some member states on nuclear deterrence – and the spread of weapons of mass destruction to other states is one aspect of this political imbalance between the non-proliferation and disarmament policies of the EU.

Another trademark of the EU's non-proliferation efforts is the practical support it gives to multilateral arms control institutions such as the International Atomic Energy Agency (IAEA), the Organisation for the Prohibition of Chemical Weapons and the Comprehensive Nuclear Test Ban Treaty Organisation. Under the CFSP, the EU has passed a number of Joint Actions which provide important political and financial support for these bodies. Given the continued erosion of political support for some of these institutions and given the lack of progress on arms control more generally such practical measures are indispensable – but at the same time fall short of the broader goal of strengthening the underlying arms control regimes. What is still lacking is a courageous, innovative and coherent European strategy to take disarmament, and in particular nuclear disarmament, forward.

It is also noteworthy that Europe is increasingly using its economic might to achieve security objectives. The EU has used economic sticks and carrots in its negotiations with Iran. The EU is also mainstreaming non-proliferation into its external policies by insisting on the inclusion of a non-proliferation clause into trade and cooperation agreements with third countries. These clauses make compliance with export controls norms a precondition for better political relations with the EU.

12 WMD Strategy, chap. 2, para. 14.

The EU, Iran & India: Test Cases for Europe's Non-Proliferation Approach

Two current non-proliferation challenges demonstrate the trends outlined above and illustrate achievements and shortcomings of Europe's non-proliferation agenda.

European negotiations with Iran have demonstrated the EU's ability to maintain a coherent position despite strong outside pressures. The US has been trying to push the EU towards a tougher stand *vis-à-vis* Iran since the beginning of the talks with Tehran in 2003. Iran, on the other hand, has been trying to lure the EU away from the US, arguing that UN Security Council referral and the possibility of sanctions would only escalate the current crisis. Even though there are substantial differences between member states on the right approach towards Iran, the EU so far has acted in a united manner. After the Iraq experience, this in itself is important progress, though it is unlikely that the model of the three largest EU states as well as the High Representative for the CFSP acting *de facto* on behalf of the 25 EU members at large, will ever be repeated.

By acting united, the EU has so far also been able to maintain transatlantic unity. But it is too early to tell whether the EU will be able to maintain its policy of engagement and dialogue while hardliners in Tehran and Washington are escalating the crisis. The EU's approach towards Tehran needs to fulfil three criteria in order to be consistent with its broader non-proliferation agenda:

- The EU should continue to engage Iran and resist US pressures to further isolate the regime in Tehran. Isolation only strengthens the hands of Iranian hardliners by weakening the hands of those Iranians who call for compromises in order to resolve the nuclear crisis.
- The EU should continue to insist that the international community's response to Tehran has to be found through the United Nations and not by "coalitions of the willing." Sanctions are not likely to convince Iran to voluntarily renounce uranium enrichment and plutonium reprocessing and will be seen as illegitimate and discriminatory by many states, in particular if they are implemented without a clear legal basis under international law.
- The EU has to renounce any military attacks on Iran. Military options are not only counterproductive and would cause immense

human suffering but would also be a breach of international law[13].

A second challenge for European non-proliferation policies has emerged since July 2005, when the Bush administration announced its intention to lift nuclear trade restrictions on India, one of three countries that have decided to remain outside the nuclear non-proliferation regime. Such a *de facto* recognition of India's nuclear weapon status would damage the NPT, fuel nuclear arms races in Asia and complicate the negotiations with Iran[14].

A recognition of India's nuclear weapon state status is possible only with the explicit consent of all 25 EU member states because a lifting of nuclear sanctions requires a change of Nuclear Suppliers Group (NSG) export guidelines. Current NSG rules restrict nuclear trade with states like India which refuse to place all their civil nuclear facilities under full-scope safeguards of the IAEA. Any change of the guidelines, however, requires consensus among the 45 NSG participants, which include all 25 EU member states.

A recognition of India's nuclear weapon status would contradict a whole range of European non-proliferation principles, some of which were outlined in response to India's five nuclear tests in May 1998 in the EU's Common Position of 26 October 1998[15]. Sacrificing long-standing non-proliferation principles for the sake of transatlantic harmony and short-term economic gains would be evidence that the EU is no longer giving multilateral approaches a high priority. In fact, Europe would follow the Bush administration's policy of applying non-proliferation norms selectively, thus undermining the very foundation of the multilateralism.

Washington decided to bring India into the nuclear club without informing or consulting even its closest European allies. Europe was

13 See Michael Brzoska, Götz Neuneck & Oliver Meier: "Diplomatic Means Have not been Exhausted: Against Alarmism in the Conflict over Iran's Nuclear Programme," Hamburger Informationen zur Friedensforschung und Sicherheitspolitik, Ausgabe 37/2006, Hamburg, March 2006, http://www.ifsh.de/pdf/publikationen/hifs/HI37_engl.pdf.

14 See for example William C. Potter: "India and the New Look of US Non-proliferation Policy," in *Non-proliferation Review*, Vol.12, No.2, July 2005, p. 343-354; Zia Mian & M.V. Ramana: "Wrong Ends, Means, and Needs: Behind the US Nuclear Deal With India," in *Arms Control Today*, Vol.36, No.1, January/February 2006, p. 11-17.

15 See Council of the European Union: Common Position on the European Union's contribution to the promotion of non-proliferation and confidence-building in the South Asian region, 98/606/CFSP, 26 October 1998.

taken by surprise and has so far been unable to articulate a coherent response of its own. The EU is clearly divided on this issue. Paris and London are following Washington's line and support a lifting of nuclear sanctions on India, mainly for economic reasons. Many EU member states, however, have reservations towards the deal with India as it stands now because they fear negative repercussions for global non-proliferation efforts. EU institutions have remained ominously silent on the issue. Javier Solana and Annalisa Giannella have not spoken on whether the EU should agree to the US proposal[16]. The inability of Europe to speak, let alone act, on such an important non-proliferation issue illustrates Europe's weakness to take action when few powerful states block consensus.

It will be a decisive test for the strength of the EU's non-proliferation policy, whether Europeans will cave in to US pressure and acquiesce to bring India into the nuclear club or whether they will come up with an independent and credible position. A European approach should make sure that a lifting of nuclear sanctions on India results in benefits for nuclear non-proliferation that exceed the damage inflicted on the broader non-proliferation. Towards this goal, EU members should not consent to a recognition of India's nuclear weapons status before:

- India has undertaken the same arms control commitments as the other recognised nuclear weapon states, including signature of the CTBT, a moratorium on the production of fissile material for nuclear weapons and a recognition of the disarmament commitments contained in Article VI of the NPT;
- New Delhi has committed itself to placing all its civil nuclear facilities, including those that are partly associated with the nuclear weapons complex, under perpetual IAEA safeguards and has concluded such safeguards agreements with the IAEA;
- India in a credible manner has outlined its plans for a "minimum nuclear deterrent" and the associated nuclear doctrine.

16 The only reference to an EU position is buried deep inside a December 2005 progress report by Annalisa Giannella, which states that "the EU should make clear by all means that this cannot be construed nor interpreted in any way as a de facto recognition of a status of nuclear weapons state." See Council of The European Union: Implementation of the EU Strategy against proliferation of WMD, 14520/05, Brussels, 5 December 2005, p. 40.

A More Effective European Non-Proliferation Policy

The EU's non-proliferation policy has become more coherent but not always more effective since the ESS and the WMD Strategy have been passed in December 2003. In two major cases – in the run-up to the 2005 NPT Review Conference and in dealing with Iran – the EU has been able to maintain its internal unity. Whether the EU will continue to act in a coherent manner *vis-à-vis* Iran's nuclear programme and whether it will be able to develop a joint approach on lifting nuclear sanctions on India will be two major tests for the effectiveness of its non-proliferation approach. More generally, there are three steps the EU could take to act more effectively on non-proliferation issues.

First, Europeans need to do their political homework on non-proliferation. This concerns on the one hand financial and institutional capacities to implement a more forceful non-proliferation policy. With the agreement on a budget framework for 2007-2013, financial planning for non-proliferation tasks has become more predictable. On average, the EU will be spending €141 million annually over the next seven years on non-proliferation, disarmament and nuclear safety. While the budget structure on non-proliferation has been somewhat simplified compared to previous budgets, non-proliferation spending will remain split between two distinct and at times competing EU institutions. The European Commission will administer funds under the new Stability Instrument and for nuclear safety activities while the Council of the European Union has its own budget for activities under the Common Foreign and Security Policy. A unified non-proliferation and disarmament budget would help to avoid unnecessary overlaps[17].

On the other hand, Europeans need to address the political differences between member states on nuclear deterrence, counter-proliferation and coercive measures to fight non-proliferation. Europe cannot be a credible proponent of non-proliferation as long as nuclear deterrence is seen by several EU member states as a useful means to provide national security. A serious and open debate about these issues among Europeans is long overdue and a prerequisite for a more coherent arms control policy.

Second, EU member states need to think more creatively about ways to get round some of the transatlantic blockades on arms control issues. European governments are still afraid to distance themselves from

17 See Stockholm International Peace Research Institute: Strengthening European Action on WMD Non-Proliferation and Disarmament: How can European Community Instruments Contribute?, Stockholm, November 2005; Oliver Meier: "EU Approves Budget Framework," in *Arms Control Today*, Vol.36, No.5, June 2006, p. 37.

Washington, even on topics where transatlantic unity cannot be reached in the foreseeable future and where an independent European approach would have broad international support.

For example, Europe could and should launch a European initiative on a Fissile Material Cut-Off and revive discussions on a biological weapons verification regime. On these issues, Europe does have a unique position that enjoys broad support internationally. The time is ripe for "coalitions of the willing" on disarmament and Europe is in an excellent position to initiate such coalitions.

Finally, the WMD Strategy states that the EU wants to address "the root causes of instability including through pursuing and enhancing its efforts in the areas of political conflicts, development assistance, reduction of poverty and promotion of human rights."[18] More can be done to place non-proliferation in the context of its external relations more generally. Mainstreaming arms control and non-proliferation into, for example, development and human rights policy holds the promise of developing a more sustainable non-proliferation approach.

In the end, Europe needs to overcome the fundamental differences that still exist between member states on the best way to prevent the spread of nuclear, biological and chemical weapons as well as their delivery systems. Pursuing a truly multilateralist approach to non-proliferation will thus require some hard choices and a willingness to also confront Washington and other major players where international consensus is not achievable.

18 WMD Strategy, chap. 2, para. 14.

Human Security

A Platform for a Common Japan-EU Agenda?

Éric REMACLE

Professor, Université libre de Bruxelles (ULB)
Visiting Professor, European Union Centre of Excellence, University of Pittsburgh

At the end of the Cold War, and even more significantly after the Kosovo War and the 9/11 attacks, both the European Union and Japan have slowly shifted from a low security profile of "civilian powers" to a tighter and a more comprehensive security role implying deployment of armed forces abroad and securitisation of civilian agenda[1]. In this context, the concept of Human Security which emerged almost at the same time, has sometimes been considered as an alternative approach to military approaches to security[2]. It is therefore useful to understand why both in Japan and Europe, this concept has gained official and civil society's support although foreign policies were also militarised.

Japan and the Human Security Agenda

The first Japanese reference to the concept of human security came from the Prime Minister Murayama in his address to the UN General Assembly in 1995 and can be considered as a part of a Japanese ap-

---

1 On this evolution see among others: É. Remacle, "The European Security Strategy and Its Impact on Europe-Japan Relations," in Ueta, T., Remacle, É. (eds.), *Japan and Enlarged Europe. Partners in Global Governance*, Brussels, P.I.E. Peter Lang, 2005, p. 35-46.; St. Keukeleire, "The European Union and Japan: Partners in global crisis management and global stabilisation?," in Ueta, T., Remacle, É. (eds.), *Japan-EU Cooperation: Ten Years after the Hague Declaration, Studia Diplomatica*, LIV (1-2), 2002, p. 159-184; H.W. Maull, *Europe and Japan. A Relationship in Search of Roles*, Tokyo, Japan Centre for International Exchange, 1996.

2 See for e.g. R. Paris, "Human Security: Paradigm Shift or Hot Air?," *International Security*, 26(2), 2001, p. 87-102; Hampson, F.E. e.a., *Madness in the Multitude. Human Security and World Disorder*, London, Oxford University Press, 2002.

proach to multilateralism[3]. His vision, followed by his successor Hashimoto, was based on two principles: on the one hand, "respect for the human rights of every citizen on earth"; on the other hand, protection from "poverty, disease, ignorance, oppression and violence"[4].

In 1998, the financial crisis in Asia led the Prime Minister (and former foreign affairs minister) Obuchi to promote the concept of "human security" in order to face Asia's new regional economic challenges and to open up a more assertive and independent international role for Japan without undermining its alliance with the United States[5]. In the meantime, human security became a real cornerstone of Japan's foreign policy and a new way to define its overseas development assistance policy. Under Obuchi's rules, Japan adopted what can be summed up as a comprehensive, multi-faceted approach to security:

> In these times, humankind is under various kinds of threat. Environmental problems such as global warming are not only highly hazardous for us but also for the next generations. In addition, transnational crimes such as illicit drugs and drug trafficking are increasing. Problems such as the exodus of refugees, violations of human rights, infectious diseases like HIV/AIDS, terrorism, anti-personnel landmines and so on, significantly threat all of us. Moreover, the problem of children in armed conflict should never be overlooked[6].

This definition of Human Security as "freedom of expression" is echoing the 1994 Human Development Report of the United Nations Development Programme (UNDP) and makes Human Security almost similar to Human Development[7]. On this basis, the Japanese government supported the establishment in 1999 of the United Nations Trust Fund for Human Security (UNTFHS) whose budget had risen to some USD 170 million by 2002 and was managed jointly by UNDP, UNESCO, UNHCR and WHO.

Although the Japanese approach to human security is based on wider principles and on a conceptual approach, it has converged with the

---

3 A. Fukushima, *Japanese Foreign Policy: The Emerging Logic of Multilateralism*, Macmillan, London, 1999.

4 D. Bosold, S. Werthes, "Human Security in Practice: Canadian and Japanese Experiences," *IPG-International Politics and Society* 1/2005, p. 84-101.

5 P.E. Evans, "Human Security and East Asia," *Journal of East Asian Studies*, Vol.4, No.2, May-August 2004, p. 263-284.

6 K. Obuchi, "Opening Remarks by Prime Minister Obuchi," *An Intellectual Dialogue on Building Asia's Tomorrow*, Tokyo, 12 December 1998.

7 See also H. Okuma, "New Directions in Japan's Official Development Assistance," in Ueta, T., Remacle, É. (eds.), *Japan and Enlarged Europe. Partners in Global Governance*, Brussels, P.I.E. Peter Lang, 2005, p. 155-172.

Canadian plea on the definition of Human Security as "freedom from fear" as promoted by the thirteen countries of the Human Security Network established in 1999 under a joint Canada-Norway initiative[8]. Both approaches have decisively inspired Kofi Annan's speech at the 2000 United Nations' Millennium Summit, as well as the Summit's final declaration though it does not directly refer to Human Security.

After the Millennium Summit, Japan initiated the Commission on Human Security (CHS) co-chaired by the former UN High Commissioner for Refugees Sadako Ogata and Nobel Economics Prize-awarded Amartya Sen, and supported the holistic security concept promoted by the CHS final report:

> the aim of human security is to protect the vital core of all human lives in ways that enhance human freedoms and human fulfilment. Human security means protecting fundamental freedoms – freedoms that are the essence of life (…) It means creating political, social, environmental, economic, military and cultural systems that together give people the building blocks of survival, livelihood and dignity[9].

The commission did also put forward a list of policy recommendations aiming at:

1. Protecting people in violent conflict.
2. Protecting people from the proliferation of arms.
3. Supporting the security of people on the move.
4. Establishing human security transition funds for post-conflict situations.
5. Encouraging fair trade and markets to benefit the extreme poor.
6. Working to provide minimum living standards everywhere.
7. According higher priority to ensuring universal access to basic health care.
8. Developing an efficient and equitable global system for patent rights.
9. Empowering all people with universal basic education.
10. Clarifying the need for a global human identity while respecting the freedom of individuals to have diverse identities and affiliations[10].

Nevertheless, the CHS report was issued just before the 9/11 attacks in the United States and its impact was considerably lowered by quick changes in the security environment. In the face of China's growing power, North Korea's nuclear ambitions, and the US war on terror,

---

8 See http://www.humansecuritynetwork.org/network-e.php.

9 Commission on Human Security, *The Final Report*, 2003, p. 4 (see http://www.humansecurity-chs.org/finalreport/).

10 *Ibid.*, p. 133-142.

Japan completely reassessed its foreign and security policies and strengthened its alliance with the USA. It actively took part into the so-called "US war on terror" and sent non-fighting troops to Iraq between 2004 and 2006. Japanese expectations of a permanent seat in the United Nations Security Council were also part of the incentives for such a change, which was nevertheless viewed as a retreat from the previous Japanese emphasis on multilateralism and the centrality of the United Nations[11].

Nevertheless, the Japanese approach to Human Security as developed by the CHS was not dropped down after the 9/11 attacks and the Iraqi War. The recommendations of the CHS led in 2003 to the deepening of the reference to Human Security among UN agencies, especially the Office for the Coordination of Humanitarian Affairs (OCHA), through the creation of an Advisory Board on Human Security (ABHS) designed for advising the UN Secretary-General on the management of the UNTFHS, on the basis of the following parameters:

- Providing concrete and sustainable benefits to people and communities threatened in their survival, livelihood and dignity.
- Implementing the "Protection and Empowerment" framework by comprehensively including both top-down protection and bottom-up empowerment measures.
- Promoting partnerships with civil society groups, NGOs and other local entities and encouraging implementation by these entities.
- Advancing integrated approaches that preferably involve more than one organisation in planning and implementation.
- Addressing the broad range of interconnected issues that take into account the multisectoral demands of human security, for example, conflict and poverty, displacement and health, education and conflict prevention.
- Concentrating on those areas of human security that are currently neglected and avoiding duplication with existing programmes and activities.
- Protecting people in conflict situations who are exposed to physical violence, discrimination, exclusion and whose destitute situation derives mostly from inequalities in treatment.
- Supporting and empowering refugees, internally displaced persons (IDPs), economic migrants and others on the move. Particular attention should be given to the socio-economic impact on the displaced and their host communities.

[11] F. Cameron, "The Enlarged EU, Japan and the United States, Partners in a New Global Order?," in Ueta, T., Remacle, É. (eds.), *Japan and Enlarged Europe. Partners in Global Governance*, Brussels, P.I.E. Peter Lang, 2005, p. 272-274.

- Protecting and empowering people in conflict situations and in transition from war to peace through the integration of humanitarian and development assistance; disarmament, demobilisation and reintegration (DDR); reconciliation and coexistence; and other processes. These activities shall also contribute to preventing the recurrence of conflicts.
- Realising minimum living standards, including assisting community-level efforts to establish mechanisms to protect people exposed to extreme poverty, sudden economic downturns and natural disasters.
- Enhancing health care and service coverage to those whom other initiatives have not reached successfully.
- Improving educational opportunities, especially for girls, emphasising universal primary education (including the emphasis on safe school environment and respect for diversity).
- Promoting and disseminating the human security concept and deepening its understanding and acceptance worldwide, including studies on key aspects of human security[12].

Japanese diplomats, CHS former members and UN agencies are playing a dominant role within the ABHS. To some extent, this successful "multilateralisation" of the Japanese Human Security concept allowed it to survive from the evolution of Japan's national foreign policy agenda towards a rather militarised threat assessment after 9/11 attacks and Iraq. Instead of being contradictory, both agendas can therefore remain complementary and even increase the diversification of Japanese foreign policy objectives and international coalitions.

The EU's Discourse on "Holistic Security"

Since the framing of its Common Foreign and Security Policy (CFSP) after 1992, the European Union has based most of its international identity on a comprehensive definition of security. The acme of this evolution was Article III-292 of the EU draft Constitution which states that the Union's external policies have to be conducted in order to:

(a) safeguard its values, fundamental interests, security, independence and integrity;

(b) consolidate and support democracy, the rule of law, human rights and the principles of international law;

(c) preserve peace, prevent conflicts and strengthen international security, in accordance with the purposes and principles of the United Nations Char-

12 Quotation from OCHA webpage: http://ochaonline.un.org/webpage.asp?MenuID=8289&Page=1503.

ter, with the principles of the Helsinki Final Act and with the aims of the Charter of Paris, including those relating to external borders;

(d) foster the sustainable economic, social and environmental development of developing countries, with the primary aim of eradicating poverty;

(e) encourage the integration of all countries into the world economy, including through the progressive abolition of restrictions on international trade;

(f) help develop international measures to preserve and improve the quality of the environment and the sustainable management of global natural resources, in order to ensure sustainable development;

(g) assist populations, countries and regions confronting natural or man-made disasters;

(h) promote an international system based on stronger multilateral cooperation and good global governance[13].

The EU's High Representative of the CFSP, Javier Solana, even considers the European approach to security as the most holistic and multi-faceted ever. The European Security Strategy adopted by the European Council on 12 December 2003 under the title *A Secure Europe in a Better World. European Security Strategy*[14] perfectly illustrates this discourse.

The strategy articulates a framework based upon a comprehensive or holistic approach to security. The underlying comprehensive security concept leads to a clear statement that the EU and its member states will co-operate to tackle their security priorities in a framework that stresses on multilateral institutions (specifically the UN and regional organisations) and the rule of law (upholding the principle of the use of force as a last resort). This means that even security 'threats' (weapons of mass destruction, regional conflicts, state failure, terrorism and organised crime) should be coped with through 'effective multilateralism'. In other words, it is necessary to support the UN system, strengthen national responses through EU synergies and address root causes such as poverty and weak governance through community instruments and regional dialogue[15].

---

13 *Treaty Establishing a Constitution for Europe*, *Official Journal of the European Union*, Series C 310, Vol.47, Brussels, 16 December 2004 (http://europa.eu.int/eur-lex/lex/JOHtml.do?uri=OJ:C:2004:310:SOM:EN:HTML).

14 See http://ue.eu.int/uedocs/cmsUpload/78367.pdf.

15 É. Remacle, "The European Security Strategy and Its Impact on Europe-Japan Relations," in Ueta, T., Remacle, É. (eds.), *Japan and Enlarged Europe. Partners in Global Governance*, Brussels, P.I.E. Peter Lang, 2005, p. 35-46.; Quille, G., "The European Security Strategy: A Framework for EU Security Interests?," *International Peacekeeping*, Vol.11, No.3, Autumn 2004, p. 1-16; S. Biscop, R. Coolsaet, *The*

Javier Solana considers indeed that this holistic approach evidences the difference between Europe and the United States. He argues, by referring to a comprehensive notion of security, that active engagement is in Europe's security interests since these are affected by poor governance, insecurity, poverty and conflict far beyond its borders. Europe must therefore meet these challenges, and it is well placed to do so with wide ranging diplomatic, development, economic, humanitarian and military instruments[16]. This is a comprehensive approach to the understanding of security shifts from a traditional military threat assessment to the identification of the 'new environment' – as described by Solana; this environment implies diffuse challenges which must be addressed by the Union including poverty, energy dependence, climate change and bad governance as key security challenges for the Union because of their role in the regional instability which in turn, affects directly and indirectly European interests, as does open violence like the Middle Eastern conflict. In addition to the 'old threat' represented by these regional conflicts, the strategy identifies 'new threats' which are a combination of traditional concerns related to the proliferation of WMD, new forms of terrorism, failed states and organised crime. It states that their novelty lies in their combination: "By bringing these different elements together – terrorism designed to create maximum violence, the availability of weapons of mass destruction and the failure of state systems – we could be confronted with a very radical threat." But the ESS always points out that the answer to such problems does not only imply the use of force but also the use of wide ranging instruments, a 'comprehensive security toolbox':

> In contrast with the massive and noticeable threat in the Cold War, none of the new threats is purely military; nor can be tackled by purely military means. Each form of threat requires a mixture of tools. Weapons of mass destruction proliferation may be contained through export controls and wiped out through political, economic and other pressures while coping with the underlying political causes. A mixture of intelligence, political, military tools and so on may be required to deal with terrorism. In failed states, military and humanitarian instruments may be needed to restore order so as to tackle the immediate crisis. Reconstruction needs for economic instruments, and civilian crisis management helps restore civil government. The Euro-

World is the Stage – A Global Security Strategy for the European Union, Paris, Notre Europe, December 2003.

16 Javier Solana, *Speech on the State of the Union*, Paris, European Union Institute for Security Studies, 30 June 2003.

pean Union is particularly well equipped to face such multi-faceted situations[17].

According to its supporters, the second originality of the European approach is the emphasis on international co-operation and multilateralism: "there are not any countries which is able to tackle entirely today's complex problems on its own." The ESS therefore emphasises the depth and primacy of the transatlantic link and collaboration, even with an unusual messianic discourse: "The European Union and the United States – in a common effort – can be a significant force for restoring the collective good in the world." It also refers to other strategic partners like the other members of the G-8 and the United Nations Security Council: Russia first, then Canada, China, Japan, and India too. The methodology of this co-operative approach is defined as an 'effective multilateralism' which aims at three strategic goals: extending the security zone around Europe; strengthening the international order; countering the threats. The first objective echoes the existing role of the EU, mostly through the enlargement process, and precisely in its wider neighbourhood. It has been recognised that the very powerful carrot of enlargement has strongly influenced the stability of the EU's periphery; but, if we consider that some time will be required for adjustment after the next round of enlargement, process needs to be invigorated in both consolidating security within the EU's enlarged borders and in extending stability beyond.

The second strategic objective provides means with which a regional multilateral actor, the EU, can extend its influence and support international responses to security challenges through "the development of a stronger international society, well functioning international institutions and a rule-based international order." This objective shows the importance of the UN system at the centre of the stage, along with the transatlantic relationship, whereby Javier Solana states: "The fundamental framework for international relations is the United Nations Charter. Strengthening the United Nations, equipping it to fulfil its responsibilities and to act effectively, must be a European priority. If we want international organisations, regimes and treaties to be effective in confronting threats to international peace and security we should be ready to act when their rules are broken"[18]. The third objective is a response to the 'new threats' and emphasises the EU's strengths based upon its response to 9/11 attacks with "a package that included the creation of a European arrest warrant, measures to attack terrorist

[17] *Ibid.*

[18] Javier Solana, *Speech on the State of the Union, op. cit.*

financing and an agreement on mutual legal assistance with the USA"[19]. Likewise it refers to existing approaches to support non-proliferation such as with its new Strategy on WMD and Action Plan which includes a commitment to the globalisation of non-proliferation, disarmament norms and regimes along with a commitment to make those regimes effective by dealing with compliance and enforcement issues. The negotiations about the Iranian nuclear programmes between the Iranian government and the representatives of the three major European states (France, Germany and the UK), together with the talks and pressure from IAEA, have been quoted as an example of the European methodology in this field[20].

The reference to an effective multilateralism allows two interpretations. The first one is that multilateralism matters: as a matter of principle, the EU strongly sticks to multilateral frameworks at global level (United Nations, World Trade Organisation), but also at regional level (NATO and the ESDP-NATO relations are quoted among the key policy implications of the ESS, and OSCE, Council of Europe, MERCOSUR, ASEAN, African Union as other key regional organisations). The other interpretation is that effectiveness matters: multilateralism does not make any sense if there is not any determination and readiness to use coercive means for implementing its decisions. According to some analysts, this implies the adoption of a 'solid' approach to Petersberg tasks and a strategic culture, whereby "the institutional confidence and processes to manage and deploy military force as part of the accepted range of legitimate and effective policy instruments, together with the general recognition of the EU's legitimacy as an international actor with military capabilities – albeit limited"[21]. Among the two focuses on 'effective multilateralism', the latter makes the EU very similar to the United States while the former contributes to shape Europe's identity as opposed to an oversimplified unilateral America. But this oversimplification does not help understanding the real incentives of states to multi-

---

19 G. Quille, St. Pullinger, "The EU Seeking Common Ground for Tackling the Threat from WMD," *Disarmament Diplomacy*, No.7, December 2003; see also Oliver Meier's contribution in this book.

20 This methodology is inspiring pleas for a new American attitude towards Iran, see: Z. Brzezinski, R.M. Gates, S. Maloney, *Iran: Time for a New Approach*, Report of an Independent Task Force sponsored by the Council on Foreign Relations, Washington DC, 2004.

21 P. Cornish, G. Edwards, "Beyond the EU/NATO Dichotomy: the beginnings of a European strategic culture," *International Affairs*, Vol.77, No.3, July 2001, p. 587-603.

lateralism[22]. And again both interpretations and their different rationales are part of a constructive ambiguity of the document and of future divergences when discussing the scope of Petersberg's tasks and military capabilities[23]. Interestingly the ESS also strikes the balance between the call for 'increasing' capabilities (by rising military expenditures) and the plea for their 'improvement' (through pooling, rationalisation, specialisation and other qualitative approaches).

A last point refers to the peculiarity of the European approach to regionalism and its impact on security. Javier Solana considers that the Union's security interests come from its ability to build a security community[24]:

> The creation of the European Union has been central to this development. It has transformed the relations between our states, and the lives of our citizens. European countries are committed to dealing peacefully with disputes and cooperating through common institutions[25].

The success of the Union's enlargement and the member sates' commitment to its institutions is pointed out in order to recognise the role of the EU in contributing to security in Europe. This regionalist/institutionalist dimension of the EU security strategy is another way of defining multilateralism. It also implies the development of enlargement and neighbouring policies as key security instruments. The extension of its own security community, the stabilisation of its environment and the promotion of a deep regional integration on other continents are considered to be inter-related institutionalist policies all dedicated to the Union's security interests in a way which is not only original but which is also inspired by the 'civilian power' approach[26].

As shown above, the EU's discourse about the holistic and comprehensive approach to security is obviously ambivalent. It might especially seem to be very paradoxical that the paragraphs which shape an EU international identity and differentiates it from the USA are those referring to the global challenges and civilian means, in the tradition of the "civilian power Europe" discourse inherited from the 1970s and

22 M.A. Pollack, "Unilateral America, multilateral Europe?," in J. Peterson, M.A. Pollack (eds.), *Europe, America, Bush. Transatlantic Relations in the Twenty-first Century*, London-New York, Routledge, 2003, p. 115-127.

23 Quille, G., "The European...," *op. cit.*, p. 10-12.

24 About security communities, see E. Adler, M. Barnett, *Security Communities*, Cambridge, Cambridge University Press, 1998.

25 Javier Solana, *Speech on the State of the Union, op. cit.*

26 M. Telò, *Europe: A Civilian Power? European Union, Global Governance, World Order*, New York, Palgrave, 2006.

1980s; while the threat assessment in the "hard security" sphere is very similar to the American one (except for the removal of the term 'pre-emption' considered as too "American" and some slight changes in the language concerning WMD)[27]. These changes and the new balance between the emphasis on challenges and threats are sufficient to appeal to various member state interests and might be one more case of constructive ambiguity as well as the seeds of future conflicts of interpretation between member states. This confirms that differences between Europe and America are not as important as both actors have themselves emphasised towards their own public opinions[28]; it also shows that the internal European diversity obliges the European security discourse to combine "civilian power" and "militarisation" approaches in order to reduce discrepancies. Interestingly, this approach started when the Helsinki European Council in December 1999 adopted on the same day the "headline goal" of the creation of a 60,000 troops' rapid reaction force and a programme for increasing its "civilian crisis management" capabilities[29].

EU's discourse on holistic security and the combination of military and civilian aspects of crisis management play *mutatis mutandis* the same role as the catch-all concept such as Human Security so that Japan helps them to build an international identity without undermining their close relationship with the United States of America.

Human Security as a Common Platform?

Some convergence between Europe and Japan can therefore be expected, but it does not require the EU to adopt formally Human Security, especially in its Japanese meaning which seems very far from the EU's dominant discourse about the need to strengthen military assets.

In Europe, a group of scholars led by Mary Kaldor, commissioned by Javier Solana and named after the Barcelona Study Group on Europe's Security Capabilities is currently promoting the adoption of the Human Security concept by the European institutions. They directly

---

27 É. Remacle, "La stratégie européenne de sécurité: plus occidentale qu'européenne," in Delcourt, B., Duez, D., Remacle, É. (eds.), *La guerre d'Irak, prélude d'un nouvel ordre international?*, Brussels, P.I.E. Peter Lang, 2004, p. 47-59.

28 M.A. Pollack, "Unilateral America, multilateral Europe?," *op. cit.*

29 See e.g. http://www.consilium.europa.eu/cms3_fo/showPage.asp?id=278&lang=fr&mode=g. For a first assessment: Nowak, A. e.a., *Civilian Crisis Management: the EU Way*, Chaillot Paper 90, Paris, Institute of Security Studies, European Union, June 2006.

refer to a neo-Kantian definition of Europe[30] – sharing and contesting paradoxically Robert Kagan's caricatural definition of the EU as a postmodern paradise[31] –, but refer more significantly to the conclusions of the Commission on Human Security and to the European Security Strategy at the same time[32]. Their rationale for supporting Human Security is justified by moral and legal dimensions, but also by an "enlightened self-interest case"[33].

Their definition of a European approach to Human Security refers to five main features: multilateralism, primacy of individuals, bottom-up approach[34], regional conflict analysis, and "appropriate methods" (not defined as "just war theory" but as Adam Roberts' views on "justifiable use of force"). Interestingly, this definition goes beyond the Japanese concept and looks closer to the Canadian approach to Human Security defined as "freedom from fear." Instead of converging with the Japanese concept, an EU approach would rather be closer to the Canadian one and contribute to "militarise" development rather than to "civilianise" security.

By putting forward a synthesis between all the previous approaches to Human Security, a combination of military and civilian capabilities together with a discourse very similar to Javier Solana's ambivalent emphasis on the holistic definition of security, the Barcelona report and its promoters might contribute to the widest catch-all security concept ever produced. Nothing proves this would increase security for anybody[35], but it would certainly help the EU to define its international profile and bridge gaps between Canadian and Japanese foreign and security policies.

---

30 M. Glasius, M. Kaldor, M. (eds.), *A Human Security Doctrine for Europe. Project, principles, practicalities*, London, Routledge, 2006, p. 3-4.

31 R. Kagan, *Of Paradise and Power: America and Europe in the New World Order*, New York, Knopf, 2003.

32 M. Glasius, M. Kaldor (eds.), *A Human Security Doctrine for Europe…*, *op. cit.*, p. 5-7.

33 *Ibid.*, p. 10.

34 Despite the creation of a "Grant Assistance for Grassroots Human Security Projects," NGOs have almost never been associated to Japanese policy formulation about Human Security (Bosold, D., Werthes, S., "Human Security in Practice: …," *op.cit.*, p. 98.

35 For critical approaches to Human Security, see Buzan, B., "A Reductionist, Idealistic Notion that Adds Little Analytical Value," *Security Dialogue* 35(3), p. 369-370; B. Saul, "The Dangers of the United Nations' 'New Security Agenda': 'Human Security' in the Asia-Pacific Region," *Asian Journal of Comparative Law* &(1), 2006.

East Asia in Search for a Region

Redefining Japan's Engagement

Tsutomu KIKUCHI

1. Introduction

For many decades, Asians have been searching for a region where they would identify themselves. In the 1960s, some Asians considered "Southeast Asia" as their collectively identifiable region, which led to cooperative efforts within the ASEAN. In the 1980s and the 1990s, almost all the Asians viewed "the Asia-Pacific" as a region where they could identify themselves, and they decided to create the APEC and the ARF. Now, Asians are looking for another definition of a region: East Asia. They have been eager to promote regional cooperation under the framework of the ASEAN+3 (APT). Indeed, in the aftermath of the Asian financial crisis, the ASEAN+3 was consolidated and institutionalised, although the APT process started as a modest undertaking. The first East Asia Summit (EAS) was held in December 2005. Have Asians finally managed to agree on the choice of their own region? How should Japan react to the need for searching a region and the community-building in Asia? These are questions to be answered in this article.

Japan, as a global nation, has huge stakes in the consolidation of global governance institutions such as UN, GATT/WTO and NPT/IAEA. To respond to transnational and global issues such as economic globalisation, spread of the WMD, and international terrorism, it is extremely important for Japan to enhance global governance institutions. Japan's bid to a permanent membership at the UN Security Council and the amendment of the Japanese Constitution – which is put on the political agenda – must be understood in this context.

At the same time, "regions" or regionalisms are increasingly getting salient concepts for managing politico-security and economic affairs in today's world. We are getting into an era of "A World of Regions."[1]

---

1 Peter J. Katzenstein, *A World of Regions*, Ithaca, Cornell University Press, 2005.

East Asia is becoming a more significant region for Japan's peace and prosperity.

An increasingly flourishing trade linked with FDI and foreign production is more closely integrating Japanese economy with East Asia. Japanese multinational firms have shifted from export to international production and reorganised their business activities. Their production networks spread over a large number of countries and involve intra-firm trade. Japanese firms are a critical part of the region-wide production networks in East Asia. This trend has created strong Japanese interests in liberalisation, guarantees for Japanese investment, and region-wide institution-building in East Asia to manage those economic relations.

Japanese firms have already established region-wide production and distribution networks in East Asia since the mid-1980s (one with Southeast Asia, and the other one with China). The pressing task of Japan consists in making two production networks closer, thereby setting up "seamless" networks of production and distribution in East Asia. The Japanese government and business community are expecting that a "seamless production and distribution networks in East Asia will greatly enhance international competitiveness of Japanese firms in a global market[2]. By using this privileged position Japan could become a 21st economic phoenix.

Politico-security issues are also getting more salient in East Asia. We have a series of insecurities ranging from traditional security issues – such as the balance of powers among the major powers, the tension across the Taiwan Strait and the conflicts in the Korean Peninsula – to non-traditional ones – such as international terrorism, the spread of weapons of mass destruction, transnational crimes, and maritime security. We need for collective endeavours to address these issues at regional level.

There are deep-seated senses of insecurity in most of the countries of the region. Geopolitical and geoeconomic transformation of the region worsens this sense. China is oscillating between the conflicting images of itself: a rising power that has been overcoming the history of humiliation and a developing country with huge internal imbalances and weaknesses. China has many kinds of vulnerabilities internally and externally. On the one hand, the economic development gives self-confidence. On the other hand, China knows how vulnerable its political, economic and social foundations for sustaining the growth are. An

---

2 See, the *Annual White Papers* published by the Japanese Ministry of Economy, Trade and Industry (METI) for the last few years.

overestimated image of China as the next superpower overtaking the USA is rising a lot of concerns among the neighbours.

ASEAN countries are facing the challenges of transforming their domestic politics. ASEAN is searching for a new role and identity in a broader East Asia in the face of growing complexities in major powers relationships and the difficult task of integrating ten members within the organisation. In spite of its huge economic power, the economic recession over a decade deprived Japan from self-confidence. Japan is struggling to sustain its status of economic superpower and regain its economic influence. Japan is also struggling to find the way to define new relationships with the neighbouring countries, especially with China in which the mantra of "Japan-China friendship" does not work any more. A great transformation of Eastern Asia sets great challenges and offers opportunities to Japan by requiring this latter to define its relationships with the neighbours and face a challenge in building up a regional community in Asia.

The article is divided as follows. The second part will ask whether any structural change has taken place in the 1990s with the purpose of establishing an "East Asian" cooperation. We can assume that a fundamental structural change occurred in politico-security and economic areas. Surprisingly, however, there were not fundamental structural changes. If so, why has the "East Asian" cooperation been getting so popular? The motives of East Asian regional cooperation will be analyzed in the third part. The fourth part touches upon the complicated strategies adopted by regional countries to respond to a strategic uncertainty, in spite of the calls for East Asia community-building. The fifth part discusses various challenges that must be faced to make an East Asian regional community successful. The last part will attempt to draw a conclusion.

2. Any Structural Changes in the Asia-Pacific? – From "Asia-Pacific" to "East Asia"

When the Asia-Pacific-wide regional institutions such as APEC and ARF were established, it was commonly understood that "the Asia-Pacific" was the most appropriate definition of a region for Asia. The United States provided Asian economies with a market, capital and technology. The US pronounced military presence, underlined by a web of alliance networks centred in Washington, has contributed to maintaining a regional peace and stability, by reducing political and military tensions within the rivalries in East Asia. Thus, the "East Asian region" has only been able to deserve the definition of a self-sustainable area when combined with the USA.

Has the situation fundamentally changed over the last decade? In terms of security, despite some tension between the USA and South Korea over the relocation of the US bases in South Korea and the role of the US forces stationing there, the USA-Japan and USA-Australia alliances got improved. Military relations between the USA and South-east Asian nations have also widened and got enhanced[3].

Economically speaking, the trade between China and the rest of Asia tremendously increased. China has been attracting huge investment from Asia as well as from other parts of the world. All these developments have been generating a newly born image of East Asia as a self-sufficient and self-sustained economy.

Concerning China's dramatic increase in trade, the CEPII (Paris) has been recently publishing interesting research papers that were based upon the detailed analysis of intra-regional trade in East Asia. The findings of CEPII's research revealed the real picture of China's trade that could not be understood through ordinary trade statistics.

According to the research carried out by CEPII, China's trade growth is attributed to China's integration into the East Asia-wide regional production and distribution networks created through an extensive foreign direct investment by foreign (not Chinese) firms. In the meantime, China's contribution in terms of added value has been limited to its role in the assembly sector. Indeed, China is importing a huge amount of expensive parts and intermediary goods from other countries such as Japan and NIES, and then just assembling them into final products for export mostly to the developed countries.

China's huge trade surplus with the USA and trade deficit with the rest of Asia only reflects its triangular trade relationships[4]. China's huge trade surplus *vis-à-vis* the USA is offset by China's huge trade deficit – in components and pieces – with other Asian economies. It can be fairly pointed out that the massive US trade deficit is held against East Asia as a whole, which has grown into an East Asia-wide giant factory with economies intertwined through extensive, region-wide production and distribution networks run by foreign firms. Thus, the situation where

3 See the US relations with the Philippines, Indonesia, Singapore, Thailand and Vietnam. In addition, the relations between the US and India have been tremendously enhanced in both security and economic areas.

4 "China in the International segmentation of Production Processes," *CEPRII Working Paper, No.2003-02, 2002.* See also Hiroya Tanikawa, "The Pitfalls of the Ideas of East Asian economic integration," RIETI (Research Institute of Economy Trade and Industry, Japan), *Column 0132*, June 2004.

East Asian economies were heavily depending upon the US market, has not changed despite the noticeable economic growth of China[5].

3. Background of "East Asian" Cooperation: Globalisation, American Hegemony and Asia

The above analysis implies that the changes have not derived from the relationships between East Asia and the USA. If so, why have the calls for "East Asian" cooperation been aired recently? There are several factors which promote the East Asian cooperation.

A. Globalisation and Regional "Self-Help" Mechanisms

The Asian financial crisis has clearly revealed both the vulnerability of the region as a whole to a financial globalisation and the regional incapacity to react to sudden shortages of liquidity. The Asian countries realised the inadequacy of contingency plans available for those countries when they have faced major economic crisis: and more especially the absence of lenders of last resort facility in case of liquidity crisis. Furthermore, those countries that underwent IMF conditionalities experienced the harsh reality of stabilisation and economic reforms under its conditions. The IMF bailout package has failed to halt a regional economic confusion. This event has pushed countries to recognise collectively the significance of building up regional (East Asian) self-help mechanisms[6].

B. Economic Globalisation and Competitiveness

There have been strong desires to enhance the economic competitiveness behind the motives of regional cooperation in East Asia. For Japan, as a matter of example, East Asian cooperation is expected to enhance the international economic competitiveness of Japanese firms. Until the late 1990s, Japan had been very reluctant to enter into regional preferential trading arrangements due to their potential negative impacts on the global liberal trading system under which Japan has successfully developed its economy. However, the economic difficulties in the 1990s changed this long-winded policy preference. Japan began to think about the way it could use regional preferential economic arrangements to enhance its global competitiveness.

---

5 See also, Edward J. Lincoln, *East Asian Economic Regionalism*, Washington, The Brookings Institution, 2004.

6 The "Chiang-Mai Initiative" for regional currency swap and the development of Asian bond market are the products of this common understanding.

For many of the ASEAN countries, regional arrangement has been one of the useful instruments for overcoming economic marginalisation[7]. Economic marginalisation represents a greater threat than the sense of security marginalisation does. The ASEAN countries have to compete with newly emerging states, especially China and India, over the foreign direct investment that has promoted the economic development of the region for the last decades. Regional cooperation in East Asia is an effective path for securing access to foreign markets, capital, investment and technology[8].

Furthermore, some governments in East Asia that try to introduce economic reform measures and face domestic opposition, enter into a regional arrangement in order to consolidate by these reforms. Regional cooperation can increase the credibility of commitments to reforms via signalling, which is crucial to attract foreign investment from outside.

C. USA Hegemony, Unilateralism and Intervention

The attitudes of East Asian countries to a unipolar world led by the USA are ambivalent. On the one hand, it is understood that the ongoing engagement and commitment of the USA to Asian affairs is essential for peace and prosperity of the region. In the face of a growing Chinese power, many countries of East Asia desperately need the US military presence in the region to hedge the risks put by China.

On the other hand, they are concerned about the US unilateralism and "hegemonic" behaviours such as the US intervention in internal affairs on the behalf of human rights protection, of the promotion of democracy and good governance together with the fight against terrorism. In that respect, East Asian regionalism constitutes an additional policy instrument to put some collective constraints on the US unilateral actions.

D. Increased Intra-East Asian Economic Connectedness

Intra-East Asian economic connectedness has endlessly increased in both trade and foreign direct investment. China is a key player in this development. Although the sharp increase in trade with China nearly

---

7 Louise Fawcett, "Regionalism in Historical Perspective," in L. Fawcett and Andrew Hurrell (eds.), *Regionalism in World Politics*, Oxford, Oxford University Press, 1995, p. 22.

8 Solingen points out; cooperative arrangements erode risk considerations and enable foreign investment, avoid potential sanctions and penalties from international private and public sectors. Etel Solingen, *Regional Order at Century's Dawn*, Princeton, Princeton University Press, 1998.

results from China's integration into the East Asia-wide regional production and distribution networks by foreign firms, and that the USA and Europe still are the main destinations of China's finished products, the expectations of Asian economies to increase further exports to China are supporting the East Asian cooperation.

4. Responding to Uncertainty: Engaging, Risk-Hedging and Soft-Balancing

Geopolitical and geoeconomic considerations – which prevail among countries in East Asia – complicate the processes of creation of a regional community. East Asia is now experiencing a great transition. The distribution of power among countries is unstable. Rapid military modernisation is underway. Most of the states in the region have territorial and/or historical conflicts with their neighbours. The relationships among the major powers lack some stability. Serious security dilemmas exist among them. Several East Asian countries are facing the challenge of transforming their authoritarian political regimes into democratic ones. Democratic transformation is often linked with domestic instabilities. Terrorism makes internal instabilities worse. Furthermore, people are not fully prepared yet to adjust themselves to the internal and external changes. Rapidly changing conditions are making people worried about their future and such concerns feed nationalism. We have already seen the disaster caused by the convergence of nationalism with populism[9].

The future of Asian economy is also uncertain. The regional economic structure has been becoming more competitive. China, ASEAN and India are competing against each other by getting foreign direct investment and searching for new markets. Japan is facing – for the first time in the modern times – a serious economic competition with other Asian nations. The way the USA is redressing the huge economic imbalance across the Pacific – whose impact will be strong on Asian economies – is unknown.

Furthermore, the future of Chinese economy is uncertain[10]. Can China sustain its growth as it did so in the past? First, as I pointed out above, the noticeable growth of the Chinese and East Asian economies

9 Peter Hays Gries, *China's New Nationalism*, Berkeley, University of California Press, 2005.

10 On the argument that massive flow of FDI that fuelled China's growth reflects China's economic weakness rather than strength, see Yasheng Huang, *Selling China: Foreign Direct Investment During the Reform Era*, Cambridge, Cambridge University Press, 2003.

(led by China) has been supported by the huge trade deficit of China with the USA. The length of sustainability of the current situation depends upon the sustainability of the huge US current account deficit. Given an increased interconnection between China and the rest of the Asian economies, the USA's current account adjustment will have a huge negative impact not only on China but also on East Asia as a whole. Secondly, there are severe concerns that stem from the distorted composition of China's aggregate demand, in which consumption only represents 40% and investment accounts for nearly the same percentage, while the total export and import values are equal to approximately 60% of GDP. Apparently this is not sustainable[11]. Thirdly, the sustainability of market mechanism under the authoritarian one-party system is also uncertain. One leading scholar on Chinese economy in Japan is now warning China that without democratisation, it may lose not only its future economic growth but also the economic assets that it has accumulated over the last decades[12]. The Chinese economy could turn out to be a mirage rather than a miracle.

All that raises a feeling of insecurity and uncertainty among political leaders and people. By echoing these feelings, East Asian countries have been simultaneously adopting a diversity of strategies to protect their own interests; those strategies range from "engagement" to "risk-hedging" and "soft-balancing," especially towards the major powers[13].

Bilateralism is another characteristic of state strategies adopted by most of the countries in the region. It has been argued for many years that East Asia has developed a regional mutually complementary economic structure. The so-called theory of "flying geese pattern of regional economic development" was advocated by many economists. However, the regional economic structure is getting more competitive.

In order to respond to an ever-hardening economic competition, many countries in the region have been actively engaged in bilateral dealings such as the conclusion of Free Trade Agreements (FTAs) with each other and with extra-regional countries. Singapore is a true example that has been eager to conclude bilateral FTAs with both intra- and

---

11 See Tanikawa's article, *op. cit.*

12 See C.H. Kwan's recent book: "Chugoku Keizai Kakumei Saisyuusyo (The Final Chapter of Chinese Economic Revolution), Tokyo, *Nihon Keizai Shinbun* (Japan Economic Journal), 2005. Dr. Kwan is chief economist at the Nomura Research Institute in Tokyo.

13 On the theory of "soft-balancing" in realist theory, see the following. T.V. Paul, James J. Wirtz and Michael Fortmann (eds.), *Balance of Powers: Theory and Practices in the 21st Century*, Stanford, Stanford University Press, 2005.

extra regional economies[14]. With the economic downturn and political instabilities of Southeast Asian nations, Singapore has desperately wanted to be distinguished from the other Southeast Asians which are running on the same boat. Singapore's FTA strategy to conclude FTAs with non-ASEAN countries evidences its willingness to "separate" itself from the rest of Southeast Asia viewed by international investors as an unstable region politically, economically and socially speaking.

FTA has both economic and security/strategic implications. For example, the conclusion of FTAs with various countries could help to anchor the presence of these countries in the region. In fact, Singapore is strongly willing to maintain the USA military, political and economic presence in the Pacific. The USA presence would help Singapore to balance the regional power politics for its own security[15].

Other Asian economies have followed Singapore's FTA initiative. Japan concluded the FTA with Singapore and Mexico; now the negotiations with the relevant countries including Thailand, Malaysia and the Philippines have almost come to an end. China has also been eager to conclude bilateral FTA with the ASEAN as a whole. At the same time, several ASEAN countries have started bilateral FTA negotiations with China. Korea has concluded its first FTA with Chile and ASEAN; it is looking now for other opportunities.

The emergence of a complex web of bilateral FTAs in East Asia will make the creation of a regional community extremely difficult. Certainly, some argue that various bilateral agreements will contribute to the consolidation of a single East Asian FTA. The ultimate goals of Japan-ASEAN and China-ASEAN FTAs are the achievement of an East Asia-wide FTAs/Economic Partnership agreements. Both are viewed as the springboard to the creation of a broader FTA covering East Asia, although the geographical scope of East Asia still has to be defined. But, these arguments are fully based upon wishful thinking. Each bilateral FTA is tailor-made (difference in scope, agenda etc.), making it all the more difficult (probably impossible) to amalgamate into a single region-wide agreement at a later stage[16]. The huge difficulties facing Latin American countries in amalgamation demonstrate this. Thus, a

14 Teofilo C. Daquila and Le Huu Huy, "Singapore and ASEAN in the Global Economy," *Asian Survey*, Vol.43, No.6, 2003, p. 908-928.

15 Teofilo C. Daquila and Le Huu Huy, *ibid.*

16 Hadi Soesastro, "Indonesia and FTAs in East Asia," *Japan Spotlight*, 17 March 2004.

further institutional fragmentation is currently being observed in East Asia[17].

A. China

China quickly responded to the emerging unipolar world led by the USA following the Cold War. China tried to make the world more multipolar where the USA's exercise of its power would be constrained by other major powers. However, China's strategy has not produced a tangible effect. Thus, for fear of the US intervention in its internal and external policies, China has tried to create various institutions with the neighbouring countries that would strengthen China's bargaining positions *vis-à-vis* the USA.

China concluded a "strategic partnership" with Russia, took the initiative in establishing the Shanghai Cooperation Organisation (SCO), and normalised the relations with India and Vietnam. China has been strengthening its relationship with its southern neighbours: ASEAN. There have been some pronounced changes in China's approach to Southeast Asia over the past decades. China signed TAC (Treaty of Amity and Cooperation), the Declaration on the Conduct of Parties in the South China Sea, pledging self-restraint. China announced its intention to sign the Protocol to the Treaty of the Southeast Asia Nuclear Weapon-Free Zone (SEANFZ). It is viewed as a confirmation of China's new and cooperative approach to the members of ASEAN. The ASEAN's approach that stresses on consensus-decision, informality, inclusiveness, and voluntarism, has been quite advantageous to China because it has prevented China from being faced with collective pressure from ASEAN as a whole. For example, ARF process led by ASEAN has contributed to prevent China from being confronted with sensitive issues such as Taiwan and the question of territorial conflict in the South China Sea[18].

China's "new" view on Japan that advocated the policy of upgrading its relationship with Japan in terms of strategic aims might be another manifestation of China's eagerness to enhance the relationships with the neighbours to face the US hegemony[19]. The Six-Party Talks that took place so as to resolve the North Korean nuclear crisis is also expected to

17 Hadi Soesastro, *Building an East Asian Community through Trade and Investment Integration*, CSIS Working Paper WPE067, Jakarta, April 2003, p. 10.

18 Kuik Cheng-Ghwee, "Multilateralism in China's ASEAN Policy: Its Evolution, Characteristics, and Aspiration," *Contemporary Southeast Asia*, 27, No.1, 2005, p. 102-22.

19 On the debates over China's new thinking on Japan, see Peter Hays Gries, "China's 'New Thinking on Japan'," *The China Quarterly*, 184, 2005, p. 831-850.

serve as an additional regional multilateralism to constrain US unilateral actions[20].

China has skilfully used the anxieties and concerns shared by the Asian countries towards the US unilateral "hegemonic" behaviours. Of course, given historically deep-seated concerns about China and the expectation – shared by the neighbouring countries – that the USA would play a constructive role in the region, it is almost impossible for China to invite the neighbouring countries into the "anti-American" joint front. Moreover, it is not in China's interest to "be in conflict" with the USA, because smooth relations with the USA are vital for China's economic development and consolidation of the CCP political power. However, China has been cleverly setting up institutions with its neighbours to balance softly the US global hegemony.

The USA's preoccupation with Iraq and the war against global terrorism, which prevents the USA from paying enough attention to other challenges faced by Asian countries, have given China an opportunity to expand its role in Southeast Asia[21]. Apparently, China's regional diplomacy is not carried out at the expense of the USA and/or Japan. But, by enlarging its political and economic influence in the region through multilateral institutions, China will make more difficult the US task of enlisting regional support against China in the future. Also, by virtue of its membership and cooperation in the regional forums, it would have ensured itself a seat in the conduct of regional affairs. In the long-run, China may have the larger ambition of forging and leading an East Asia community. China's enhanced relations with ASEAN will serve as a foundation stone of a broader regional community.

B. ASEAN

ASEAN countries have also adopted complex strategies of engagement, risk-hedging and soft-balancing against the major powers[22].

---

20 Tsutomu Kikuchi, "Institutional Linkages and Security Order in Northeast Asia," a paper presented at the United Nations University=Aoyama-Gakuin University Workshop on "Institutionalizing Northeast Asia: Making the Impossible Possible," held from 20-22 September 2005 at the UNU Headquarter in Tokyo.

21 China's approach to the neighbouring countries was to share the basic principles of organising the world and regional affairs, together with providing economic benefits. Trough the conclusion of various joint declarations and statements, China confirmed with the neighbouring countries the fundamental principles organising world affairs such as respect for sovereign equality, non-intervention in internal affairs, different courses of nation-building, the supreme role of the United Nations in global peace and security so forth.

22 Yuen Foong Khong, "Coping with Strategic Uncertainty: The Role of Institutions and Soft Balancing in Southeast Asia's Post Cold War Strategy," Allen Carlson,

Many countries are engaging China and the USA economically to generate profits. Indeed, they are enhancing economic relations with both China and the USA through such means as the conclusion of the FTAs and investment agreements. In the meantime, they are diversifying their respective economic relations to avoid an undue economic dependence and to hedge the risks of economic uncertainty. This is clearly shown in the recent conclusion of the bilateral FTA with both intra and extra East Asian partners. ASEAN has accepted the offer of concluding FTA with China, but at the same time, ASEAN started the negotiations with other countries such as Japan, Australia and India.

They are concluding agreements with China in the field of security. But, meanwhile, they are improving their respective security relations with the USA to hedge the security risks likely to be caused by the "rise of China." They are entering into agreements with the USA in Asia in the political and military fields. Malaysia and Singapore provide military facilities and access to the US Navy and air forces and are also committed to practicing bilateral and multilateral joint military exercises with the USA.

At the same time, they are deeply concerned about the US unilateralism and the USA's "interference" in their internal affairs on the behalf of promoting freedom, democracy, human rights and good governance. Therefore, they are enhancing their relations with their neighbours to protect themselves against the US unilateral behaviour. For some ASEAN members, East Asian cooperation is viewed as an instrument to protect themselves from the US "hegemonic" behaviour[23].

C. The United States

The United States has also been engaging China in international and regional societies, which were demonstrated in the USA's efforts over the last decades to encourage China to become a member of the international and regional institutions such as GATT/WTO, NPT, APEC and

---

Peter Katzenstein, and J.J. Suh (eds.), *Rethinking Security in East Asia: Identity, Power, and Efficiency*, Stanford, Stanford University Press, 2004; Evelyn Goh, "Great Powers and Southeast Asian Regional Security Strategies: Omni-Enmeshment, Balancing and Hierarchical Order," *Working Paper No.84*, July 2005, Singapore, Institute of Defence and Strategic Studies.

23 Singapore is the most typical case of taking complex diplomatic strategies. On the one hand, it is seeking to enhance economic relations with China. However, Singapore also concluded the bilateral FTA with the US, Japan, Australia, India, EFTA etc to diversify their economic relations. In security, Singapore has military contacts with China, but at the same time, enhanced its security relations with other countries including the US, Japan and Australia.

ARF. Now the economic relationships between the USA and China have been dramatically expanding. Today, the Bush administration compels China to be a "responsible stakeholder" in international systems; it forces China to take more responsibility for maintaining the international system, going beyond its membership to the international society[24]. Meanwhile, the USA seems to be worried about the increase in Chinese influence in Asia that may reduce the influence and power of the United States. So, the USA has been expanding its economic and security relationships with various countries in Asia. The United States has been improving its alliance with Japan and Australia and widening security cooperation with some of the ASEAN countries through joint exercises, military training program, supply of military hardware and access arrangements for the US armed forces. In the economic field, the USA carries on concluding FTAs with some of the Southeast Asian countries under the Enterprise of ASEAN Initiatives. The negotiation of a FTA with South Korea has already started.

D. Japan

Japan has been actively setting agreements with China in international and regional societies At the same time, Japan has been hedging risks caused by the uncertainty of China's future, given such facts as Chinese military modernisation, possible domestic instabilities and "assertiveness" in Chinese foreign policies towards Japan. China still attracts huge Japanese investments, but, Japanese companies are now looking for other appropriate places for investment in other regions. "Risk-hedging" is a key element for Japanese business.

The most pronounced change in the relations with China is the adoption by Tokyo of a more assertive stance towards Beijing, by dropping the long-winded policy which aimed at avoiding an open confrontation with China under the banner of "Japan-China friendship." Both Japan and China have not realised yet that two powers coexist in East Asia. Historically speaking it was not the case because Japan suspected China to erode its power and influence.

However, Japan does not view the "rise" of China as a threat but as an opportunity and a challenge to face. Economically speaking, China is not threatening Japan but gives Japan plenty of opportunities. China is not an economic competitor for Japan in the foreseeable future. The argument that Japan is concerned about and even jealous of China's economic growth is fundamentally flawed, because it does not take into

---

24 See Robert Zoellick' speech "Wither China: Membership or Responsibility?," at the US-China Commission on 21 September 2005.

account the fundamental changes in the economic relations throughout East Asia over the last decades.

As mentioned above, Japan urgently have to make two production networks – one with Southeast Asia, the other with China – closer, thereby creating "seamless" networks of production and distribution in East Asia. In this respect, contrary to the general view, the government and business community of Japan are mostly happy with the recent venture between China and ASEAN to conclude a FTA. Japan will be indeed the largest beneficiary of the FTA between China and ASEAN. Rather, Japan is concerned about the potential failure of China and ASEAN in concluding a deeper FTA with a substantial opening of the respective economies.

Today goods "made in China" are actually made by assembling parts and intermediate goods made elsewhere through the cross-border networks for production led by multinational companies including Japanese ones. "Made in China" should be properly called "assembled in China." Japanese and other multinational companies are largely "invisible" behind the "Chinese" factories and produce a large amount of tradable goods. About 60% of China's exports are controlled by foreign companies. They are reaping the bulk of profits resulting from exports from China[25].

With the emergence of an ageing society, Japan must generate profit overseas by using efficiently the accumulated assets. Japan desperately needs for fruitful overseas markets for investment from which it would get profit[26]. China's growth provides Japan with excellent opportunities for investment. Furthermore, without a painful domestic restructuration, Japan could relocate industries that have lost international competitiveness to China and restructure the Japanese economic structure, thereby enhancing further the Japanese economic competitiveness. There is not any reason why Japan should be worried about China's development. Japan is rather concerned about the domestic instability and economic confusion in China which is caused by social unrest and the lack of economic governance.

At the same time, Japan does not take for granted the peacefulness of China's rise. China is a young nation-state with a disparate desire to regain some leadership in the world. China remains a potential destabi-

---

25 David Barboza, "Some Assembly Needed: China as Asian Factory," *The New York Times*, 9 February 2006.

26 Japanese income profit transferred from oversea to Japan is approximately equal to trade surplus. Japan is becoming a matured economy where gains from overseas investment are crucial for economic prosperity.

lising factor until it becomes a mature nation-state, which will develop political institutions and culture to solve disputes peacefully and pave the way to pluralistic political values. China may make a strategic choice in its attempt to contain the American influence by keeping the USA out of the region and driving a wedge between the USA and Japan. Thus, Japan has been hedging "China risks" by strengthening its alliance with the United States.

5. Major Challenges towards an Enhanced Cooperation in East Asia

There are many ideas and concrete joint actions among East Asia countries to promote East Asian cooperation. In the next years, East Asian countries will expand further its areas of cooperation. In fact, the ASEAN+3 has been widening its cooperative activities in many areas such as currency, bond market, investment, energy, food, non-traditional security (terrorism, piracy, drug-trafficking, human-trafficking, disease) and so forth.

But, the pending question is the "quality of cooperation": it is asked whether East Asian cooperation will develop more effective regional mechanisms to tackle the pressing issues faced by the region. Institutionalising and organising regional cooperation do matter. Increasing interactions among East Asians will not necessarily contribute to the creation of an East Asian Community. In this respect, it is still uncertain whether the ASEAN's norms of non-interference, informality and consensus that have generally been accepted in the region as normative premises for managing regional institutions can produce tangible results, which overcome the major barriers to community-building in East Asia.

There are many serious challenges to face for achieving a Eastern Asian regional institution so as to develop it into a more efficient and useful regional mechanism.

A. Competing Norms/Principles Organising International Relations in Asia

There are fundamental differences among East Asia countries in their way to establish international relations. To put it in a nutshell, there are four distinct concepts on which are based the organisation of international relations in the region.

Organising Norms/Principles of International Relations

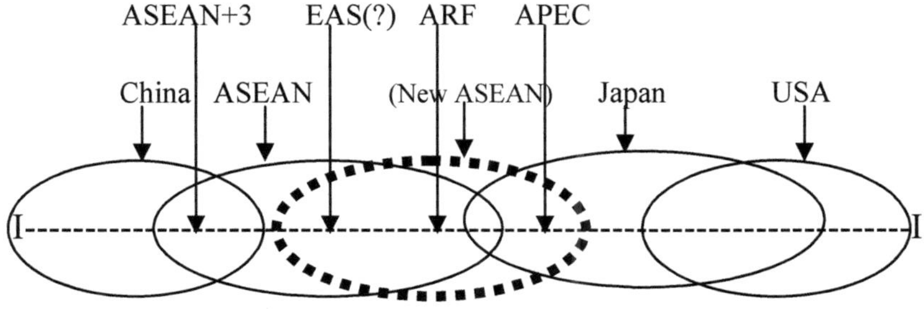

"External" Norms/Principles	**"Internal" Norms/Principles**
Sovereignty,	Democracy, Human Right,
Non-Intervention in internal affairs	Harmonisation of domestic institutions
Different nation-building processes	Good Governance
State Security	Human Security
Border Measures (tariff etc.)	

The first one is the "ASEAN way." The most pronounced feature of the traditional "ASEAN Way" is its emphasis on state sovereignty and the principle of non-interference in internal affairs. The strict interpretation of these norms and principle regulating the relationship among the members has certainly worked well in stabilising the state-to-state relationships.

The second one is the Chinese way. The "New Security Concept" and the concept of "Peaceful Rise/ Development" were recently added to the Five Principles of Peaceful Co-Existence[27]. Although these concepts stress on various new concepts such as mutual trust, mutual benefit, dialogue, confidence-building and cooperation, they are basically Westphalian ones.

China's norms and principles are mostly related to "external" dimensions that define inter-state relations. As for "internal" matters, China firmly sticks to the traditional concepts of national sovereignty and non-interference principles. In fact, if we examine closely the Chinese concepts such as "Peaceful Development" and "New Security Concept," we find that there is nothing about collective engagement in "internal" matters. China's new concepts are only applied in inter-state (not intra-

27 Speech by Zheng Bijian, *China's New Road of Peaceful Rise and China-US Relations*, 16 June 2005, Washington, The Brookings Institution. See also *China's Peaceful Development Road*, Information Office, China's State Council, 22 December 2005.

state) affairs. Indeed, China's recent approach to the neighbouring countries was to share these basic norms and principles. Through joint declarations and statements with these countries, China tried to confirm with them these Westphalian principles. In cooperation with ASEAN, China has tried to avoid such sensitive issues such as Taiwan case, human rights, political liberalisation, military transparency, deeper integration issues touching upon domestic institutional adjustment.

The third one is the American way which emphasises "internal" norms and principles together with the harmonisation of domestic institutions under liberal doctrines. As the US president Bush has clearly shown in his speeches at his second inauguration and also in Kyoto (Japan) in November 2005, democracy, freedom, human rights and good governance are the key principles that should underline international relations in the region[28].

According to the USA's views, the setting up of a regional cooperative framework does not only require an economic liberalisation but a political one as well. A new regional cooperation is no longer defined as a mere mutual liberalisation of trade but as a harmonisation and possibly a coordination of economic policies and domestic institutions. An enhanced confidence-building among countries requires common democratic and transparent domestic institutions at regional scale.

Japan's stance represents the fourth way. We may call this a "hybrid" kind of concept. On the one hand, Japan has been supporting ASEAN's way. On the other hand, Japan is pursuing more intrusive and binding regional arrangements that could touch upon internal matters such as democracy, human rights, transparency and harmonisation of internal regulatory systems. It is in the interest of Japan that East Asian countries share some basic understanding on norms regulating domestic affairs. It is in this context that Japan has been pushing India, Australia and New Zealand into joining the East Asia Summit processes. The participation of those three countries is expected to facilitate the negotiation of more intrusive arrangements in the region.

Nowadays, East Asia needs stronger and more intrusive regional institutions that touch upon domestic affairs so as to tackle the pressing political, security, economic and social issues faced by the region. Political openness and liberalisation are decisive to increase transparency on the respective internal affairs. The lack of transparency causes misunderstanding and mutual suspicion, while aggravating further the security dilemma. The complexity of modern economies requires a well

---

28 "President Bush Discusses Freedom and Democracy in Kyoto, Japan, 16 November 2005," http://www.whitehouse.gov/news/releases/2005/11/20051116-6html#.

detailed set of common laws and regulations for global market relations to work. The focus has shifted from border measures to the harmonisation of domestic institutions and business rules. For example, we need to develop some common procedures to regulate bilateral FTAs. This must include deeper integration issues that could make the domestic institutional arrangements compatible with each other.

Achieving common rules of conduct and entering into reciprocal commitments and obligations need some degree of "like-mindedness" among the states concerned. Social organisations and values commonly shared, together with the convergence of political and security interests make it easier altogether to accept necessary levels of intrusive management.

Japan is mostly concerned about an East Asian cooperation which would be organised under converged principles and norms resulting from China's way and the old-fashioned ASEAN way; it means that this cooperation would mostly deal with the "external" dimension of state-to-state relations and leave internal matters out of the agenda of regional cooperation.

B. ASEAN+X: Making of ASEAN-Centred Institutions

Fearing that Southeast Asia becomes a strategic buffer zone, or a bone of contention between the big powers, ASEAN has tried to give itself a steering role in East Asian community building[29]. Competition among the major powers has allowed the ASEAN to grip the opportunity to draw Tokyo, Beijing, New Delhi and Canberra into a bidding competition over the hearts and minds of ASEAN. ASEAN is coming back to the central stage of regional institution building in East Asia.

Active approaches adopted by the major powers to establish more comprehensive partnerships with ASEAN have led to the construction of ASEAN-centred institutional arrangements. ASEAN+X institutional arrangements were established. We have now ASEAN+3 (Japan, China and South Korea), ASEAN+2 (Australia, New Zealand), ASEAN+1 (India and Russia respectively). The East Asia Summit is viewed as a part of the ASEAN-centred institutional arrangement[30].

Based upon the "ASEAN+X" institutional framework, ASEAN has been "transplanting" their basic principles and norms ("ASEAN ways") to East Asia as a whole. This has been shown in the recent ASEAN's

---

[29] Michael Vatikiotis, "Three cheers for East Asian Summit: A Bullish view of Asian regionalism", *The Jakarta Post*, 20 December 2005.

[30] The East Asia Summit was originally designed as a forum where East Asian countries participate on an equal footing, not an ASEAN centred one.

endeavours of inviting non-ASEA countries to sign the TAC. The signature of TAC is considered as a prerequisite to join the East Asia Summit[31].

ASEAN's ambition to play the leading role for creating an East Asian community would not be fulfilled without being accompanied by the modification of the existing premises underlying the ASEAN cooperation. Even if it implies hardships and difficulties, a renovated ASEAN is eligible for leading the East Asian cooperation. In this regard, it is worth noting that the ASEAN countries are modifying, to some extent, the long-winded normative premises of cooperation under the recognition that they are not conductive to face transnational security threats and the problems generated by economic globalisation. The "Myanmar problem" puts additional stimulus to this process. The ASEAN countries are now considering that democratic governance, civil society, human security and human rights should be legally binding in common guiding principles among the members. The ASEAN Charter which is currently under consideration will be the first test to know whether ASEAN could succeed in modifying the normative premises[32].

Indeed, East Asia needs a more intrusive regional framework of cooperation in dealing with the security, political, economic and social challenges facing the region. In order to realise this, East Asia does require a deeper international harmonisation among the members based upon a detailed set of commonly accepted values, laws and regulations. This is clearly illustrated by the extensive legal frameworks drawn up for regional markets such as the negotiation of the Single European Market and NAFTA. At the WTO and OECD, the focus of their activities has shifted to the harmonisation of domestic competition and business rules.

This is not easy for East Asia at all. Firstly, states are not firmly established. Most of the countries in East Asia are clearly at the modernist stage of development, which is still defined by strong government control over society and a restrictive attitude towards openness and pluralist concepts of a society. Contemporary regional cooperation that focuses on more "intrusive" aspects may not be acceptable to them, because it causes the "erosion" of the traditional national sovereignty. Secondly, several Asian countries are facing the challenge of greatly transforming the political regimes from authoritarian to democratic

31 Kuala Lumpur Declaration on the East Asian Summit, 14 December 2005.

32 See *ASEAN-ISIS Memorandum, The ASEAN Charter: An Opportunity Not to Be Missed*, Bali, Indonesia, 17 April 2006.

ones. Democratic transformations are not necessarily smooth in some countries, which generate many national instabilities and confusions. Economic hardships and terrorism increase further instabilities. The extent to which regional cooperation can contribute to the development is likely to depend very heavily on the coherence and viability of the open and liberal states and state structures within a specific region. The domestic instabilities in several East Asian countries make the process of region-building extremely difficult.

C. Reconciling East Asia with the Asia-Pacific and Global Institutions

A genuine desire of Asians to build up their own region must be respected. At the same time, it is true that an East Asian region could be constructed in the context of institutional reconciliation with the Asia-Pacific and global institutions. The United States has been and will be playing the decisive role for peace and prosperity in Asia. The "East Asian" cooperation must proceed in tandem with the "Asia-Pacific" cooperation which includes the USA.

Given the role of the US-Japan alliance – in ensuring the public good of security – that provide stabilising forces in this conflicting region, it is quite appropriate for Japan to improve its alliance with the USA. At the same time, however, Japan has to be sensitive to different views among the countries of the region, on the unipolar world or the US hegemony in a contemporary world. The confrontation with the emerging power of China and the security concerns about North Korea's nuclear and missile development makes the alliance with the United States more relevant for Japan's security. In this respect, the whole Japan is happy with US-led unipolar world. In a way, Japan is seeking to manage jointly US power and influence in East Asia.

The attitudes of other Asian nations are more ambivalent in this matter. We can identify such ambivalence in ASEAN countries and South Korea. On the one hand, it is commonly understood that the ongoing engagement and commitment of the USA to Asia is essential for the region. Concerning the uncertainty about China's changes, many countries from East Asia needs for the US military and economic presence in the region to hedge risks put by China.

On the other hand, however, as I pointed out above, they are worrying about the USA's unilateral intervention in their internal affairs under the banner of promoting human rights, democracy, good governance and the capacity of fighting terrorism. The USA's military doctrine which advocates the preventive strike as a legitimate sovereign right increase further these concerns. They criticise the US unilateral "hegemonic" behaviours. Thus, some of the ASEAN countries need for a collective mechanism to protect themselves from an "undue intervention" of the USA. In South Korea, the anti-American nationalism and the populist leadership are strengthening each other. They are also concerned about the growing tensions between China and the USA-Japan alliance that is prepared to meet strategic complexities in East Asia mainly caused by China. Most of the countries in East Asia clearly understand that the US forward military presence in Asia underlined by the US-Japan alliance has been and will be contributing to regional peace and stability. However, at the same time, Japan should not take for granted that ASEAN countries and South Korea fully support the alliance. Japan should be aware that the US global power generates lot of resistance at regional and local level, and that the US global power is not necessarily automatically transferred into its influence in Asia.

East Asian community-building must also be underlined by norms and principles compatible with global ones. Given the prospect that East Asia will needs some time to lay down its own new norms and principles related to regional cooperation, the improvement of a regional structure for cooperation could result from an association of East Asia with global institutions. Global institutions provide East Asia with a variety of "tight" norms and binding rules to enhance a deeper integration in East Asia.

D. Who Are East Asians? – Definition of "East Asia"

The creation of ASEAN-centred regional institutional networks may bring about a new definition of the geographical scope of "East Asia." It is usual to define regions from a geographical perspective. However, a region can be defined in terms of function. Regions reflect interactions among their components. The density of interdependence is usually the key factor to distinguish a region from the rest of the international system. To speak about a region, the intensity of interdependence should be sufficient to mark it out as a distinctive subsystem in some significant way. Barry Buzan describes a regional security complex as a set of states with significant and distinctive networks of security relations that ensure a high level of interdependence on security to the members: a group of states whose primary security concerns link them together sufficiently closely so that their individual national security cannot realistically be viewed apart from one to another[33].

---

[33] Barry Buzan, *People, States, and Fear: An Agenda for International Security Studies in the Post-Cold War Era*, 2nd ed., Boulder, Lynne Rienner, 1991. See also various articles included in David A. Lake and Patrick Morgan (eds.), *Regional Orders: Building Security in a New World*, PA, Pennsylvania University Press, 1998.

If we follow the definition of a region, the geographical scope of "East Asia" may expand or get narrower, contingent upon the intensity of interdependence in a specific functional area. For example, the USA and Europe are parts of "East Asian financial interdependence." Taiwan is an essential part of regional financial transactions. The USA is an indispensable part in the East Asian security complex.

This argument may imply that East Asian cooperation should not be confined to the "ASEAN+3." East Asian cooperation should be extended to include additional 'intra-regional' actors such as Taiwan and "extra-regional" actors such as EU.

6. Conclusion

East Asia needs norms and principles that promote much deeper cooperation to face challenges experienced by the region. Functional cooperation – despite an increase in the number of cooperative exercises – would not produce tangible results without being accompanied of normative changes of which countries in the region have been deprived. Furthermore, changes in the existing premises is not an easy task for East Asia, given the deep-seated differences in the organising norms and principles related to international relations and the complex geopolitical and geoeconomic factors prevailing in East Asia. Given the complex diplomatic strategies adopted by the regional countries, the progress of East Asian cooperation will need some time at best. Asian people will still have a long trip to find a commonly identified region in the further decades.

In the meantime, Japan which suffered from deep feelings of insecurity and uncertainty must recognise that it has the capability and responsibility to transform East Asia into a stable and prosperous region. Japan's future is closely intertwined with that of East Asia, given their political, economic and security interdependence. The alliance with the USA is essential not only for ensuring Japanese security but also for the security of the whole East Asia. But, Japan should neither escape from facing challenges nor evade into a comfortable shelter of its alliance with the USA. Japan must face and react to the challenges, even if this demands a painful rethinking of Japan's past and future role in the region.

Epilogue

The EU and Japan as Strategic Partners

His Excellency Takekazu KAWAMURA

Ambassador of Japan to the European Union[1]
at the Trans European Policy Studies Association (TEPSA)
International Conference on 27 November 2006

I. Introduction

Good afternoon, ladies and gentlemen,

First of all, I would like to extend my sincere thanks to Professor Franck (TEPSA), Professor Remacle (ULB), Professor Telò (ULB) and Professor Ueta (ICU), for their joint efforts in organising this event.

It is a great pleasure for me to be able to address the TEPSA international conference again, and share views with you.

For this second session of the conference, I was given the theme of "the EU and Japan as strategic partners". I will focus my intervention on the Japan-EU partnership in tackling global challenges.

As one year has passed since I was appointed as Ambassador to the EU, I have come to realise that people in Europe no longer talk about "Japan" or "Japanese economy" as they used to do. Japan is no longer a miracle, or a threat. Instead, Japan is a global partner of the EU. Both Japan and the EU understand the benefits of multilateralism, and share fundamental values such as democracy, market economy, the rule of law, and human rights. As global partners, Japan and the EU have been making serious efforts in tackling global problems and challenges from similar, if not identical, perspectives for the same goals.

Such strong Japan-EU partnership can be seen in various areas. I would like to touch upon four areas, namely, intellectual property rights,

1 This speech opened the EU-Japan Conference organized by TEPSA, ULB, ICU and GARNET on 27 November 2006

climate change, energy, as well as security in East Asia and Central Asia, as concrete examples to demonstrate how we are strategic partners.

II. Intellectual Property Rights

1. Protection of Intellectual Property Rights

The protection of Intellectual Property Rights, or IPR, is one of the major global concerns.

IPR issues vary from harmonisation and quality to enforcement. Particularly high on the Japan-EU agenda are counterfeiting and piracy. Counterfeiting and piracy weaken the motivation for innovation and creativity, and undermine competitiveness. They might also threaten the health and safety of consumers. Fake Gucci bags or songs of Britney Spears copied without licence are few examples.

In the year 2005, Japanese Customs seized more than one million counterfeit and pirated goods. In the same year, EU Customs seized more than 75 million such articles. The damage has been increasing as more sophisticated technology has become readily available and distribution has become easier, by a wide usage of the internet, for example.

Against such a background, at the 2006 G8 Summit, the leaders adopted a statement on "Combating IPR Piracy and Counterfeiting". It gave priority to such actions as (i) promoting and upholding laws, regulations and/or procedures to strengthen IPR enforcement, (ii) raising awareness in civil society and in the business community of legal ways to protect and enforce IPR and of the threats of piracy and counterfeiting, and (iii) providing technical assistance in that area to developing countries. The leaders also agreed that close cooperation between law enforcement agencies, including customs authorities, is of great importance.

2. Efforts in Japan and the EU

Both Japan and the EU have been actively engaged in IPR protection and enforcement.

(1) Japan

In Japan, with the economic recession continuing after the collapse of the so-called bubble economy, awareness has been widely shared since the late 1990s, that Japan should take nationwide measures to create, protect, and use intellectual property so as to revitalise its economy.

Prime Minister Koizumi, in his policy speech at the Diet in February 2002, set a national goal to strategically protect, and utilise, the results of research activities and creative endeavours as intellectual properties, and to enhance the international competitiveness of Japanese industries. His speech was followed by the establishment of the Strategic Council on Intellectual Property in March 2002, and the Intellectual Property Policy Headquarters in the Cabinet in March 2003. One of the noteworthy developments the Headquarters promoted is the establishment in April 2005 of the IP High Court, with a view to reinforcing the dispute resolution function, and to proclaiming the national policy that intellectual property was one of the top priorities.

The "Intellectual Property Strategic Program 2006", announced by the Headquarters in June 2006, is to promote such actions as (i) achieving early adoption of an international Treaty on the Non-proliferation of counterfeit and pirated goods; (ii) strengthening measures against, and cooperation with, countries and regions where infringements have been exposed; (iii) reinforcing countermeasures in foreign markets through cooperation with the United States and Europe; (iv) tightening regulations at the national borders, and in the country; and (v) strengthening cooperation between public and private sectors.

(2) The EU

The EU, on its part, set a strategic goal in 2000 to become "the most competitive and dynamic knowledge-based economy in the world capable of sustainable economic growth with more and better jobs and greater social cohesion".

In 2005, the EU presented an Action Plan to combat counterfeiting and piracy. In order for Customs to tackle counterfeit and pirated goods more effectively, for example, the Action Plan sets forth a package of measures to (i) increase Community level protection through improved legislation and operational controls; (ii) strengthen the customs/business partnership; and (iii) reinforce international cooperation in this area.

3. Japan-EU Cooperation

Japan and the EU have been engaged in various cooperation on the counterfeiting and piracy issue.

The 2004 Japan-EU Summit adopted the "Japan-EU Joint Initiative for the Enforcement of IPR in Asia". This initiative was to strengthen our cooperation for combating counterfeiting and piracy goods in Asia. It focused on, among others, (i) closely following-up Asian countries' progress in the fight against counterfeiting and piracy, and (ii) exchanging information on technical cooperation projects. Subsequently in October in the same year, an EU-Japan IP Seminar was held in China.

In October 2006, in support of the EC's approach on IPR enforcement in the WTO Council of the TRIPs (Agreement on Trade-Related Aspects of Intellectual Property Rights), Japan, together with the EC, the US and Switzerland, presented a Joint Communication on IPR enforcement to the TRIPs Council. The purpose of this communication is to anchor the enforcement issue in the TRIPs Council debate and serve as a basis for further substantive discussions.

Japan-EU cooperation in IPR protection and enforcement is also active at the business level. In February 2005, senior representatives from the US Chamber of Commerce, the IPR Protection Forum from Japan, UNICE, and the International Chamber of Commerce met in Brussels to discuss how they could work closely together to address the growing global threat of counterfeiting, piracy and IPR violations. Announcing a declaration, they agreed to join efforts to further cooperate and develop coordinated actions to address this issue.

III. Climate Change

1. Commitment to Reducing CO2 Emissions

Climate Change is another global concern. As regards the CO2 emissions, Japan accounted for 4.9 % of the total global emissions in 2003, while the EU 15 Member States emitted 13.6% of the CO2 in the world. (The US accounted for 22.8%, China for 16.4%, Russia for 6.3% and India for 4.3%, respectively)

Under the Kyoto Protocol, which is an agreement made under the United Nations Framework Convention on Climate Change, and entered into force in February 2005, Japan agreed to reduce its emissions of greenhouse gases during the 2008 to 2012 period by 6% below their 1990 levels, and the EU 15 Member States by 8%.

2. Efforts in Japan and the EU

The Government of Japan adopted the "Kyoto Protocol Target Achievement Plan" in 2005. It is considered not easy for Japan to reach this goal as Japan had already made considerable progress in energy conservation at the time of 1990, and the reduction, according to the Protocol, is to be measured against the base year of 1990. Nevertheless, based on this Plan, the Government is making every effort to achieve the Kyoto's 6% reduction target through a series of measures. These measures include: making social and economic systems, including transportation infrastructure, more environmentally friendly; reducing the volume of waste materials; and facilitating forestation and reforestation.

The EU established the European Climate Change Programme (ECCP) in 2000, with the aim of meeting its target of reducing emissions under the Kyoto Protocol. Since then, the EU and Member States have been initiating a series of measures to cut greenhouse gas emissions both at the national and EU levels. In January 2005, the EU became the forerunner worldwide in initiating the EU-Emission Trading Scheme. With this system, large industrial companies exceeding their CO2 emissions quota are allowed to buy additional allowances from more environmentally friendly companies, in order to release excessive emissions.

3. Japan-EU Cooperation

About a week ago, meetings of the United Nations Climate Change Conference were held in Nairobi. (6- 17 November, the 12th session of the Conference of the Parties to the UN Framework Convention on Climate Change and the second meeting of the Parties to Kyoto Protocol)

Post-2012 was discussed during the meetings, and a detailed work plan was decided. Japan and the EU are one in that it is essential for all major players, including the United States, China, and India, to join our efforts in reducing CO2 emissions globally. We will continue to explore ways and means to realise our common objectives, sharing our views and experiences.

IV. Energy

Discussions here in Europe centre particularly on energy these days. This year, the Commission published a "Green Paper on a European Strategy for Sustainable, Competitive and Secure Energy" in March. Subsequently in October, it released an "Action Plan for Energy Efficiency", and set a goal of saving 20% of the energy by 2020. Behind these actions is the energy security issue, the importance of which was highlighted over a concrete case between Russia and Ukraine earlier this year. Members of the EU were reminded of the significance of cooperation among themselves, and dialogue with energy producing countries.

1. The Energy Policy of Japan

What is Japan doing in the meantime?

Three months after the Commission presented its Green Paper on energy, in May, the Japanese government announced a "New National Energy Strategy". The principles of this Strategy, among others, are (a) to maintain and further develop a state-of-the-art structure of energy demand and supply, and (b) to strengthen international cooperation in both energy and the environment.

a) The "state-of-the-art" demand/supply structure would require the improvement of energy efficiency; and diversification of energy sources in both source and country. Discussions on diversification are old and familiar. Let me talk a little about energy efficiency.

Japan has made considerable progress in energy efficiency. The first energy crisis in 1973 urged Japan to establish appropriate energy conservation measures. Japan's use of energy has become highly efficient, compared with other leading industrialised countries. To give you an idea, when Japan's energy consumption (crude oil equivalent in kiloliters) per real GDP is set at 1, Germany's consumption per real GDP is 1.7, France 1.9, United Kingdom 1.4 , and the United States 2.7 (2005 OECD figures).

Furthermore, that of (Cf. Russia is 19.7, China 9.6 and India 9.6 while the world average 3.0)

Japan's current level of energy use efficiency is approximately 37% improvement since the Oil Shock of 1973. In the May Strategy, the Japanese government has adopted the "Energy Conservation Frontrunner Plan", and set forth a goal of further improving the energy consumption efficiency by at least another 30% by 2030, through technological innovations and changes in social systems (e.g. road networks).

Japan is actively engaged in R&D for efficient and environmentally friendly use of energy resources. One such example is R&D and dissemination of liquefaction technology of natural gas, which will enable expanded and more environmentally friendly use of natural gas. These new liquid fuels, called gas-to-liquid, or, GTL, and dimethyl ether, or DME, are expected to provide fuel for transport and industry in the future.

Another technological development that Japan and other advanced industrialised nations, including members of the EU, are engaged in is called "clean coal technologies", and these will reduce the adverse environmental impact of using coals.

b) The National Energy Strategy stresses the importance of an integrated approach towards energy and the environment. As regards energy, the Strategy emphasises the importance of dialogue and cooperation through such international frameworks as the International Energy Agency (IEA) and the International Energy Forum (IEF).

One of the critical issues in this respect is the continuation and expansion of investment in energy producing countries such as Russia and the Middle East countries. Trade, transit and investment are all important issues for a stable supply of energy. In this regard, let me also mention another international framework, the Energy Charter Treaty that addresses all these three issues.

On November 20th, fifty-one member countries and the EC of the Energy Charter Conference elected me as Chairperson of the Conference, beginning in January 2007. I wish to commit myself to serving the interests of global energy security.

2. Japan-EU Cooperation

Japan and the EU are both committed to the Kyoto Protocol, the reduction of greenhouse gas emissions. We are seriously engaged in R&D on energy conservation and new energy, and in their actual introduction into the market. Both Japan and the EU are working on the liberalisation of electricity and gas markets.

Europe started such areas as the liberalisation of electricity and gas markets, and the introduction of non-fossil fuel, or bio-fuel, such as bio-ethanol and Bio Diesel Fuel, earlier than other industrialised countries. In this respect, Japan can draw upon European experiences.

At the same time, Europe could learn from Japan's experience in importing LNG (liquid natural gas). In addition, as oil prices rise, Europe has started re-evaluating coal. One day in the future, Japanese experience in developing "clean coal technologies", might be of some use in Europe.

As global partners sharing common views and perspectives on energy, I am certain that Japan and the EU could further reinforce our energy cooperation.

V. Japan-EU strategic dialogues in East Asia and Central Asia

The EU plays an increasingly important and responsible role for peace and stability, as well as for prosperity, within the international community. The political and economic evolution in East Asia is thus a subject of particular interest to the EU.

The basic strategy that guides all EC actions in Asia is contained in the 2001 Commission Communication entitled 'Europe and Asia: A Strategic Framework for Enhanced Partnerships'. The basic strategy endorsed by the General Affairs Council identified six objectives. One of them is to contribute to peace and security in the East Asia region and globally, through a broadening of the engagement with the region.

You can see examples of such European engagement in Ache, Sri Lanka, and the Korean Peninsula, to mention a few.

At the 2005 Japan-EU Summit, the leaders agreed that strategic dialogue between Japan and the EU on security in East Asia should be enhanced. The agreement coincided with the period when the discussion in Europe was centring on the lifting of arms embargo against China.

Four months later, in September 2005, the first Japan-EU Dialogue on the East Asian Security Environment was held in Brussels.

It cannot be denied that, until recently, there was a strong tendency in Europe to regard East Asia mainly as an economic market. There was not enough understanding as to the security situation in the region. East Asia is not without some security and political problems and challenges. Furthermore, the Cold War may have ended with the fall of the Berlin Wall in 1989, but remnants of that period persist at the other end of the Eurasian Continent, most notably on the Korean Peninsula. One of such examples was the nuclear test conducted on October 9th by North Korea, which is still under the typical, Cold War era, dictatorial communist regime. Through our dialogues, however, the EU has come to better understand the security situation in East Asia.

Realising the importance of continuing such a dialogue, and reaffirming our desire to strengthen the partnership between Japan and the EU, at the Japan-EU Summit in April of this year, the leaders again endorsed enhancement and continuation of the dialogue. The second Dialogue was just convened in June 2006 to the satisfaction of both sides. At the Summit, the leaders also recognised Central Asia as the region of mutual interest, and agreed to develop a similar dialogue on this part of Asia, which took place in July 11th this year.

As strategic partners sharing values, interests and concerns, Japan and the EU should continue to work closely in this part of the world for global peace and security.

VI. Conclusion

The areas of Japan-EU cooperation that I have touched upon today were just a few examples. As global partner tackling issues of IPR, climate change, energy, and security in Asia, it is increasingly important that Japan and the EU further deepen our dialogues and share our experiences and information.

In this respect, exchanging views and knowledge through symposiums and conferences like today's TEPSA conference, is crucial. As Ambassador of Japan to the EU, I hope to be the one who will continue to contribute to further facilitating Japan-EU cooperation.

Thank you for your attention.

ANNEXES

1st Conference

Seminar on EU-Japan Interests in a Globalized World

Organised by
Trans European Policy Studies Association (TEPSA)
International Christian University
Institute for European Studies, Université libre de Bruxelles(ULB)
and Sponsored by the Japan Foundation

Brussels, 29 June 1998, Fondation universitaire
11 rue d'Egmont, 1000 Brussels

PROGRAMME

Morning

8.30: Arrival of the participants

9.00: Welcome addresses by:

– H.E. Ambassador Atsushi TOKINOYA, Head of Mission of Japan to the EU
– Baron GODEAUX, Former Governor of the National Bank of Belgium, Former President of the Committee of Governors of Central Bank of the Member States of the European Communities

9.30 – 11.00: Session 1: ***EU-Japan common economic interests and economic interdependence***

Topics include: 1. Trade issues in EU-Japan relations.
2. Monetary issues (including the role of the EURO and the YEN on the world scene).
3. Relationships of the EU and Japan with the US and their impact on EU-Japan common interests.
4. Economic developments/crisis in East and South-East Asia and EU-Japan co-operation towards this situation.

Chair: Dr. Guy VENHAEVERBEKE, Secretary General of TEPSA

Introductions by:

– Prof. Toru NAKAKITA, Director of the Economic Research Institute, Toyo University
Subject: "Financial and Monetary Crisis in East and South East Asia and its Implications for the Present Japan"

– Prof. Kjell ELIASSEN, Centre for European and Asian Studies, Norwegian School of Management & Université libre de Bruxelles (ULB)
Subject: "Trade issues in EU-Japan Relations (ex. telecommunications)"

– Prof. Yorizumi WATANABE, Otsuma Women's University and Special Assistant, Japan Mission to the EU
Subject: "Trade Regionalism and the WTO System"

Round Table Discussion with:

– Ms. Yolanda FERNANDEZ LOMMEN, Centro Español de Relaciones Internacionales
– Dr. Andras HERNADI, Institute of World Economics, Hungarian Academy of Sciences
– Mr. Wolfgang PAPE, Forward Studies Unit, European Commission
– Dr. Willem VAN DER GEEST, Research Director, European Institute for Asian Studies, Brussels
– Mr. Richard WRIGHT, Head of Japan Unit, European Commission

11.15 – 12.45: Session 2: ***EU-Japan common security interests and security interdependence***

Topics include:
1. Comparison between European and East-Asian security, including respective roles of the EU and Japan.
2. Japanese contribution to the EU and the OSCE space.
3. European contribution to East-Asian security.
4. EU's and Japan's position towards US predominance in regional security systems.
5. EU's and Japan's relationships with Russia and China.

Chair: Dr. Guy VANHAEVERBEKE, Secretary General of TEPSA

Introduction by:

– Prof. Seiichiro TAKAGI, National Graduate Institute for Policy Studies
Subject: "Japan's Relationship with China and East-Asian security."

– Prof. Éric REMACLE, Director, Institute for European Studies, Université libre de Bruxelles (ULB)
Subject: "Transatlantic Relations after Amsterdam"

– Prof. Takako UETA, International Christian University
Subject: "Japan-EU Common Security Interests and Security Interdependence"

Round Table Discussion with:

– Mrs. Daniela DICORRADO, Principal Administrator, European Commission
– Dr. Paul LUIF, Austrian Institute for International Affairs
– Prof. Reimund SEIDELMANN, Giessen University and Université libre de Bruxelles (ULB)

Afternoon

15.00: Session 3: ***EU-Japan common interests in global governance***

Topics include:
1. The reform of the UN Security Council.
2. G-7/G-8 as the core for a global governance system.
3. EU-Japan co-operation in addressing global challenges (environmental issues, poverty, underdevelopment, drugs, terrorism, organised crime).

Chair: Prof. Yorizumi WATANABE, Otsuma Women's University and Special Assistant, Japan Mission to the EU

Introductions by:

– Prof. Yasuyuki KOKUBO, Shizuoka Kenritsu University
Subject: "A Labyrinth of EU and its Impacts on the Relationship"

– Mr. Yasunobu SATO, Former Counsel, European Bank for Reconstruction and Development, Institute of Advanced Legal Studies, University of London
Subject: "Japan's Initiative for the Law Reform Technical Co-operation: Experience in UNTAC and EBRD"

– Prof. Simon NUTTALL, College of Europe, Bruges & former Director for Far East Relations, European Commission
Subject: "EU-Japan co-operation in addressing global Challenges"

– Prof. Mario TELÒ, Université libre de Bruxelles (ULB)
Subject: "Globalisation and Regionalism: a Framework for Analysis"

Round Table Discussion with:

– Véronique ARNAULT, Head of Analysis and Policy Planning, DGI, European Commission
– Miguel SANTOS, Head of the Asia Programme, Instituto de Estudos Estrategicos e Internacionais

– Yoichiro YAMADA, First Secretary, Japan Mission to the EU

16.30: Conclusions by Laurens-Jan BRINKHORST, Member of European Parliament, Former Head of Delegation of the EU to Japan

17.00: Reception offered by the Japanese Mission to the EU

2nd Conference

The EU's Changing Role in the World and Its Partners: towards New Trilateral Relations – EU, Japan and USA

Organised by
Trans European Policy Studies Association (TEPSA)
in Cooperation with International Christian University, Tokyo
Institute for European Studies, Université libre de Bruxelles (ULB)
(Brussels Jean Monnet European Centre of Excellence)
and Sponsored by the Japan Foundation

Brussels, 2 December 1999

PROGRAMME

9.00 – 9.30:

Chair: Baron GODEAUX, Former Governor of the National Bank of Belgium

Welcome: Dr. Guy VANHAEVERBEKE, Secretary General of TEPSA

Opening remarks: Ambassador Takayuki KIMURA, Head of the Japanese Mission to the EU

9.30 – 10.45: Session 1: ***External Relations and the Changing Role of Alliances***

Chair: Ambassador Hisashi OWADA, President of the Japan Institute of International Affairs

Presentations by:

– Todd BECKER, Political Minister Counsellor, US Mission to the EU
Subject: "EU-US Relations"

– Michael RÜHLE, Senior Planning Officer, Policy Planning and Speechwriting Section, NATO
Subject: "NATO and ESDI"

– Prof. Matake KAMIYA, National Defence Academy,
Subject: "Japan-US Alliances"

Discussion

11.00 – 12.15: Session 2: ***Towards a New Trilateral Partnership***

Chair: Prof. Mario TELÒ, Jean Monnet Chair, Université libre de Bruxelles (ULB)

Presentations by:

– Prof. Simon NUTTALL, College of Europe and former Director for Far East Relations, European Commission
Subject: "A European View"

– Prof. Emil KIRCHNER, University of Essex and Université libre de Bruxelles (ULB)
Subject: "A European View"

– David FOUQUET, Freelance Journalist & Researcher
Subject: "An American View"

– Ambassador Hisashi OWADA, President of the Japan Institute of International Affairs
Subject: "A Japanese View"

Discussion

14.00 – 15.15: Session 3: ***Japan-EU Relations for Crisis Management: Russia and the Korean Peninsula***

Chair: Prof. Reimund SEIDELMANN, Justus-Liebig Universität Giessen and Université libre de Bruxelles (ULB)

Presentations by:

– Prof. Katlijn MALFLIET, Catholic University of Leuven
Subject: "The Case of Russia"
Comment by Ambassador Nagao Hyodo, Ambassador of Japan to Belgium
Comment by Dr. Tuomas FORSBERG, Director of the Finnish Institute of International Affairs

– Prof. Hideya KURATA, Fuji College
Subject: "The Case of Korea"
Comment by Mr. Jonathan HATWELL, Desk Officer for Korea, European Commission

15.30 – 16.45: Session 4: ***Enhanced Common Foreign and Security Policy – The Case of Kosovo***

Chair: Prof. Stelios STAVRIDIS, University of Reading and Université libre de Bruxelles (ULB)

Presentations by:

– Prof. Éric REMACLE, Université libre de Bruxelles (ULB)
Subject: "A European View"

– Georges ZAVVOS, Adviser, DGIA, European Commission
– Andrew LEVI, Deputy Head of Cabinet of the special coordinator for the Stability Pact for South-East Europe
Subject: "The Stability Pact"

– Prof. Takako UETA, International Christian University
Subject: "Japan and the Kosovo Crisis"

Discussion

17.00 – 18.00: Session 5: ***General Discussion and Concluding Session***

Chair: Prof. Éric REMACLE, Université libre de Bruxelles (ULB) & Prof. Takako UETA, International Christian University

Speakers: Mr. Richard WRIGHT, Head of Unit, DGI, European Commission
Mr. Pierre Schori, MEP, President of the Delegation for Relations with Japan
Prof. Yorizumi WATANABE, Ohtsuma University

18.00: Reception hosted by Ambassador Takayuki Kimura

3rd Conference

EU – Japan – US: Ten years after the Hague Declaration

Organised by
Trans European Policy Studies Association (TEPSA)
in Cooperation with International Christian University, Tokyo
Institute for European Studies, Université libre de Bruxelles (ULB)
(Brussels Jean Monnet European Centre of Excellence)
and Sponsored by the Japan Foundation

23-24 November 2000

PROGRAMME

Thursday 23 November 2000

9.30 – 10.00: Opening of the conference

Welcome: Prof. Christian FRANCK, Secretary General of TEPSA

Opening remarks: Ambassador Takayuki KIMURA, Head of the Japanese Mission to the EU

10.30 – 12.00: Session 1: ***Justice and Home Affairs***

Chair: Prof. Mario TELÒ, Institute for European Studies, Université libre de Bruxelles (ULB)

Panel: Mr. Daisuke MORIYAMA, Justice Attaché of the Japanese Mission to the EU
Mr. Gilles DE KERKHOVE, Director, DG for Justice and Home Affairs, Council of the EU
Mr. Marc RICHARD, Head of the Legal Section of the US Mission to the EU
Prof. Stelios PERRAKIS, Pantheon University, Greek Centre of European Studies and Research

General Discussion

14.00 – 18.00: Session 2: ***Foreign and Security Policy***

14.00 – 16.00: A. Crisis Management

Chair: Prof. Éric REMACLE, Director of the Institute for European Studies, Université libre de Bruxelles (ULB)

Panel: Mr. Christoph HEUSGEN, Director, Policy Unit, Secretariat of the Council of the EU
- Prof. Stéphane KEUKELEIRE, Catholic University of Leuven
- Prof. Takako UETA, International Christian University
- Prof. Matake, KAMIYA, National Defence University
- Prof. Emil KIRCHNER, University of Essex and Université libre de Bruxelles (ULB)

General Discussion

16.30 – 18.00: B. The Case of Russia

Chair: Prof. Reimund SEIDELMANN, Justus-Liebig Universität Giessen and Université libre de Bruxelles (ULB)

Panel: Prof. Motohide SAITO, Kyorin University
- Mr. Seamus GILLESPIE. Head of Japan Unit, European Commission
- Prof. Sergei MEDVEDEV, The George C. Marshall Center for Security Studies
- Mr. Paul HOFHEINZ, *Wall Street Journal Europe*

General Discussion

18.00: Reception hosted by Ambassador KIMURA, Head of the Japanese Mission

Friday 24 November 2000

9.00 – 13.00: Session 3: ***Economic, Trade and Financial Issues***

9.00 – 10.30: A. World Trade Organisation: Prospects for the New Round

Chair: Mr. Hans BESELER, Honorary Director General of the European Commission

Panel: Mr. Taro ISHIBASHI, Deputy Head of the Japanese Mission to the EU
- Mr. Hans LABOHM, The Netherlands Institute of International Relations, Clingendael
- Prof. James MATHIS, University of Amsterdam

General Discussion

11.00 – 12.30: B. Monetary and Financial Issues

Chair: Mr. Michel VANDEN ABEELE, Director General at the European Commission and Vice-President of the Institute for European Studies, Université libre de Bruxelles (ULB)

Panel: Prof. Sahoko KAJI, Keio University
- Mr. Roy GENTRY, EU Affairs of the American Chamber of Commerce
- Mr. Karsten SKJALM, Danish Institute of International Affairs

General Discussion

12.30: **Wrap-up of the discussions:** Prof. Simon NUTTALL, College of Europe, Bruges

13.00: Lunch offered by the Japanese Mission

Chair: Baron Jacques GROOTHAERT, Chairman of the Francqui Foundation, Honorary Ambassador of Belgium

Keynote Speeches: by Amb. Hisashi OWADA, President of the Japan Institute of International Affairs
by Amb. Thomas FOLEY, Ambassador of the US to Japan

Trilateral discussion to follow

4th Conference

A Decade of Japan-EU Co-operation

Organised by
Study Group for European Policies(SEP)
in Cooperation with International Christian University, Tokyo
Institute for European Studies, Université libre de Bruxelles (ULB)
with the support of the Japan Foundation

26-27 November 2001
European Parliament, Brussels

Programme outline

The EU and Japan: Expanding our cooperation
Japan is the EU's second-largest market (after the US), and a major investor in the EU. A healthy Japanese economy is of critical importance for our own prosperity as well as that of their regional neighbours. But our relations with Japan go far beyond the purely economic, with an increasing cooperation on global and regional issues, expressed in particular in the new "Action Plan" to be adopted at the 2001 EU-Japan Summit. Building on this, our task in the coming years will be to express this global partnership in concrete terms, whether in the political, economic or social field, both in multilateral institutions and in our bilateral relations.

Source: Communication from the European Commission "Europe and Asia: A Strategic Framework for Enhanced Partnerships" (September 4, 2001).

The main items of the International Conference, in the light of the abovementioned Communication and referring to the increasing relations between Japan and the EU since the signing of the Joint Declaration in 1991 and the forthcoming Joint Action Plan, should be structured around the following basic questions. How can the EU and Japan:

– cope with global and societal challenges, f.i. through a further development of the multilateral system, through growing awareness of shared interests in solving common challenges such as environmental degradations and ageing society and in defending common values such as the rule of law and human rights(Monday-afternoon session);

– contribute more, regionally and globally, to peace and security (Tuesday session I);

– strengthen their dialogue on economic and financial policy and on mutual trade and investment (Tuesday session II-part I)

– strengthen their dialogue on social policy issues and in particular their efforts towards poverty (Tuesday session II-part II)

– build a closer partnership in appropriate international fora to help address both the challenges and opportunities offered by globalisation and the global environmental and security issues (concluding session).

Monday 26 November 2001

14.00: Arrival of the participants

14.30 – 15.30: Opening of the Conference

Opening remarks: ***Prof. Jean-Victor LOUIS, President of the Studygroup for European Policy & Université libre de Bruxelles (ULB)***

– Mr. Willy DE CLERCQ, Minister of State and Member of the European Parliament
– Ambassador Takayuki KIMURA, Head of the Japanese Mission to the European Union
– Ambassador Frans VAN DAELE, Permanent Representative of Belgium to the European Union

15.30 – 17.30: Coping with Global and Societal Challenges

Chair: Prof. Christian FRANCK, Catholic University of Louvain (UCL), Secretary-General of TEPSA

Panel: Prof. Hiroshi OHTA, Aoyama Gakuin University, Tokyo
Dr. Maria KARAZINSKA-FENDLER, Foundation for European Studies, Lodz and Université libre de Bruxelles (ULB)
Mr. Eberhart RHEIN, Former Director of the European Commission (External Relations)

General Discussion

Tuesday 27 November 2001

10.00 – 12.00: Session 1: *Promoting Peace and Security*

The Role of Civilian Powers (Japan and EU) and Crisis Management

Chair: Prof. Éric REMACLE, Université libre de Bruxelles (ULB)

Panel: Jean-Arthur RÉGIBEAU, Federal Ministry of Defence, Belgian Government, Diplomatic Advisor
Prof. Takako UETA, International Christian University, Tokyo
Prof. Hiroshi OHTA, Aoyamagakuin University
Prof. Stephan KEUKELEIRE, Catholic University of Leuven, College of Europe

General Discussion

12.30 – 14.00: Lunch at the European Parliament, offered by the Japanese Mission to the European Union

14.00 – 18.00: Session 2: ***Strengthening Economic and Trade Partnership Utilising the Dynamism of Globalisation for the Benefit of All***

14.00 – 16.00: *Part I: Monetary situation, Economic and Trade Partnership*

Chair: Prof. Franklin DEHOUSSE, University of Liège

Introduction

– Mr. Didier REYNDERS, Minister of Finance

Subject: "The role of the Euro"

Panel: Mr. Pierre DEFRAIGNE, Head of Cabinet of Commissioner Lamy, European Commission
Prof. André SAPIR, Université libre de Bruxelles (ULB)
Mr.Toshihiro FUJII, Secretary General, Japanese Business Council Europe
Mr. Julien GUERRIER, Director of the EU-Japan Centre for Industrial Cooperation

General Discussion

16.30 – 18.00: *Part II: Development and Fight against Poverty: "A Social Model"*

Chair: Prof. Laurent VAN DEPOELE, Vice-President SEP

Panel: Prof. Hiroshi OKUMA, Seijo University
Mr. Claus SØRENSEN, Head of Cabinet of Poul Nielson, European Commission
Prof. Philippe POCHET, Observatoire Social Européen
Prof. Mario TELÒ, Université libre de Bruxelles (ULB)

General Discussion

18.00 – 19.00: Concluding Session

Chair: Prof. Simon NUTTAL, College of Europe

Speakers: Mr. Koji KAKIZAWA, Former Minister of Foreign Affairs of Japan, Member of Parliament
Mr. Seams GILLESPIE, Representing Director Percy Westerlund, DG Relex (the European Commission's Negotiator for the Action Plan)

19.00: Reception offered by the Information office of the European Parliament for Belgium

5th Conference

EU and Japan

Facing the Challenge of Global Governance

Organised by
Study Group for European Policy (SEP/GEPE)
in Cooperation with International Christian University, Tokyo
Institute for European Studies, Université libre de Bruxelles (ULB)
with the Support of the Japan Foundation

Brussels, 28-29 November 2002

Thursday 28 November 2002

14.00 – 14.30: Arrival and registration of the participants

14.30: Welcome by:

– Prof. Jean-Victor LOUIS, President of the Studygroup for European Policies and Professor at the Université libre de Bruxelles (ULB)
– Welcome by the Japanese Mission to the EU

14.45 – 16.00: Session 1: ***Civilian Powers: Models of Regional and Global Governance***

President: Prof. Christian FRANCK, UCL

Speakers: Prof. Mario TELÓ, ULB
Mr. Pierre DEFRAIGNE, Deputy Director-General for Trade, European Commission
Prof. Hiroshi OKUMA, Seijo University

Discussion

16.00 – 16.15: Coffee break

16.15 – 17.30: Session 2: ***A New Security Agenda***

President: Prof. Reimund SEIDELMANN, ULB & Giessen University

Speakers: Prof. Takako UETA, International Christian University
Prof. Luc REYCHLER, Catholic University of Leuven
Prof. Éric REMACLE, ULB

Discussion

Friday 29 November 2002

9.45 – 11.15: Session 3: ***New Social and Economic Challenges (Corporate governance, trade and co-operation with developing countries)***

President: Prof. Sylvain PLASSCHAERT, SEP/GEPE
Speakers: Mr. Kenjiro MONJI, Minister, Japanese Mission to the EU
Ms. Maria CARRILHO, Member European Parliament
Mr. Thierry BECHET, Deputy Head of Cabinet of Commissioner Poul NIELSON

Discussion

11.15 – 11.30: Coffee break

11.30 – 13.00: Session 4: ***Humanitarian Challenges: Immigration, Democratic Citizenship, Cultural Identities and Social Dimensions***

President: Prof. J. VANDAMME, Honorary Chairman SEP/GEPE
Speakers: Ms. Naoko HIROBE, IEE-ULB
Prof. Dimitri VANOVERBEKE, Catholic University of Leuven
Mr. Reiner HOFFMANN, Director-General of the European Trade Union Institute
Mr. Jean-Claude KOEUNE, Secretary-General of the European League for Economic Co-operation

Discussion

13.00 – 15.00: Lunch

15.00 – 17.00: Session 5: ***The Reform of Multilateral Organisations: Improving Efficiency. Political Conclusions***

President: Prof. L. VAN DEPOELE, Catholic University of Leuven

Speakers: Prof. Juichi INADA, Senshu University
Prof. Nicolas ANGELET, ULB
Mr. Seamus GILLESPIE, European Commission
Mr. Jim FOSTER, Deputy Head of US Mission to the EU and Chargé d'Affaires

17.00: Reception

6th Conference

Enlarged EU and EU-Japan Relations

Organised by
Study Group for European Policies (SEP)
in Cooperation with Social Science Research Institute and Coe Programme of the International Christian University, Tokyo
Institute for European Studies, Université libre de Bruxelles (ULB)
With the Support of the Japan foundation

Brussels, 24-25 November 2003

PROGRAMME

The aim of the Conference is to discuss two main objectives of the 2001 Action Plan in the context of the enlargement of the European Union and its Constitutional reform

Monday 24 November 2003

9.30 – 10.00: Opening Session

– Prof. Jean-Victor LOUIS, Professor ULB
– Ambassador Kazuo ASAKAI, Japanese Mission to EU

10.00 – 12.30: Promoting Peace and Security
The Building of a European Security and Defence Policy

President: Prof. Reimund SEIDELMANN, ULB & Giessen University

– Prof. Takako UETA, International Christian University Tokyo
– Prof. Kjell ELIASSEN, Director, Centre of European and Asian Studies, Business Institute, Oslo and Professor ULB
– Prof. Jean-Victor LOUIS, Professor ULB
– Prof. Éric REMACLE, ULB
– Dr. Fraser CAMERON, Director of the European Policy Centre
– Mr. Armand DE DECKER, President of the Belgian Senate (invited)

Lunch

14.00 – 16.30: Future Members and New Neighbours

President: Prof. Em. Sylvain PLASSCHAERT

– Prof. Shigeo MUTSUSHIKA, Shizuoka Prefectural University
– Prof. Vladimir BARANOVSKY, University of Moscow (invited)
– Dr. Arkady MOSHES, Senior Researcher, Finnish Institute of International Affairs (invited)
– Dr. Pal DUNAY, Geneva Centre for Security Policy
– Prof. Mathias JOPP, Director, Institut für Europäische Politik, Berlin

Tuesday 25 November 2003

Economic Partnership and Trade

9.00 – 10.15: Enlargement and the Doha agenda

President: Prof. Christian FRANCK, Catholic University of Louvain

– Pr. Takayuki KIMURA, Visiting Professor of the International Christian University, Former Japanese Ambassador to the EU
– Pr. Pierre DEFRAIGNE, Deputy director-general for Trade, European Commission
– Prof. Luk VAN LANGENHOVE, Director, UNU Programme on Comparative Regional Integration Studies, College of Europe, Bruges
– Prof. Maria KARASINSKA-FENDLER, IEE, ULB & European Institute, Lodz, Poland
– Prof. Willem VAN DER GEEST, Director, European Institute for Asian Studies, Associate Lecturer ULB (invited)
– Prof. Alain DE CROMBRUGGHE, University Faculties of Namur

10.15 – 11.15: The Implementation of the Kyoto Protocol

President: Prof. Em. Jacques VANDAMME, honorary president of the Study Group for European Policies

– Prof. Hiroshi OHTA, Aoyama Gakuin University
– Prof. Marc PALLEMAERTS, Professor Faculty of Law, ULB and VUB, Senior Research Fellow, Institute for European Studies, VUB
– Mr. Jos DELBEKE, Director, European Commission, DG Environment

11.45 – 13.15-30: Concluding Session: ***Japan and the EU: Facing Common Challenges***

President: Prof. Laurent VAN DEPOELE, Vice-President of the Study Group for European Policies

– Ambassador Takayuki KIMURA, Visiting Professor of the International Christian University, Former Japanese Ambassador to the EU
– Dr. Jim FOSTER, Deputy Head of US Mission to EU
–Mr. Seamus GILLESPIE, European Commission
– Prof. Mario TELÒ, ULB

7th Conference

EU-Japan Relations at the Time of the EU Constitution and Enlargement

Organised by
Trans European Policy Studies Association
in Cooperation with the Social Science Research Institute and the Coe Programme of the International Christian University, Tokyo
Université libre de Bruxelles (ULB) (Institute for European Studies and Solvay Business School)
With the Support of the Japan Foundation

Brussels, 22-23 November 2004

Venue: Université libre de Bruxelles (ULB), Main Library, Building NB, "Salle de Vision" (Floor 2), Campus "Solbosch", Avenue Paul Héger, B-1050 Brussels

PROGRAMME

Monday 22 November 2004

9.00: Arrival of participants and registration

9.30: Opening Session:
Opening Remarks: Prof. Christian FRANCK (TEPSA/UCL)
Ambassador Kazuo ASAKAI (Mission of Japan to the EU)

10.00 – 12.30: Session 1: ***Economic Partnership and Global Governance***

Trade remains an important part of the agenda for co-operation between Japan and the European Union. How can the EU and Japan promote global governance to bring the Doha Development Agenda forward? This question is important since the Doha-round has demonstrated that the trade agenda is closely connected to other global economic issues like sustainable development, the fight against poverty, economic and social security, and the future of the G-8's role in global governance. Another important area for the EU-Japan economic relationship concerns the opportunities and challenges for trade and investment created by enlargement of the European Union. These will also be considered in this session.

Chairperson: Prof. Mario TELÒ (ULB)

– Ambassador Takayuki KIMURA, Visiting Professor, International Christian University
Subject: "Japan-EU and the WTO Agenda"

– Prof. Petros MAVROIDIS, Université libre de Bruxelles (ULB)
Subject: "EU-Japan and the WTO Agenda"

– Mr Pierre DEFRAIGNE, Deputy Director General, DG Trade, European Commission
Subject: "DDA Negotiations: The Role of Developed Countries in Promoting Global Governance through International Trade"

– Dr. Kalman DEZSERI, Institute for World Economics, Budapest
Subject: "Enlargement and the patterns of Trade and Investment"

– Mr. Georg JARZEMBOWSKI, MEP Chairman, European Parliament Delegation for relations with Japan
Subject: "EU-Japan Cooperation in the World: Challenges and Prospects"

– Prof. Bruno Van POTTELSBERGHE, Solvay Business School, Université libre de Bruxelles (ULB)
Subject: "New Technologies and Knowledge Based Economy; The Challenges for Japan and Europe"

– Prof. Richard HIGGOTT, Warwick University
Subject: "Global Governance: a Challenge for Europe and Asia"

14.30 – 17.00: Session 2: ***Bringing Together People and Cultures: Expanding the Action Plan Agenda***

The partnership between Europe and Japan can be enhanced by developing people to people contacts. In light of the 2005 EU-Japan Year of People to People Exchanges, in this session we will assess what has been done in this field (educational exchanges, business dialogues, and cultural and scientific cooperation for example), including within the context of the EU-Japan Action Plan, as well as what more can be done.

Chairperson: Prof. Laurent Van DEPOELE, SEP & KULeuven

– Mr. Seamus GILLESPIE, Head of Unit Japan, Korea, Australia and New Zealand, DG RELEX, European Commission
Subject: "Implementation of the Action Plan's Fourth objective: Bringing together peoples and cultures"

– Dr. Nobuyuki HIRATSUKA, Secretary General of the Japan Business Council Europe

– Mrs. Diane Van BOCKSTAL (Director of EU-Japan Centre for Industrial Cooperation)
Subject: "People to People Business Dialogue"

– Prof. Yuichi MORII, University of Tokyo
Subject: "The Activities of German and European Studies in Komaba"

– Dr. Cesar DE PRADO YEPES, Research Fellow, United Nations University, Bruges
Subject: "Converging the regionalisation of higher education in Europe and East Asia"

Tuesday 23 November 2004

10.00 – 12.30: Session 3: ***Political Challenges in the EU-Japan Co-operation***

Security and stability on the world stage is becoming a key dimension of co-operation between Japan and the European Union. The definition of threats and security agendas is part of our bilateral relations and involvement in world affairs. The geographical expansion of the EU has reinforced its interest in promoting stability and good governance in its neighbourhood. The EU is implementing its own security strategy. Therefore EU-Japan co-operation for world security is a central concern.

Chairperson and Introductory Remarks by: Prof. Takako UETA (ICU, Japan)

– Prof. Hiroshi OHTA, Aoyamagakuin University, Japan
Subject: "Japan on the Way to Multilateralism? Japan-US Security Alliance and the United Nations"

Comment by: Dr. Axel BERKOFSKY, Senior Policy Analyst, The European Policy Centre

– Mr. Seiichi OTSUKA, Minister, Mission of Japan to the EU
Subject: "Policy Cooperation and Coordination between Japan and the EU"

– Mr. Alexander ZAFIRIOU, European Council, General Secretariat
Subject: "Neighbourhood Policy"

– Prof. Éric REMACLE, Université libre de Bruxelles (ULB)
Subject: "The European Constitution: A view from Europe"

Concluding Remarks

8th Conference

International Conference: "Global Actorness of the European Union and Japan in the Era of Knowledge-based Society"

TRANS EUROPEAN POLICY STUDIES ASSOCIATION

In Cooperation with
The Social Science Research Institute and the COE Programme of the International Christian University, Tokyo
Université libre de Bruxelles (ULB)
(Institute for European Studies, Solvay Business School and REPI, Réseau d'études en politique internationale)
Garnet-Globalisation and Regionalism Network
(Network of Excellence, EU Commission 6th FP on R&D)
with the financial support of the Japan Foundation

Brussels, 28-29 November 2005

Venue: Monday 28 November: Fondation universitaire, 11 rue d'Egmont, 1000 Brussels, Tuesday 29 November: Université libre de Bruxelles (ULB), Institute for European Studies, Classroom III (round floor), 39 avenue Franklin Roosevelt, 1050 Brussels

PROGRAMME

This event has been selected to be part of 2005 Japan-EU year of People-to-People Exchange

Monday 28 November, Fondation universitaire

14.00 – 14.30: Welcome and registration of the participants

14.30 – 14.35: Opening remarks:

- Prof. Christian FRANCK, Secretary General of TEPSA, President UCL-IEE

14.35 – 14.55: Introductory remarks on Session 1: ***Lisbon Agenda and Japan***

– Ambassador Takekazu KAWAMURA, Japanese Ambassador to the European Union

14.55 – 16.20: Session 1: ***Preparing the transition to a competitive, dynamic and knowledge-based economy***

Chairman: Prof. Christian FRANCK, Secretary General of TEPSA, President UCL-IEE

Speakers:

– Prof. Eiji OGAWA, Hitotsubashi University
Subject: "AMU Deviation Indicator for Coordinated Exchange Rate Policies in East Asia"
– Prof. Philippe POCHET, Observatoire social européen, ULB-IEE
Subject: "Employment and competitiveness in Europe"
– Dr. Maria KARASINSKA-FENDLER, Foundation for European Studies, Lodz, ULB-IEE
Subject: "Enlarged Europe in a knowledge-based economy"

16.20 – 16.40: Debate with the audience

16.40 – 17.00: Coffee break and registration for the keynote speech

17.00 – 19.00: Keynote speech: The Lisbon agenda

Speakers: Prof. Pierre DEFRAIGNE, UCL-IEE, ULB-IEE
Prof. Mathias DEWATRIPONT, ULB, ECARES, European Centre for Advanced Research in Economics and Statistics

19.00 – 19.15: Conclusions by:

– Prof. Éric DE KEULENEER (ULB/SBS)

This event will be followed by a reception.

Tuesday 29 November 2005, ULB

9.30 – 10.00: Registration

10.00 – 10.05: Opening remarks:

– Prof. Mario TELÒ, President of the ULB-IEE

10.05 – 12.00: Session 2: ***EU-Japan relationship in the context of global economy***

Chairman: Prof. Mario TELÒ, President of the ULB-IEE

Speakers:

– Prof. Shinichi OKA, Meijigakuin University
Subject: "EU Social Model Viewed from Japan"

– Dr Michael PULCH, European Commission, DG Relex, Japan, Korea, Australia, and NZ Unit
Subject: "Advancing the EU-Japan relationship: Common challenges – joint responses?"

Commentator:
– Prof. Kalman DEZSERI, Institute for World Economics, Budapest

12.00 – 12.30: Debate with the audience

12.30 – 14.00: Lunch break

14.00 – 16.00: Session 3: ***External Actions Pillar: EU-Japan Global Action for World Stability***

Chairperson: Prof. Takako UETA, International Christian University, Tokyo
Subject: "Introductory remarks"

Speakers:
– Prof. Ryo OSHIBA, Hitotsubashi University
Subject: "Japan and the UN"
– Prof. Éric REMACLE, ULB/IEE-REPI
Subject: "Security and development policies: towards a Japan-EU agenda?"

Commentator:
– Prof. Michel LIÉGEOIS, UCL

16.00 – 16.30: Debate with the audience

16.30 – 16.45: Concluding Remarks:
– Ambassador Takayuki KIMURA, Visiting Professor, International Christian University

9th Conference

TRANS EUROPEAN POLICY STUDIES ASSOCIATION

International Conference:"EU and Japan: the emerging challenges for the middle of the decade 2000-2010"

In cooperation with

The Social Science Research Institute and the COE Programme of the INTERNATIONAL CHRISTIAN UNIVERSITY, TOKYO
&
UNIVERSITE LIBRE DE BRUXELLES
(Institut d'Etudes européennes, Solvay Business School and REPI, Réseau d'Etudes en Politique Internationale)

GARNET-GLOBALIZATION AND REGIONALISM NETWORK
(Network of Excellence, EU Commission 6th FP on R&D)

With the support of the JAPAN FOUNDATION

Brussels, 27-28 November 2006,
Venue: Monday 27 November: Fondation universitaire, 11 rue d'Egmont, 1000 Brussels, Tuesday 28 November: Université libre de Bruxelles (ULB), Institute for European Studies, Classroom III (round floor), 39 avenue Franklin Roosevelt, 1050 Brussels

PROGRAMME

Monday 24 November 2006 (Fondation universitaire)

14:00 – 14:30: Welcome and registration of the participants

14:30 – 14:35: Opening remarks

– Prof. Christian Franck, Secretary General of TEPSA, President UCL IEE

14:35 – 16:35: Session 1: ***The internal challenges faced by the EU and Japan***

Chairman: Prof. Christian Franck, Secretary General of TEPSA, President UCL-IEE

Speakers:

– Prof. Shinichi Oka, Meijigakuin University
Subject: "The challenge of Japan through the social and welfare reforms"
– Prof. Iain Begg, London School of Economics
Subject: "Are the EU financial perspectives adapted to the challenges?"
– Dr Mojmir Mrak, University of Ljubljana, Slovenia
Subject: "The challenge for the extension of the EMU"

Commentator: Prof. Janine Goetschy, Centre National pour la Recherche Scientifique, Paris, IEE-ULB

16:35 – 16:55: Open discussion

16:55 – 17:15: Coffee break and registration for Session 2

17:15 – 19:00: Session 2: ***the EU and Japan as Strategic Partners***

Chairman: Ambassador Takayuki Kimura, International Christian University

Speakers:

– Ambassador Takekazu Kawamura, Japanese Ambassador to the European Union
– Mr Jonathan Hatwell, Deputy Head, European Commission, DG Relex, Japan Korea, Australia and New Zealand Unit

19:00: Reception

Tuesday 28 November (ULB)

09:00 – 09:30: Registration

09:30 – 12:00: Session 3: ***The external security challenges***

Chairman: Prof. Carolyn Ban, University of Pittsburgh,
Visiting Professor IEE-ULB

Speakers:

– Mr Sukeyuki Ichimasa, The Japan Institute for International Affairs, Non-Proliferation Center
Subject: "Japan and the International Efforts on Non-Proliferation"
– Dr Gerrard Quille, EP's Committee on Foreign, Security and Defence Policy
Subject: "The EU and International Efforts for Non-Proliferation"
– Prof. Eric Remacle (ULB/IEE-REPI)
Subject: "The OECD, a new Western Security Institution"

Commentator: Prof. Gustaaf Geeraerts, VUB

12:00 – 12:15: Open discussion

12:15 – 13:30: Lunch break

13.30 – 15.15: Session 4: ***The non-military security challenges***

Chairperson: Prof. Eric Remacle

Speakers:

– Dr Ken Koyama, Institute of Energy Economics, Japan
Subject: "Energy security in Japan"
– Prof. Michel Liégeois, UCL-IEE
Subject : "The challenge of terrorism"

15:15 – 15:30: Coffee break

15:30-17:30: Session 5: ***Towards an East Asia Community?***

Chairperson: Prof. Takato Ueta, International Christian University

Speakers:

– Prof. Tsutomu Kikuchi, Aoyamagakuin University
Subject: "East Asia Community viewed from Japan"
– Prof. Dimitri Van Overbeke, KUL and Mr Frederik Ponjaert, FNRS-ULB
Subject: "East Asia Community viewed from Europe"

Commentators: Prof. Karoline Postel-Vinay, Sciences-Po, Paris

17:30 – 17:45: Concluding Remarks

– Prof. Mario Telò, President ULB-IEE
– Ambassador Takayuki Kimura, Visiting Professor, International Christian University

Contributors

Pierre Defraigne is Economist and Director of Eur-IFRI in Brussels. He is also Associate Professor at the Catholic University of Louvain (UCL) and the Université libre de Bruxelles (ULB). He has served the European Commission as Deputy Director-General of DG Trade (2002-2005), Commissioner Pascal Lamy's Chef de cabinet (1999-2002), Director for North-South Relations at DG External Relations (1985-1999), and Commissioner Etienne Davignon's Chef de cabinet (1977-1983). He has also been Fellow at the Center for International Affairs, Harvard University. His research fields are international economic policies, political economy and EU's relations with developing countries.

Kálmán Dezséri is Senior Research Fellow at the Institute for World Economics of the Hungarian Academy of Sciences (VKI) in Budapest, and especially in its European integration research centre. He has authored extensively about international monetary and trade issues, transatlantic economic relations, EU's integration and enlargement, neighbourhood policy, financial issues and Economic and Monetary Union.

Christian Franck is Professor of Political Science at the Catholic University of Louvain (UCL), President of UCL's Institut d'études européennes and Secretary-General of the Trans European Policy Studies Association (TEPSA), one of the partner institutions organising the annual Japan-EU seminars in Brussels. He has also been Guest professor at the Diplomatic Academy in Vienna, Alcala Henares University, Institute for Political Studies in Katowice, Bratislava University and Hassan-II University in Casablanca. He has extensively published about Belgium's European and foreign policy and about EU's institutional dynamics and external policy. He is editor of the annual chronicle about Belgium for *La Documentation française.*

Richard Higgott is Professor of Politics and International Studies at the University of Warwick, where he was Foundation Director of the Centre for the Study of Globalisation and Regionalism (CSGR) and is now Senior Scientist and Director of the EU Framework 6 Network of Excellence on Global Governance, Regionalism and Regulation (GARNET), one of the partner institutions organising the annual Japan-EU seminars in Brussels. Previous chair level appointments and visiting positions have been held at the University of Manchester, in the Research School of Pacific and Asian Studies at the Australian National University, at the Fondation Nationale des Sciences Politiques (first holder of 'la Chaire Asie') and at the Hungarian Institute of Advanced Study: Collegium Budapest. He is editor of *The Pacific Review* and the author/editor of some 16 books or monographs and 100 or so refereed articles and book chapters in the areas of international politics and development studies. His current general interests focus on the post Washington Consensus era global governance agenda with specific reference to the politics of international economic relations in the Asia Pacific region and debates about monetary regionalism after the Asian financial crises.

Sukeyuki Ichimasa is Research Fellow at Centre for Promotion of Disarmament and Non-Proliferation, Japan Institute of International Affairs in Tokyo. He was educated at International Christian University (ICU) and Osaka School of Public Policy (OSIPP), Osaka University. He is former Special Advisor of Permanent Mission of Japan to the International Organisations in Vienna (2002-2004) and later served as COE Research Assistant of ICU (2004-2005). Since 2002, he has been a member of Japanese delegation to the Comprehensive Nuclear Test-Ban Treaty (CTBT) Working Group B. His most recent work concerns On-Site Inspection regime of CTBT, especially focuses on information management.

Takekazu Kawamura is Ambassador of Japan to the EU. He was Ambassador to the Islamic Republic of Iran (2002-2004), Ambassador and Consul-General in New York (1999-2002), the Chief of Protocol in the Ministry of Foreign Affairs (1997-1999), Ambassador and Director-General in charge of the arms control and scientific affairs in Tokyo (1995-1997). He was also Minister in the Embassy of Japan in France (1991-1995).

Tsutomu Kikuchi is Professor of International Political Economy at Aoyama-Gakuin University, Tokyo. He is also Adjunct Senior Fellow at the Japan Institute of International Affairs. He has published many books and articles on political economy of the Asia-Pacific, especially regional institution-building. He was visiting fellow at Australian National University and Institute of Southeast Asian Studies, and visiting professor at British Columbia University.

Azèle Mathieu is Research Fellow in the Innovation & Technology Research Unit of the Centre Émile Bernheim, at the Solvay Business School (Université libre de Bruxelles, ULB, Belgium) since October 2004. She has a Master of Sciences in management from the Solvay Business School. Her research covers mainly the determinants of R&D

intensity in the OECD countries and knowledge transfers from universities to the business sector.

Oliver Meier (PhD in Political Science, Free University of Berlin) is currently expert for the Arms Control Association (ACA), based in Berlin. He was a fellow at the Center for Arms Control and International Security at Stanford University. Most recently, Meier has served on the staff of Uta Zapf, who is a member of the Foreign Relations Committee and chairperson of the subcommittee on disarmament, arms control and non-proliferation in the German Bundestag. From 1999-2002, he was (Senior) Arms Control and Disarmament Researcher with the Verification Research, Training and Information Centre (VERTIC) in London. He has previously served as a consultant to several non-governmental organisations, including the Arms Control Association and the BioWeapons Prevention Project. His expertise includes control of nuclear, chemical and biological weapons, multilateral disarmament and non-proliferation, Iran's nuclear program, as well as European security issues.

Eiji Ogawa is Professor of International Finance at the Graduate School of Commerce and Management, Hitotsubashi University in Tokyo. He is also Deputy Director of EU Institute in Japan (EUIJ) Tokyo Consortium and Faculty Fellow of Research Institute of Economic, Trade and Industry (RIETI) in Tokyo. He obtained PhD from Hitotsubashi University. He was Visiting Scholar at Harvard University, University of California at Berkeley, and the International Monetary Fund. His research focuses on the euro related issues and regional monetary coordination in East Asia. He has published his works in many academic journals such as *JJIE*, *JAE*, *AEJ*, *Japan and the World Economy*, and *the World Economy*.

Shinichi Emile Oka is Professor of Social Security at the Meiji Gakuin University, Tokyo. He received PhD in Legal Science from Catholic University of Leuven (KUL) in 1986. He participated in the collaborative research projects in 1990-1991 and 1992-1993 in KUL when he was Associate Professor at the Oita University. He is the guest professor (KUL) in 2006-2007. He is also holder of Doctor in Commercial Science from Waseda University, Tokyo. His researches have focused on the international comparative study of Welfare States. In particular ha has a strong interest on international relations in social security.

Ryo Oshiba was born in 1954. Graduated from Hitotsubashi University and Graduate School of Law, Hitotsubashi University. He received his PhD in Political Science from Yale University. He was Visiting Fellow at University of Oxford and Princeton University. He is currently Dean of School of International and Public Policy, Hitotsubashi University, and President of Japan Association of International Relations. He is the author of *Political Economy of International Organisations* (1994, in Japanese), *Introduction to International Political Economy* (co-author, 1996, in Japanese), *American Democracy Analyzed: Its Universality, Uniqueness, and Interweaving Influences* (co-edited with Chieko Kitagawa Otsuru, 2000), and *Pearl Harbor as Memory* (co-editor with Chihiro Hosoya and Akira Iriye, 2004, in Japanese). E-mail: r.oshiba@srv.cc.hit-u.ac.jp.

Frederik Ponjaert is grant-holder ("Aspirant") at the Fonds national de la recherche scientifique (FNRS) in Brussels and at the Université libre de Bruxelles (ULB), Institute for European Studies, where he also assists Professor Mario Telò for the organisation of the GARNET Network of PhD Schools. His PhD thesis will be dedicated to the comparison between regionalism in Europe and Asia and the respective roles of Germany and Japan.

Éric Remacle is Professor of Political Science at the Université libre de Bruxelles (ULB), based at the Institute for European Studies (IEE), Director of the Pôle Bernheim d'Études sur la Paix et la Citoyenneté and Réseau d'études en politique internationale. He is also Visiting professor at the University of Pittsburgh, USA, and the Université Panthéon-Assas (Paris-II, France). He has published books and articles about the European Union's foreign and security policy, peace studies and conflict analysis. As one of the main organisers of the annual Japan-EU seminars in Brussels, he has co-edited with Takako Ueta several publications about Japan-Europe relations.

Takako Ueta is Deputy Chief of the Mission of Japan to the European Union. Her academic career includes positions as Director of the Social Science Research Institute (SSRI) and full professor of the International Christian University, visiting professor of the Graduate School of the University of Tokyo, the University of Air, the Institute of European Studies (IEE) of the Université libre de Bruxelles (ULB), and visiting research fellow of the Graduate Institute of International Studies, Geneva. She was special assistant to the Embassy of Japan to Belgium. As an advisor to the Japanese Delegation, she has attended major CSCE/OSCE meetings including: the summit meetings from Helsinki in 1992 to Istanbul in 1999. She has published many books and articles on European security and Japan-Europe relations in English and in Japanese.

Bruno van Pottelsberghe de la Potterie is Chief Economist of the European Patent Office (EPO) since December 2005. His task is to inform EPO policy for economic related matters and to conduct studies and projects on economic aspects of patenting in Europe. He has been professor at the Université libre de Bruxelles (ULB) since September 1999. As holder of the *Solvay S.A. Chair of Innovation* he teaches courses related to the economics and management of innovation and intellectual property. He has been visiting researcher/professor, at the following institutions: Columbia Business School (NYC), the Research Institute of the METI (Tokyo), the Institute of Innovation Research of Hitotsubashi University (Tokyo), the University of Stellenbosh Business School (Cape Town), the Open University of Ho Chi Minh City, and the National Economics University of Hanoi.

International Insights

International Insights brings together studies from various and mixed disciplines to put forward new analyses of issues and developments on the world stage. This series seeks to address in an open-minded and critical manner both theoretical and empirical questions arising from the major shaping forces at work in the modern world. The series will deal with the following subjects: armed conflict and wars in the 21st century, globalisation and transnational developments, new forms of world and regional organisation, political applications of international law and the transformation of the role of the state in international relations.

International Insights is a crucible of debate concerning the key questions discussed by researchers and students of international relations. The series will publish reference texts as well as theoretical and empirical studies.

The series gratefully acknowledges the logistical support of the Réseau d'Études en Politique internationale (REPI) (Network of Studies in International Politics) and of the Pole Bernheim for Peace and Citizenship Studies at the Université libre de Bruxelles.

SERIES TITLES

N° 1 – Pierre CALAME, Benjamin DENIS & Éric REMACLE (dir.), *L'Art de la Paix. Approche transdisciplinaire*, 2004, 363 p.

No. 2 – Gustaaf GEERAERTS, Natalie PAUWELS & Éric REMACLE (eds.), *Dimensions of Peace and Security. A Reader*, 2006.

N° 3 – Yves DENÉCHÈRE (dir.), *Femmes et diplomatie. France – XXe siècle*, 2004, 200 p.

No. 4 – Takako UETA & Éric REMACLE (eds.), *Japan and Enlarged Europe. Partners in Global Governance*, 2005, 288 p.

N° 5 – Barbara DELCOURT, Denis DUEZ & Éric REMACLE (dir.), *La guerre d'Irak. Prélude d'un nouvel ordre international ?*, 2005, 259 p.

N°6 – Claude SERFATI (dir.), *Mondialisation et déséquilibres Nord-Sud*, 2006, 354 p.

No. 7 – Takako UETA & Éric REMACLE (eds.), *Tokyo-Brussels Partnership. Security, Development and Knowledge-based Society*, 2008, 315 p.